Advance praise for *F*

"Mind-stretching!"
– Clifford Pickover, Ph.D., author of *A Beginner's Guide to Immortality: Extraordinary People, Alien Brains, and Quantum Resurrection*

"This book has the inventiveness and prose of a novel, but it's good, honest observation and speculation. From lambasting fakery to closing in on the true paranormal, Mac Tonnies takes us on a wild trip. He was mysterious, maybe because he always had an eye and ear for the mystery underlying our strange existence."
– John Shirley, author of *Gurdjieff: An Introduction to his Life and Ideas* and the *A Song Called Youth* trilogy

"*Posthuman Blues* is of a piece with the Lost Generation of the 1920s and the Beat Generation of the 1950s. Tonnies spoke for his generation with passion, eloquence, and a rare insight. If this is your first exposure to his work, welcome: you're in for a treat."
– Aaron John Gulyas, author of *Extraterrestrials and the American Zeigeist*

"I was changed. You will be changed. Listen to Mac Tonnies as he mutates your preconceptions. Who knew all this strange stuff was so intimately connected?"
– Greg Bishop, author of *Project Beta* and host of *Radio Misterioso*

"*Posthuman Blues* is an important document of the first decade of the 21st century, written by a complex and thoughtful man who dared to confront his life and times head on with no compromises."
– Paul Kimball, filmmaker and author of *The Other Side of Truth*

Posthuman Blues

Mac Tonnies

Redstar Books

dispatches from a world on the cusp of terminal dissolution

volume I (2003 – 2004)

ISBN: 978-0991697526

Published by Redstar Books, a division of Redstar Films Limited
www.redstarfilmtv.com/books
2541 Robie Street, Halifax, NS B3K 4N3

For Bob & Dana Tonnies

Contents

Acknowledgments

Greg Bishop, Nick Redfern, Mark Plattner, Dia Sobin, Sarah Cashmore, Rita J. King, Joshua Fouts, Mike Clelland, Kate Sherrod, Karen Totten, John Shirley, Elan Levitan, Greg Taylor, Tim Binnall, David Biedny, Errol Bruce-Knapp, David Peeples, Bryan and Andrea Ring, Lane Van Ham, Harold Washington, Becky Jackson, George Noory, Michael Garrett, Michael MacDonald, Rob Walker, Aaron John Gulyas, Christina Cuffari, Linda Wood, Reg & Betty Kimball, Clifford Pickover, Katie Martin, Patrick Huyghe, Zorgrot, Spook & Ebe.

And of course Natalie Portman and Morrissey!

Editor's Note

Paul Kimball

Mac Tonnies was one of my best friends, a fellow traveler and a kindred spirit. If I ever arrive at the gates of Valhalla, I know that he'll be there waiting for me.

That makes editing his blog *Posthuman Blues* into a series of books both a true pleasure, and a daunting challenge. The pleasure comes from knowing that my friend's work will find its proper place as a significant document of life and thought in the early 21st century. The challenge is to find the best balance between his ideas and his experiences, all while avoiding the repetition and cultural driftwood that inevitably creeps into a journal (whether in print or on-line) over a period of two years, which is the time frame that this first volume covers.

Inevitably, choices had to be made. Mac's blog was a pastiche of many things, which can be grouped into three very broad categories: (1) his original work, (2) his reflections on his day-to-day life, and the world around him, and (3) his posts of an eclectic range of on-line material that he found interesting, from news items and music videos to photos of famous models and sci-fi comic book covers of women in test tubes. The first two categories are the ones that I have focused on, although some of the commentary he offered on the links he posted (many of which are no longer active) have also found their way into this collection when they represent Mac's responses as opposed to the original material.

The books that Mac cites can be found in the bibliography, not in the footnotes, which I have tried to keep to a minimum (and which are written by me, and not by Mac).

As Aaron Gulyas notes in his insightful foreword, the Mac

Tonnies that you will meet in *Posthuman Blues* might seem different than the one that you heard on radio shows, or even the one found in his books *After The Martian Apocalypse* and *The Cryptoterrestrials*. I knew him as well as anyone, and even I have discovered new things about him as I've revisited his early blog postings. He was a complex individual, living in complex times, who dared to confront life head on, with no compromises. We should all be so courageous. I hope I've done him justice, and presented as complete a portrait of my friend as one can glean from the material.

In the end, it's impossible for any editor to not inject himself into the story, if for no other reason than the choices he makes of what to include or not include will naturally be subjective. But as Mac was part of my story, and I was part of his, it seems only fitting that there is an echo of me in this work, even as there will always be a very real echo of him in my own.

- Paul Kimball, 20 October 2012

Foreword
By Aaron John Gulyas

**"There's an itch in my mind, but I
can only find it occasionally."**

Paul Kimball has done historians a great service by assembling this
collection of Mac Tonnics' writings from the *Posthuman Blues* blog.
What you are holding in your hands is a valuable resource for
understanding the early twenty-first century. That's a pretty massive
statement, I know, but it is within the context of history that I tend
to examine Tonnies' writings – which is why, I suspect, that Kimball
asked me to write this Foreword. Professionally, I'm a history teacher
first, and a devotee of the paranormal only incidentally. My treatment
of the paranormal, in print or in conversation, tends to focus on
placing "The Weird" within the larger context of the human past.

What this has to do with a collection of Tonnies's online writing
may not be readily apparent to some. To the thousands who think of
him primarily as the man behind the "Cryptoterrestrial Hypothesis,"
or the person who offered the sanest approach to alleged Martian
anomalies, much of this book will be a revelation.

It was the Cryptoterrestrial Hypothesis with which he was, for
good or ill, becoming increasingly identified at the time of his death
in 2009.[1] The essence of these ideas can be found in *The*

---

[1] Tonnies speculated that UFOs and other paranormal phenomena could
possibly be explained as the work of secretive races of earthly origin. These
races have existed upon Earth for at least as long as humanity, and are
described as presenting themselves as extraterrestrials or occult beings.

Cryptoterrestrials, which was published posthumously This *Posthuman Blues* collection, however, is an entirely different beast, for Tonnies had a wide-ranging intellect. He was an artist and a writer of fiction as well as a critically aware devotee of design and music. Most importantly for the historian, he was also a product of his times.

Tonnies and I were born within a few months of each other in 1975. We shared many of the same interests. We went to similar small, Midwestern liberal arts colleges. In 2003 and 2004 we were both trapped in jobs that we did well but didn't fully utilize our talents or training. From the beginning of my readings of Tonnies' work, I identified with him. We both existed at the tail end of Generation X, struggling through the ennui of a world which failed to meet our expectations.

"What the hell is this? My psyche eviscerated? An extended confession for never-committed crimes? An elitist soapbox? A simple plea for attention?"

Within the stories of reading, blind dates, workaday dead-ends, and endless amounts of caffeine ingestion, a thread of anger and frustration emerges. Tonnies clearly found himself frustrated by the middlebrow trappings of life in the American Midwest. Often, he comes across to the reader as more misanthropic than a man in his late twenties should be. While he is always engaging and erudite, Tonnies is *not* always nice. There's an edge to his tone, as he vents his frustration at a world in which he doesn't seem to fit.

Like many of our generation, he comes across as nostalgic for a world which never was and, indeed, never can be. His laments on the moribund nature of the American space program, for example, are partly a function of his age, as he watched the space vehicles of his childhood worked far beyond their limits, slowly disintegrating with no future in sight. In many ways, this dismay about human space exploration is a reflection of his dismay with other aspects of American and Western culture.

xvi

Taken in the context of the 1990s, Tonnies' diarizing would have been an obvious companion to the Douglas Coupland's late twentieth century works such as *Generation X* or *MicroSerfs*. Tonnies, however, was writing in the twenty-first century. Specifically, he was writing after the watershed moment of the September 11, 2001 terror attacks on the United States, an event that changed everything.

"Your mind is a battleground.
And I'm not talking about aliens."

This first year of Mac's online blogging is deeply enmeshed in the post-9/11 world. As the United States and its allies fought one war in Afghanistan, the Bush administration began making a public case for a concurrent war against Iraq. The invasion of that country began on March 20, 2003, and the war would continue until finally ended by the Obama administration in December, 2011.

Throughout the run-up to the invasion, Tonnies' disdain for the Bush administration's warmongering is apparent. Also clear is the unease with which he viewed the wider monoculture which emerged after the 2001 terror attacks on the United States. It was, and in many ways still is, a culture which prized banal sloganeering rather than nuanced debate; a culture in which emotive assertions increasingly replaced careful logic and argument. As Tonnies put it on August 11, 2003:

> In the post-September 11 zeitgeist, isolating truth is just too difficult and confusing for most people. The military-industrial-entertainment complex's answer is to bind politically expedient myth and predigested "facts" into an unenlightening but market-friendly chimera. It's cheap, vulgar candy. But man, does it sell.

Like members of previous generations who struggled to find a place in the world after significant cultural and political change, Tonnies perceived the transitional nature of the times in which he lived. His work and thought is of a piece with the lost generation of the 1920s, and the Beat generation of the 1950s. This awareness of being in a time of change, I believe, was one of the factors fueling his fascination with both the posthuman future and his speculation on the fate of Martian life and civilization. In a time of change, there are always forks in the road. In 2003, Tonnies saw a number of potential directions for the United States and humanity as a whole.

Tonnies was not, however, quite as concerned with the future as he might have seemed. On his *Posthuman Blues* blog he addressed the increasingly science fictional condition of our Western world, but science fiction is not necessarily meant to anticipate the future or predict what might be coming next. Rather, it uses the tools and trappings of futurism to make statements about the world in which the writer lives. This is what Tonnies did. The word "Posthuman" is almost misleading. *Posthuman Blues* is a window into the early twenty-first century through the eyes of a thoughtful and perceptive man living in those turbulent times.

Tonnies' day to day explication of the post-9/11 American condition is a valuable component of his overall contribution to the unfolding history of the century. Historians, contrary to what most people think, are often just as concerned with the lives of individuals as they are the workings of governments and corporations. These narratives help fill in the context of the larger political, social, and cultural trends which shape the human story. While the Internet age has provided a wealth of bloggers and commentators, few were as eloquent as Mac Tonnies.

"I take special pains to purge my brain of the ordinary."

His contribution, of course, has largely been defined through his connection to the paranormal. One of the fascinating things about reading through *Posthuman Blues* from the beginning is the development of Tonnies' thinking. The various trains of thought which would, eventually, lead to the theorizing about the "cryptoterrestrials" and the deeper connections between the paranormal and the posthuman have their genesis here.

The intellectual journey that Tonnies took blended the worlds of alternative archaeology (particularly the work of Michael Cremo) with more traditional paranormal figures like Whitley Strieber. Crucially, Tonnies merged these influences with the work of science fiction authors like Philip K. Dick, John Shirley and Rudy Rucker. The roots of Mac's paranormal thought were deeply entrenched in a variety of subcultures, which is one of the factors that makes his work so compelling.

As Tonnies and his blog moved into 2004, the tone began to change. The anger over the political realities of the Bush administration faded into a grudging resignation, and his focus moved increasingly toward explorations of the paranormal. Part of this was, I assume, to guide readers to the upcoming release of *After the Martian Apocalypse*, but I also think that Tonnies' cynicism was building a protective shell around his mind, which led him to focus his attention on more esoteric concerns. Here we see the origins of what would become the Cryptoterrestrial hypothesism, which would come to fruition in 2005 and 2006. I understand Tonnies' mindset on this issue much better after revisiting these earliest explorations of the topics. Through 2003 and 2004, the years covered in this inaugural volume, his attitude toward paranormal phenomena is more tentative, as he explored the edges of the field with curiosity and an open mind. Later he would involve himself more fully and wildly in the anomalous.

I have a hunch that "reality" is the ultimate con.

But that was in the future. Mac's first two years of public journaling (which is what a blog is, after all) represents a window into a world which has now moved from "current events" to "recent history." This collection is a source of ideas and emotions from a profound thinker who left us far too soon. Mac Tonnies is gone, but his words remain to hold a mirror to American society. We have changed far too little in the years since Tonnies wrote *Posthuman Blues*. Our culture, whether one considers this nation's policies or the state of discussion centering on the paranormal, has fulfilled his often dark and pessimistic vision.

Mac Tonnies was not one to take a soft approach. Those whose view of him was shaped by his radio and podcast interviews or his books rather than his blog may be surprised by the hard-edged tone in his critiques of the America of a decade ago. If this is your first exposure to his work, welcome: you're in for a treat. If you are familiar with his writings, keep your mind and eyes open. Seeing these words in a new print context is enlightening in a way that is different from the online experience. Every time I read his words, I find something new, some coincidental connection to something I had never noticed before. Examine his ideas again with fresh eyes and a fresh mind, and remember that he spoke for a generation with passion, eloquence, and a rare and valuable insight.

Aaron John Gulyas has a Master's Degree in history from Indiana University-Purdue University Indianapolis, and is an Associate Professor of History at Mott Community College in Flint, Michigan. He is the author of *Extraterrestrials and the American Zeitgeist*, and maintains a blog called *History, Teaching and The Strange* at www.ajgulyas.com.

Introduction

Last night I dreamed I was an android. Someone told me, very casually. I wasn't particularly surprised, but the revelation left me with a vague sense of existential unease.

Speaking of dreams, that's one very good reason for creating a blog that I hadn't thought of moments before, when it just seemed like a Cool Thing To Do. A dynamic medium like this welcomes dreams. In 30 years, we'll be carrying around personal dream recorders and thrusting them into the faces of friends saying, "Watch this!" But everyone will be too engaged in their own half-forgotten Technicolor reveries to pay much attention.

Given the opportunity, I defend Wim Wenders' *Until the End of the World*, with its moody globalized milieu and Sterling-esque attachment to blobjects and gizmos. And the orchestral soundtrack is truly great.

Dreams as addiction. Claire (pleadingly, frantic, like a child with a malfunctioning Game Boy): "Make it work!"

Why create a web log?

What's the point?

Speaking only for myself: to write. I have stacks of notebooks to be typed into readable form, but they're languishing. I fully intend to buy a laptop, so hopefully my collection of wire-bound journals will shrivel and die.

You *there*.

Reading *this*.

You don't have to, you know. William Gibson's blog is almost certainly more interesting than this (yes, he has a blog now, and a pretty good website).

This isn't intended for an audience, per se. Then again, that seems to be part of the cyber-chic/geek-appeal of this whole "blogging" thing: that reader and author are merged in an illicit conceptual pact, eavesdropping on otherwise uninteresting bouts of creative self-indulgence.

Why "Posthuman Blues"?

Jack Kerouac's *Book of Blues* contains some essentially worthless poetry, but if he'd toted a palmtop instead of a ruled notepad, his output would likely find a small but fervent niche audience. His *Book of Blues* is rich blogging material, written as one would scribble postcards to one's own clone or multidimensional counterpart.

I've always admired Kerouac and the Beats, so consider this blog my book of "posthuman" blues – dispatches from the edge of a world on the cusp of terminal dissolution.

So here's the semi-official invitation to come look over my virtual shoulder:

Dear person on my mailing list, I have succumbed to the narcotic tentacles of blogging and will likely be posting a daily mishmash of uncategorical mental rubbish to appease my strange and obscure urges to populate the info-sphere with my creative spoor.

And thanks to the Web, you can be there as it happens!

It's even better than reality-based television!

I'll probably give it up after a week.

– Mac Tonnies, 26 January 2003

CHAPTER 1
JANUARY 2003

27 JANUARY

We visualize space probes as delicate, tiny conglomerations of solar panels, instrument packages and radio dishes. Probes like Viking and Magellan, which orbited and mapped Venus, last a matter of years before exhausting themselves and falling inert.

But a probe launched by a mature, far-sighted culture might be very different. Instead of a brittle observation platform designed to last all of three years, we might expect self-repairing (or even self-replicating) *interactive* machines that might easily pass our criteria for "intelligence." Communicating with such an artifact, if it chose to communicate at all, could take bewildering forms (for example, "theatre," as opposed to swapping lists of prime numbers). And time might be irrelevant. A suitably equipped alien probe could outlast entire civilizations, shrugging off cosmic rays and whiling its time in a show of godlike sentience.

28 JANUARY

I think America's infatuation with cell-phones and Palm Pilots is symptomatic of a profound loss of identity. Supposedly these devices make life easier, and there's no question that, in the right hands, they do. But I see hordes of people meandering along sidewalks and in the aisles of stores speaking avidly into their "designer" headsets and stroking LCD screens with ergonomic styli and I'm forced to conclude that this is an *illness*.

Listen to these people. They have nothing to say.

They make arbitrary (and usually lengthy) "field reports" to their spouses, telling them precisely where they are, why they're there, and how long they intend to be there. Then they request the same information from the person on the other end of the connection.

This isn't interactivity.

This isn't rational behavior in an information ecology.

It's an exercise in applied banality, an attempt to automate existence into post-cerebral oblivion.

Maybe, given enough time, human brains will atrophy to accommodate handheld communications devices. Everyone will wander the Starbucks-infested landscape bristling with GPS gear, pedometers, cell phones (and their endless color-coordinated accessories), digital cameras, and palmtop computers (all of which, of course, are obsolete in approximately three and a half days).

The brain will no longer be needed. Like the victim of William S. Burroughs' "talking asshole," their eyes will take on the dull, incognizant luster of a crab's at the end of a stalk.

29 JANUARY

Do we really need more fat, pretentious novels about crack-heads and junkies?

This is a defining trend in "literary" publishing, as witnessed by *Trainspotting* (which I haven't read) and a procession of others by "hip" young authors. This stale obsession with rejects and outcasts is stifling, yet it continues. There's a new one coming out by some guy who thinks it's really subversive to use "fuck" in virtually every sentence during interviews. Oh, yeah, and he has a cryptic tattoo.

The angst!

Don't expect innovation from the new generation of would-be Pynchons who attempt to infuse their autobiographical novels with William Burroughs' iconoclastic hipster panache. Expect literary innovation from the likes of William Gibson and Bruce Sterling. *Pattern Recognition* is Gibson's first non-SF novel, and has the potential to invigorate the mainstream literary scene with some fresh ideas. We'll see.

Arthur C. Clarke is famous for his maxim, "Any sufficiently

advanced technology is indistinguishable from magic."

Let's take this further. A pervasive, "arbitrarily advanced civilization" (a term coined by Kip Thorne) could alter the universe so radically that we would perceive its workings as physical law. Quantum mechanics seems contradictory and weird to us. Maybe it's because we've reached the threshold of our universe's resolution. Stare too closely at a television screen and you can see the individual pixels; the image dissolves into a stew of glowing points.

Human experience is inherently conspiratorial. The data that my brain interprets as "reality" has already passed through an array of biological filtering mechanisms. Photons are converted into images; waves in the atmosphere are assembled into "sounds"; diffuse molecules become "smells," etc.

The human body is a highly selective sensory environment – an interface between what we choose to call our "selves" and whatever seething weirdness lurks beyond our membrane of skin. Virtual reality is the *only* reality.

Our posthuman descendants will be able to modulate experience. I imagine them as wispy stick-figures with thatches of cilia for hands. Some of them have heads; others don't. Their mentational substrate is distributed throughout their bodies so that trauma won't endanger their identity. Like starfish, they're able to regenerate. And they're so light they can take to the air like bits of refuse in a strong breeze.

Maybe I was being too harsh about wannabe authors. Philip K. Dick and William Gibson's novels are peopled by oddballs and addicts of various sorts. And what of J.G. Ballard's roster of psychotics?

Still, the "Infinite Jest" thing is played. I'm tired of it. And I'm tired of science fiction being marginalized by stodgy academics.

30 JANUARY

Internet buzz-words are the linguistic versions of Bruce Sterling's user-friendly, touchy-feely "blobjects." Yahoo. Google. Blogger. It's hipsterized baby-talk, fun to pronounce. Ridiculous-sounding names like this are like the flimsy translucent casing around a disposable calculator, rendering ubiquitous tech into unthreatening conceptual baubles.

31 JANUARY

I wish I had a flying car. It's a frequent fantasy of mine when stuck in traffic. There's a particular scene in *Blade Runner* that is the quintessence of my flying car dream. Harrison Ford is parked outside a decrepit hotel and a hovering police car, called a "spinner" in the production notes but never referred to as such in the film, drops into view while its driver checks on Ford's ID.

There's a misconception among *Blade Runner* watchers that Ford's character has his own "spinner." He doesn't. He drives an old-fashioned ground-car that looks a bit like the Honda Insight hybrid crossed with a DeLorean. There's even a brief discussion in a *Seinfeld* episode in which Jerry mentions Harrison Ford's "cool" flying car. My impression from the film is that the spinners, far from being common, are toys of the postindustrial elite.

I would love to tool around Kansas City in a Moller Skycar. Supposedly these things will become reasonably affordable by 2015, although if I had a choice, I'd prefer a force-propelled flying saucer.

Chapter 2

FEBRUARY 2003

1 FEBRUARY

This morning a friend called to let me know that the space shuttle *Columbia* had disintegrated before a scheduled landing. Somehow, this news came as more of a punch in the face than when I learned of the terrorist attacks of 2001. Flawed and short-sighted as it is, NASA is a uniquely American institution capable of doing truly awe-inspiring things given the budget and initiative. The recent announcement of Project Prometheus, a long-overdue effort to use nuclear energy in space in the peaceful pursuit of knowledge, is an example.

Columbia's disintegration is a profound loss that raises important questions about the future of our already tenuous manned presence in space. It could be argued that better technology could have prevented this setback; the shuttle program utilizes laughably obsolete craft that properly belong in the Smithsonian Air and Space Museum. The loss of the *Columbia*'s crew is a monumental waste of human potential that transcends national boundaries. The seven astronauts killed in the mishap were humanity's envoys, avatars of our inherent exploratory spirit. We badly need more people like them.

The demise of the *Columbia* and its crew shouldn't hold us back. Their death should be a rallying call for new, more efficient and more reliable space transportation systems. The space shuttle concept, as presently manifested by NASA, begs replacement. The time has surely come to broaden our conception of space and the definition of our role in its uncompromising vastness.

Perhaps I'm being foolishly optimistic about this. The loss of

Columbia was a grotesque blow. But maybe NASA needs a grotesque blow to wake it up to the fact that it's using risky hardware and getting very little in return.

The shuttle program is largely a charade, a manned spaceflight program in permanent standby mode. Yes, it's better than nothing at all, but now we're seeing how fragile it really is. This could be a chance to introduce a real reusable shuttle instead of the cumbersome, wasteful, horribly inefficient mutation we call the Space Shuttle.

But will we rise to the challenge, or revert to the status quo?

Let's continue to expand, establishing permanent beachheads in the sky, never holding back for the sake of bureaucratic whim or political myopia.

2 FEBRUARY

Great weather today. Gibsonian dead television sky. Two functioning fountains; receding ice. This weekend was criminally short. Ominous contrails on the covers of newspapers, the smell of thawing sewage hovering like a painful memory above Brush Creek.

I feel poised in the brink of a familiar existential malaise. A vague sense of nostalgia and vertiginous longing like the prescient tickle in the back of your throat when a cold's coming on.

I received a wall-mounted clock today. It's square and features a cup of coffee with the words "Best Coffee in Town." Here's the weird part: this thing actually ticks. It makes audible, almost Victorian sounds as it performs its designated function of informing me of the time. This is in stark contrast to all the other electric devices I own, with their mute LCD displays and anonymous plastic carapaces, i.e., my Sharp microwave oven, alarm clocks, stereo system, printer, computer. I like the ticking; it's oddly reassuring, like a healthy heartbeat.

Meanwhile, here's a fiction fragment that's been gathering dust (or its informational equivalent) on my hard drive. The intention here is shock value, à la William S. Burroughs' *Naked Lunch*. I wanted to render a weird science-fictional environment without being hindered by machinations such as plot and character; it's a decent writing exercise that forces you to think organically. Here we go:

The habitat's docking spires pierce the vast canopy of green membrane, needles through the viscera of an embryonic city. Gaping bone-white shafts lead to the atmosphere generators deep underground; passersby lounge at their rims, plucking drinks and syringes from the backs of giant modified insects. Multi-level stores and endless restaurants huddle around the spires, connected by translucent skywalks that shine with the membrane's jade glow. The sun is a blotch of eye-stinging yellow-green, like a phosphorescent lesion on some exotic deep-sea fish.

Every available surface is thronged with a mishmash of pedestrians and small, unassuming vehicles that clamber over one another with adhesive tires, leaving trails of noxious resin that degrades into fine blue powder. Silvery robotic cameras dart about like birds, bobbing and weaving in vertiginous flocks before exhausting their fuel and falling to the ground, where they burst and are scooped up by patient custodial insects. Prostitutes with animated tattoos beckon from automatic sidewalks, striking poses, feigning copulation with ambling waist-high beetles with bar-coded shells.

Zoom out. The membrane flashes by and recedes into a dappled disk-shape, like an algal pond seen from a great height. All around it is red-orange desert and scattered rock. The spires poke through the disk's surface like hermetic wands, tips bristling with parked vehicles. Spindly helicopters with impossibly stretched rotors ply the yellow sky in winking convoys, their shadows thin and insubstantial on the Martian surface. Blimps, pendulous with imported coffees and raw meat and choice microelectronics, extend resinous antennae that curl around the docking spires like the arms of a drowning man around a passing tree-limb.

The membrane habitats dot the landscape, encapsulating craters, interconnected by satellite uplinks and whispering monorails.

3 FEBRUARY

Lava lamp observations:

When turned on, nothing happens for a while as the wax heats up. Then, abruptly, jagged, organic-looking tendrils and stalks shoot up from the lump of puddled wax at the bottom of the flask like synapses in an eager brain.

As the heat increases, the stalks collapse and settle to the bottom, where they melt into oblivion. Soon, myriad spheres are seen moving up and down, only to fuse into a single tentacular column that exchanges mass with its hemispherical counterpart floating above.

Given time, this column prevails against smaller bits of molten wax. It's like watching a patient, peristaltic mollusk. The amoeboid shapes inside the flask act out a sort of pre-biological evolution.

5 FEBRUARY

Kindness is a cheap commodity. All too often, compassion takes the form of a "patriotic" bumper-sticker or theatrical "peace rally." It's a most convincing show, but that's all it is.

Activism obviously has its place, but don't try to pass it off as heartfelt and genuine.

It's sentimental politics, nothing more.

8 FEBRUARY

My digital answering machine recorded nine beeps today (or possibly very late last night). The odd thing is that no one had called. The phone never rang; the beeps (accompanied by modulated static) were somehow recorded directly into the memory chip.

In UFO lore, this might qualify as a "phantom phone call." Similar calls are sometimes received by close encounter witnesses (see John Keel's *The Mothman Prophecies* for post-encounter weirdness galore).

But what interests me is that I knew how many beeps there would be before counting them.

In *Transformation* Whitley Strieber recounts how he was startled to hear "nine knocks" high on the wall of his cabin in New York. This spurred him to try to discover not only how the impossibly high knocks had occurred, but what the knocks represented – if anything.

Strieber's knocks occurred in three sets of three. My mystery beeps didn't. Strieber, if he is telling the truth, has a history of unusual encounters with apparent nonhuman beings. I don't. However, the beeps took place in what I can only describe as a synchronistic framework.

Months ago, right after reading Keel's book, I received my first mystery call (and although I thought it was weird, I erased the "message" before counting the beeps).

Today's call was the second one I've ever received. The first incident took place in the midst of an alarming, albeit subjective, degree of synchronicity. Today's occurred while finishing a book that specifically dealt with phantom phone calls, so one could argue that there's an acausal relationship there, a Jungian "meaningful coincidence."

Or just possibly something stranger.

10 FEBRUARY

I've had online run-ins with members of the self-proclaimed transhumanist elite: embarrassingly shallow, thick-skulled collectivists who have simply substituted "cyberspace" for the archaic notion of "heaven." The vocabulary has changed, but the Will to Believe persists, evolving as certainly as demons and fairy-folk morph into extraterrestrial visitors to camouflage themselves among our expectations.

11 FEBRUARY

Whitley Strieber has posted a disturbing piece on his site with respect to a massive proposed expansion of the "Patriot Act." An

American dictatorship? Why not? It's not nearly as implausible as it sounds. Strieber makes an emotional show of it, as always, but I really don't blame him.

I've become an NPR listener sometime in the last couple months. The spoken word editorials are a blast; I crank up the volume for those. I'm a terrible orator. I skip from topic to topic, sever my own arguments in mid-sentence and apologize on behalf of the person/political entity I'm attacking only to realize that I'm allowing myself to be manipulated, which makes me bitter and vindictive. I prefer to hover at the margins, taking it all in like a holographic camera, letting it settle and ferment of its own volition. I'm a locus of weird memes, a biohazard, an ambiguous and decidedly nonpartisan singularity.

Bureaucracy is a parasitic life form. It will continue feeding until human existence is a mere shuffle of commodity and idiotic smiles.

A splinter faction must enter space. Escape before the planet goes nova. Burroughs and Leary. Gerard O'Neill and Robert Zubrin. Their memes must survive long after the bureaucrats are so much radioactive bone meal.

12 FEBRUARY

The future isn't an inevitability; it's a process. It reaches back in time with delicate, enveloping fingers and beckons. We proceed like slender pseudo-pods straining to break free of a parent cell. The transition is amorphic, dangerous and continuous. We are always on the front lines, waging temporal war within the privacy of our own skulls. The future is not ours, although it can be.

Maybe this is what a multiversal intelligence seeks: not the chatter of electromagnetic transmissions, but the intricate lacing that occurs when space-time is tempered with conscious intent. Finding us, it insinuates itself into our ontological flow. It replicates until its presence is so familiar we cease to even notice. We are silent partners, weaving new matrices of causality.

More NPR listening today. Great driving material. Nukes in North

Korea, heightened terror alerts, mystery tapes from a quasi-mythical bad guy, and hysterically out-of-place commentary on books I'll never read and obscure restaurants. Quite the spectacle.

The millennium didn't really begin on Jan. 1, 2001. It began on Sep. 11, 2001. The fall of the towers was a fittingly bleak celebration, ushering in a national paranoia worthy of Philip K. Dick.

No follow-up "phantom phone calls" or mystery beeps. In fact, the power in my apartment went off while I was away yesterday and the digital recording of the nine beeps (see earlier entry) was erased. Thankfully I'm not paranoid enough to attribute this to snooping ultra-terrestrials.

I'm off to get a latte and read some Neal Stephenson.

13 FEBRUARY

I nominate David Icke as a prototype 21st century man.[2] He's got the necessary survival skills for today's post-*X-Files* zeitgeist. He's even politically correct inasmuch as his disdain for Jews is masked by a loathing for inter-dimensional reptiles.

Icke, like John Edward, is a smarmy pseudo-prophet who delights in smearing his own face across his publications. Image is everything; Icke knows this, realizes it with an acuity that the politicians he despises only sense from a distance. He knows how to package idiocy, and it's the package, not the contents, that is so eagerly swallowed. The covers of his books have all of the graphic subtlety of a box of laundry detergent. His audience is a reeling mass of paranoid media symbionts: the human aftermath of the Heaven's Gate suicides, late-night radio conspiracies and the shoot-out death of professional doom-monger Bill Cooper.[3]

---

[2] David Icke, *David Icke Website*. www.davidicke.com.

[3] William Cooper was a far right conspiracist who was shot and killed by police in 2001 after he opened fire on them when they tried to arrest him. His website is still active, at www.hourofthetime.com.

15 FEBRUARY

I just read some disturbing news. It turns out that if the Authorities detect a global-killer asteroid heading our way, and there's absolutely no way of averting it, then the populace will be kept in blissful ignorance. The reasoning is that there will be nothing that anyone can do, so we might as well avoid mass panic.

I can't help but feel strangely cheated. If there's a big chunk of rock about to collide with Earth and exterminate all life except for some nano-bacteria, I want everyone to know.

I want to see some panic in the streets. I want looting, screaming, mass suicides, rampant craziness. Religious goofballs waiting to be "saved." Stupefied suburbanites hoarding groceries. That sort of thing.

The public has a right to know!

16 FEBRUARY

I strolled down to the Memorial Fountain today to meet a friend at Kansas City's big antiwar protest. I never found her, but was swept along the Country Club Plaza by a stew of protesters with signs and banners, all coolly scrutinized by news cameras. Relentless honking from passing cars was accompanied by approving cheers.

Some endearing slogans: "No More Bu$hit," "Drop Bush, Not Bombs," "Eat the Patriarchy."

I swilled a cup of coffee and attempted to read, but the swarm of marchers rendered concentration impossible. Plus, I felt rude by ignoring the demonstration. Someone might think it was deliberate and decide to brain me with a "No Blood for Oil" placard.

So I drifted back into the chanting crowds, brandishing Neal Stephenson's *Cryptonomicon* like some subversive piece of anti-war propaganda, fingers growing steadily numb. A news helicopter circled overhead like a metallic gnat, taking in the throngs though darkened windows. Theoretically, at least, I might be on TV.

Bruce Sterling has referred to the Bush regime as a post-ideological technocracy. But I think the sickness runs deeper. Dubbya appears to lack genuine empathy or reason, like a junkie desperate for a fix and willing to suspend higher brain functions until he gets it. Cheap patriotic sentiment and clever slogans aside, the pending war is sickeningly wrong.

But can protest really avert it? Stooping to examine a newspaper vending machine, I was slightly heartened by the sheer numbers of war opponents taking to the streets.

18 FEBRUARY

Real events, as opposed to confabulated or hypnotically synthesized events, leave an unmistakable sensory signature in the brain that can be detected using PET scan technology. When events are "relived" verbally, brain centers responsible for processing input at the time of the event become active. This can't be faked as far as neuroscientists can tell. Whitley Strieber and others have suggested using this technique to see if alleged alien abductees are telling objective truth and not merely recounting fantasies.

Potentially, a single abductee with appropriate neural feedback could prove that close encounters are real. But would aliens intent on spreading confusion have an answer to PET scan reality-testing and operate on a mental or dream level, bypassing the brain's sensory input indicators?

We know little about consciousness and telepathy, let alone technologies that might exploit latent psi ability. Maybe visiting aliens have anticipated our high-tech efforts to separate truth from fiction. Maybe when they reportedly stick clinical-looking objects up people's sinuses and eye cavities they're shunting evidence of their intervention into the regions of the brain that govern imagination, like fastidious burglars making sure there's no evidence that could lead to their apprehension.

Your mind is a battleground. And I'm not talking about aliens.

19 FEBRUARY

So it's like this: although my answering machine is up-to-date, fully digital, and user-friendly, it contains old-fashioned chips that cause it to give a nine-beep "low backup battery" warning.

This is superfluous, as it gives me a battery warning in a human voice every time I check my messages.

Needless to say, this anachronism isn't in the instruction books; evidently the chips serve some other purpose and the manufacturer decided to leave them alone rather than scrap them, hoping they wouldn't cause any confusion.

So guess what woke me up in the middle of the night? Loud beeping from my phone! I was too out of it to count them but I think it's a safe bet there were nine of the damned things.

20 FEBRUARY

The Department of Homeland Security (or whatever it calls itself) has unveiled *www.ready.gov*, your one-stop online source for endless anxiety.

Don't have time to wade through the government's meandering list of precautions? Try these simple steps instead!

1. In case of a terrorist nuclear strike, run screaming into the streets brandishing bibles and frothing at the mouth.

2. In case of a terrorist chemical strike, run screaming into the streets brandishing bibles and frothing at the mouth.

3. In case nothing at all happens, run screaming into the streets brandishing bibles and frothing at the mouth.

But most of all – be ready!

21 FEBRUARY

Friday. At last. My mind-body interface feels weak. A slight fatigue shadows my movements, or is that just caffeine-augmented awkwardness?

I had a flavored latte last night for the first time in probably over a year. Usually I just get them plain. Espresso, when blended with steamed milk, actually calms me incredibly, and transports me into an agreeable meditative state. Plain coffee, on the other hand, gives me a slight buzz if I drink a lot of it.

Reality is the ultimate anesthetic. I think we are all congenital amnesiacs; we're missing out on something of excrutiating importance, like the cubicle-dwelling drones in *The Matrix*. There's an itch in my mind, but I can only find it occasionally. It's like rummaging through a box of ancient refuse and incomprehensible knick-knacks and suddenly feeling the two-pronged bite of a snake between your fingers; you recoil, shrieking, but your curiosity is irreversibly piqued. You want to empty the box into the light of day regardless of the danger – or maybe even because of it.

The fabric of waking reality is lacking. I feel like a drill has been shoved through my brain, excavating some essential neural hardware and leaving the wound to fill in with bland synaptic meat. Jacques Vallee professed to harboring a "strange urge" to unveil his ufological conditioning system, revealing an existential disquiet as probing as Camus'. Rats pressing levers. Blind, maniacal clockwork spitting out gamma rays and diners, wisecracking technocrats and quantum foam, "orange" alert levels, Pentium chips, and faddish authors.

We cling to "reality," which dutifully adapts to our quaint definitions. Are we drafting our own experiential cryptosystem as we go, subconsciously confident that we'll never have to get too close to the projection booth?

22 FEBRUARY

I slept in late today and suffered a bout of recurring dreams: something about a train ride through a surreal and devastated Germany: fungal statuary emerging from the ground like drowning relics under a gray sky.

Then I got up and lingeringly checked my email, managed to put together something vaguely resembling breakfast, and sat on my futon in not-entirely-unpleasant existential stupor. This is typical Saturday morning behavior.

The temperature drops. I'm at loose ends, wondering whether or not to brave the weekend crowd and enjoy a cinnamon latte. I ate

Mexican tonight in a place evidently designed by midgets.

Pinatas grazing my forehead like imbecilic cherubs, chairs and tables like furniture designed for use in a tin-can Moon base. Ranks of ceramic pigs with ironic smiles.

23 FEBRUARY

It's snowing, the flakes listing sideways and even veering up, like flecks of debris riding the slick veneer that encases your pupil. Spook the Cat is fascinated, her head twitching in an attempt to take it all in. Tiny airborne mice?

The anti-war protesters have made a valiant showing, but they're almost invisible, hidden behind a screen of languid snow like figures half-glimpsed through a fog of sleep deprivation. I read all afternoon and stopped when I realized I was starving. Brain crackling with coffee-induced lucidity, I trudged back to my apartment, ritualistically turned on the lava lamp, and plugged in the space-heater. I love the draft of ozone it gives off after staying unplugged all night.

25 FEBRUARY

Despite SETI's good intentions, we have no way of knowing what an alien transmission might hold in store for us. This calls SETI's international protocol into question. In the event that we receive an impartial beacon consisting of prime numbers or a digital schematic of the aliens' domain within the galactic disk, there would be little problem democratizing the transmission.

On the other hand, what if the extraterrestrials sent a more ambitious message our way? Instead of sending us a series of conspicuous beeps, an alien civilization might feel inclined to help emerging civilizations by supplying "blueprints" for new technologies, offering new paradigms for communication, energy extraction, medicine, or even artistic expression.

Conceivably, any message encompassing unknown technologies would fall under the domain of national security. Suppose an ET message contained a coherent primer for extracting the fabled zero-point energy of the vacuum. Few would argue that a global, utopian society would eagerly accept such wisdom. But the Earth of the 21st century is far from utopian; the nation in possession of such knowledge would stand to benefit enormously in both economic and military spheres.

SETI's protocol sounds completely just, but it naively assumes that incoming signals from faraway civilizations will be little more than cosmic Hallmark Greetings of no possible strategic importance.

Would the United States openly share information leading to new energy sources to, say, Iraq or North Korea if it could be used to create new and more destructive weapons?

28 FEBRUARY

Is consciousness analogue or digital?

Chapter 3
MARCH 2003

1 MARCH

Cinematic snowfall; flakes adhere to my jacket like white fractal spiders. Children hand me gospel literature as I attempt to navigate the intersection near Barnes & Noble.

"Thank you," I mutter. I'm carrying a cup of steaming coffee which I could easily empty on their heads, but, being considerate, I refrain. Besides, it's the father with the "REPENT" placard I really want to get at. Push him in front of a car, maybe.

Quick poem...

Caffeine
perennial mushroom cloud blimp-like,
ponderous over horizon
holographically rendered
an amalgam of emission angles and
lasers
the gaseous curvatures of unknown architects
asleep in newsprint bunkers
reems of ciphers
metallic overcast
night skies
benign radiations
inundate the sleeping city

2 MARCH

The ATM is "unable to fulfill my request" – again. What makes these things so damned temperamental? The machine isn't broken. Evidently it just doesn't especially feel like disgorging money, which I direly need if I'm going to eat something besides an overpriced bag of vending machine chips for lunch tomorrow.

3 MARCH

Someone dumped a few boxes of old textbooks into my building's dumpster. I retrieved *The Complete Book of Progressive Knitting*. I hadn't realized there was such a thing. I assumed knitting was knitting. The possibility of knitting being "progressive" – even by knitting standards – had simply never occurred to me.

4 MARCH

Months ago, I made a silent pact not to get particularly upset over stupid politicians. This wasn't the same thing as proclaiming pacifism; I merely felt that politicians made too easy a target. Everyone gets irate over politics. It's amusing to an extent, but nothing I wanted to indulge in. But the Bush Regime threatens to dissolve my personal pact as certainly as the White House's behavior has tarred the international reputation of the United States.

Bush is a quintessential addict/tyrant, madly setting the stage for petrochemical apocalypse. Bush's war-lust goes beyond bad politics and into the domain of psychopathology. He is a frothing-at-the-mouth aggressor, all unrequited id, mulish obstinance and hideous posturing. The man is sick; his agenda is even worse. To the Bush Regime, Iraq's initial reluctance to destroy its arsenal was a mean-spirited game of "chicken." But now the truly unthinkable is happening: they're complying! They're beginning to cooperate! Damn them!

Bush fills Washington's corridors with a foul reptile stink. He's followed by a nastily persistent haze that leaves his opponents gasping for breath. His mind operates with the subtlety of hardwired circuitry; machine-like, he sees in the garish green sub-spectrum of night-vision goggles.

Facing Bush's mania is roughly as difficult as going up against James Cameron's "Terminator" bare-handed, and just as exhausting.

6 MARCH

So, will the human race survive the next 1,000 years? Stephen Hawking, for one, doesn't think we will unless we expand into space. It's sad commentary on our predicament when a week's worth of precision bombing in Iraq could have financed a manned Mars exploration program. Will humans make the evolutionary cut? Almost certainly not. But that doesn't exclude our descendants, who may or may not be human-like in any recognizable sense.

I sense that we are treading a vast and portentous ontological gulf; it's crunch time. The next few hundred years will be absolutely decisive. Either the Earth becomes a planetary mass grave or it becomes a fondly remembered home, or an abstract notion. Post-humanity will take on a variety of forms; almost by definition, it will be multiplex, vastly intelligent, and as tenacious as any virus or prion.

A thousand years, in geological time, is less than an eye-blink. A mere century can be viewed as a single defining event. If so, it's not unreasonable to expect that our flailing attempts at ascension, burdened as they are with superstition and bureaucracy, are being watched by others in the space-time neighborhood. We might be quite amusing to them. Or quite sickening.

People invariably ask me about my "beliefs" in aliens. The point I try to make is this: If extraterrestrials exist – which they probably do – then it doesn't logically follow that they're here (although they very well might be). Secondly, aliens are not likely to think in terms of 1950s sci-fi films. I doubt there are too many cosmic altruists out there, like the blatantly messianic "Mr. Carpenter" from *The Day the Earth Stood Still*. On the up-side, I don't think malevolently xenophobic civilizations are too common, either. Why destroy or enslave another civilization when posthuman reasoning suggests that advanced ET intelligences will be able to provide for themselves without assistance?

I really don't want to be an alarmist, but time is running out. Our weather patterns are showing ominous new trends; global warming continues; deforestation – and its brutal cousin, desertification – are hacking away at our biosphere's roots with the unheeding avarice of out-of-control clockwork. An ecological 9-11 might get our attention, but it also might consume too much of it: while we feebly try to restore order, an un-catalogued asteroid might be racing silently our way. Or the rain forests will unleash an airborne Ebola in an attempt to maintain some semblance of homeostasis.

Earth is dying under what William S. Burroughs aptly referred to as a mudslide of "devalued human stock." Don't think it won't fight back, even if its weapons seem initially superficial or quaint compared to humankind's iconic nuclear stockpiles.

I watch our planet steered by soulless multinational corporations and bigoted governments whose "future" is as reassuringly near as next month's NASDAQ or voter opinion polls. Is this how it ends, snuffed out into petrochemical oblivion before we make the critical move off-planet? Our space shuttles crash because they're obsolete, fragile museum pieces. But our smart-bombs are cutting edge: gleaming chrome and laser-light, avatars of technological cunning.

8 MARCH

The street preacher I encountered last week was at it again, his children dutifully handing out inane little pamphlets to embarrassed passersby. It was bitterly cold out. This son of a bitch should be locked up for child abuse.

9 MARCH

Looks like the antiwar protest is coagulating as I write, like a strange attractor in some lavishly holographic CGI representation; an abstraction clothed in flesh and bristling with cardboard sentimentality. I must descend to street-level to enjoy overpriced (but very good) coffee despite the slicing cold.

11 MARCH

I indulged at the used-book store after work. I could bore you with lists of books, but I won't.

I'm thoroughly disgusted with our government. I didn't think it would be this bad. Frankly, I figured Dubbya's installation as President would amount to stagnant, uninspired "business as usual" — apparently I "misunderestimated" my own unwitting prescience.

The world is full of worthless shits and mired in the apocalyptic fallacy that faith in the supernatural is a virtue; religion is more deadly than any nuclear stockpile, more obdurate than mere egomania. Arthur C. Clarke has called religion a "disease of infancy," implying that we have a chance of growing out of it. Which, of course, we must. And, biologically speaking, soon.

Bumper sticker concept: "LOSE YOUR RELIGION."

This sort of disgust can't be healthy.

12 MARCH

Nodal points
islands of stability
in binary neural fugue
livid and pulsating
Vegas psychedelia
LCDs and phosphors
left in the wake of an escaped singularity
endless screens
and calculated departures
an unnoted hush
encompassing vinyl
and cool glass partitions
resinous extruded signs
chrome railings marred
with anonymous DNA

13 MARCH

Blank computer screen like electro-fluorescent egg yolk.

I bought a massive case for my CD collection after work. This could keep my busy for a while.

Also, I can no longer claim that I don't own a television. Someone gave me one, unasked, the other day because it has a built-in VCR. So now I can watch videos, and possibly *Seinfeld* reruns.

Coffee tonight? I'm thinking yes. A double espresso would go well with Nietzsche's *The Antichrist*, which I bought on my lunch break.

15 MARCH

Something I really can't stand: Urbanites who drive Humvees. Do these brain-addled yuppie opportunists, and their even more pathetic middle-aged counterparts, really need military-spec vehicles to haul their fat asses across town?

The "reasoning" at work here seems to be that boosting gas consumption is penultimately manly: "I have so much money I can afford to fuel a military assault vehicle even at wartime gasoline prices!"

The vehicle itself certainly isn't anything to look at: it's cumbersome and ugly, like some extruded plastic Tonka toy built to withstand years of generalized pounding by some hyperactive toddler.

Other vehicles I hate: the "PT Cruiser." These aren't cars; they're massive dung-beetles with wheels. The streets are seething with automotive vermin. I also detest the "Mini Cooper," BMW's attempt at vehicular cuteness. The result is a garish, comical farce that looks more like high-priced athletic footwear than something you can actually drive – assuming you'd be caught dead behind the wheel of one of these soulless metal pods. There's something singularly disturbing about petroleum-fueled kitsch.

On a more somber note, I learned today that a high-school teacher of mine – who I liked very much – died in an accident (not car-related). I consider myself more acutely sensitive than most to the fact that death can happen anywhere at any time, without warning. I'm almost numb to it (aren't we all?). Still, I don't like ugly surprises anymore than anyone else. If one person's needless death can shock and terrify, magnify that horror by a factor of half a million or more. These are the numbers of "ugly surprises" enthusiastically plotted by the Bush Regime – for Iraq's own good, mind you.

Oil? Doesn't even enter the picture. This is about helping Iraq. Try as I might, I still can't wrap my mind around that concept. I suppose I'm terminally "un-American," and instead of chiding the hedonistic shitheads who like to be seen manning their (mercifully weaponless) Humvees, I should instead aspire to own one as soon as financially possible.

One large order of "Freedom Fries" to go, please.

16 MARCH

I just ate Chinese. Now I'm doing laundry and bemoaning the fact that my weekend is perishing by the second. I'm trying to siphon enjoyment from the remaining few hours like a spider draining the fluids from a paralyzed fly.

I'm reading Peter Watts' *Maelstrom*, a sequel to his first novel, *Starfish*. Watts is a singular talent who does a convincing job of rendering a believably catastrophic near-future. And his website is unusually entertaining.[4]

There is a candlelight antiwar vigil easily visible from my floor. Flames like the fuses of unseen bombs.

17 MARCH

I'm in a fairly dark mood. Learning of incipient war didn't exactly help. I feel like someone's rammed a dental instrument into my head and it's slowly easing its way out, leaving a wake of neurological scar tissue.

18 MARCH

I seem to be developing carpal tunnel syndrome, or something disturbingly like it. The dental instrument that had embedded itself in

---

4 Peter Watts. www.rifters.com.

my skull fell out overnight; I discovered it, bloodied and sheathed in coagulated pus, next to my pillow.

I'm in a generally foul mood. Why? I tire too easily. I find prolonged contact with other people oppressive. It's all I can do to limp through a week in order to spend time by myself reading over the weekend, which is becoming my only genuine pleasure.

Right now I'm reading John Keel's *The Complete Guide to Mysterious Beings*. I find the familiar voices on NPR increasingly annoying. More than ever, I'm a character in a Franz Kafka novel, displaced and alienated; the utter apocalyptic stupidity of Bush's pet war, *Columbia* disintegrating in flames, the death of old acquaintances, the death of Fred Rogers, you name it.

I must look on the bright side: William S. Burroughs' enduring canon, *Zippy the Pinhead*, William Gibson, espresso, R. Crumb, Portishead – Happy postmodern thoughts.

20 MARCH

Another gray day. The garish juxtaposition of bursting artillery against the mossy green of night-vision Baghdad; Dubya "talkin' smack" on TV, gazing wincingly at the teleprompter.

Somewhere, in a terminally abstracted parallel universe, people die.

"Christianity," wrote Thomas Jefferson, "is the most perverted system that ever shone on man."

Quotes like these from our "founding fathers" are a dime a dozen, yet windbags like Jerry Falwell have helped build an industry committed to America's alleged "Christian roots." The notion that the United States is a fundamentally Christian nation is a blatant lie perpetuated by the intellectually impaired.

Yet the mythos of Falwell, Robertson, et al gathers momentum. It has apocalyptic appeal; it's irresistibly simplistic. In a landscape propelled (and pummeled) by information, the quickest, easiest reality-tunnels become the most desirable. History becomes a sub-textual ink-blot. Reason perishes to make way for reassurance.

Religion – in all forms – is humankind's deadly legacy, infinitely more frightening than all the chemical warfare stockpiles on the planet. Weapons inspectors scour musty Mid-East basements in search of missiles and anthrax while oblivion incubates in their skulls, unnoticed.

If we ever manage to leave our planetary womb we cannot allow ourselves to take our debasing metaphysics with us. Perhaps vaguely anticipating a better (albeit unthinkably god-free) future, the Vatican actually has an assembly of priests devoted to "converting" possible extraterrestrials. Maybe the aliens will have a more robust sense of irony than I do and we'll be spared an *Independence Day*-style extermination.

21 MARCH

Support our troops; bring them home immediately.

22 MARCH

I bought Stephen King's *Dreamcatcher* tonight. I couldn't help myself; apparently it's King's take on the contemporary "alien menace" mythos. It's great fun to see how this particular meme spreads and mutates, and whether the commodification of the archetypal "alien" has anything to do with the close encounter phenomenon.

There are "real" aliens, and there are the aliens in our heads, ready to burst forth like hungry lizards from thick-skinned eggs.

How do we determine the difference?

Let me be clear: I think it's genuinely possible that we're being invaded by something "otherworldly." "Invasion" is almost certainly a shallow, imperfect term – especially since it appears to have been going on since prehistory. If "they" merely wanted to take over the world, "they" ("it"?) would have done so by now.

Something altogether weirder is happening. I suspect we lack the vocabulary to describe it. Are we getting closer? Possibly.

I succumbed and bought R.E.M.'s *Fables of the Reconstruction* tonight. This is a CD I had lost. My email dialogue with fellow R.E.M. fan and science fiction writer Peter Watts necessitated this purchase. I have an almost visceral need to hear "Maps and Legends." "Old Man Kensey" is playing as I type. I'd missed this one, too.

Today was devoted to reading 1.) *Maelstrom* and 2.) Keel's *Complete Guide to Mysterious Beings*. Keel suggests, fairly convincingly, that the UFO/paranormal intelligence wages a kind of psychological warfare against humans. Its primary motive appears to be deception. But to what end? Is this "intelligence" really intelligent in any meaningful sense of the word, or is it simply the by-product of Vallee's "unattended clockwork"? If we inhabit a computer simulation, as argued by Peter Gersten, then a built-in psychosocial conditioning system might be necessary to keep us from learning the Horrible Truth.[5]

Upon learning What's Really Going On – i.e., that we don't exist in any sort of ontologically palatable form – we just might shed the confines of Gersten's "Cosmic Computer System" and go on to infect some unthinkably vast cosmic Internet.

Perhaps terrestrial intelligence is akin to a sample of isolated germs used for occasional research purposes. Or maybe we're being allowed to evolve into something more hardy and virulent.

"Someone else" – in this case, a kind of godlike hacker – might have big plans for us.

23 MARCH

Large humanoid rabbits have once again infested the Plaza, the microcosmic consumer-culture observatory where I live (nine floors above the insolent, bag-toting crowds). I hate these damned things.

---

[5] Gersten is a lawyer based in Sedona, Arizona. He was a founder in the late 1990s of the advocacy group CAUS (Citizens Against UFO Secrecy). His website is www.pagenews.info. For his views on the "Cosmic Computer System," see "Peter Gersten – Part I," *Redstar Films YouTube Channel*, 9 October 2007. www.youtu.be/32f9PsI33BQ.

This year they're equipped with durable eyeballs that, presumably, won't be plucked from their sockets by idiot tourists. Somehow I'm not convinced.

I attended today's war protest briefly. Now that bombs are actually being dropped (as we all knew they would), the atmosphere is much less "hippie" and much more militant, with factions committed to accepting Dubbya's every whim. There were the obligatory "Support Our Troops" people there; I have no problem with supporting our troops, although my personal method of "supporting" them would be to get them the hell out of Iraq, not urging them on to some ugly corporate "victory" over mythologized "evil-doers."

I certainly support our troops. But I don't support the war they've been commanded to fight. Amazingly (well, perhaps not that "amazingly"), there's a large demographic that doesn't get the distinction. Apparently they think that antiwar activists secretly hope that our armed forces perish. American binary thought at its ignorant best – "Love it or leave it."

What about changing it for the better?

Is that an option?

Apparently Americans won't entertain any sentiment that can't be reproduced on a bumper-sticker.

Make no mistake: a large portion of the pro-war crowd likes this pyrotechnic display of force. They're getting off on it. And isn't it a bit curious that Iraq has yet to counter Allied devastation with those "weapons of mass destruction" that supposedly precipitated this thing to begin with? As a friend reminded me, we'll find them eventually. Even if we have to plant them ourselves.

Any pretense that "Operation Iraqi Freedom" (I think they're actually calling it this) is about anything but oil and geo-economic control has evaporated into utter nothingness. But now that we're safely committed to wholesale slaughter, minor considerations like this have predictably faded into the background, like mute, red-shifted stars.

24 MARCH

This evening I finally signed the official contract for my book, *After the Martian Apocalypse*. It will be published by Paraview Pocket Books, a recent imprint of Simon & Schuster dedicated to weird phenomena, in early 2004. I'm getting paid for this, obviously, but to my surprise I'm also getting 50 free copies. And I get royalties, too. This is certainly a step in the right direction, and I'm excited.

25 MARCH

Does the new century/decade have a flavor yet? The 80s and 90s certainly did. Presumably the 70s did too, but I was only around for five years of them and remember very little. I could have been raised by aliens and I'd never know it. Actually, that would explain a lot.

My internal calendar is marked by offbeat "defining events." The first was 1987, when Whitley Strieber's *Communion* was published, even though I didn't read it until much later. In 1991, R.E.M.'s *Out of Time* came out, and that set the tone for my high-school existence; *Monster*, released in '95, kicked off my college experience (or lack thereof).

Since 1998 or so it's been a blind and unheeding dive into adulthood, punctuated with bursts of existential panic. I feel simultaneously about 10 and about 90.

26 MARCH

Dubbya is, without argument, the most ardent, sincere humanitarian history has ever seen. How else to explain his otherwise inexplicable actions? Dismissing the prospect of geo-economic control as wild-eyed nonsense, he claims his war is solely to liberate Iraq from the dystopian regime of Saddam Hussein. Certainly a noble ideal.

And Dubbya is a president who stands by his ideals in the face of opposition. Dubbya abandoned the United Nations' attempts at diplomacy – which were beginning to reap fruit – to begin his war as soon as possible. This act may seem puzzling until one remembers his outspoken commitment to the liberation of the people of Iraq. Possibly more difficult to understand (at least to those who haven't recognized Dubbya's stringent, consummately humanitarian standards) is the strange fact that Dubbya has ordered an all-out "liberation" assault despite protests from the Iraqi people themselves.

Foolish commentators who don't understand Dubbya's utterly selfless principles might assume that the people of Iraq have a clearer perspective with which to weigh the damages of war than a bone-headed American technocrat; after all, they've lived under Hussein's rule and frankly acknowledge that they want a change, just not under conditions of violence perpetrated by imperialist outsiders. But those commentators would be wrong. Dubbya's devout humanitarianism will not be dampened by something as inconsequential as lost human lives. His principles are, after all, arbitrarily lofty, quite possibly beyond reach of mere mortals. "Liberation of Iraq" must proceed!

Today an "errant missile" killed 30 civilians as they went about their business. The fortunate ones were literally blown to pieces, their brains and severed hands angrily wielded by the explosion's survivors, who had the insolence to condemn Dubbya's humanitarian crusade of liberation in a pitiful – and frankly quite sickening – show of ingratitude. There will doubtlessly be more sacrifices in the next weeks, followed by more whiny condemnations of the United States' arrogance and brutality.

One eventually wonders how Dubbya's passion for Iraqi liberation can possibly persist in the face of such blatant military error.

One is almost tempted to wonder if there are other, unspoken factors at play.

But no. Impossible.

Dubbya is simply the first of a disconcerting new breed of humanitarian; to question his acumen is to join the ranks of the suffering Iraqi people who, in their merely temporary distress, dare to question (or denounce) his self-proclaimed rule.

27 MARCH

Instead of a uniform, coherent "I," a multiplex identity consisting of the mere sum of its parts: incognizant subroutines going through their mentational labors. A dysfunctional "society of the mind." Clockwork gristle. Dueling peptides. A frothing neural regime governing context, Self, external/internal. Reality shivers and freezes; a cold trickle of awareness plotting escape to more flexible substrates.

Tonight I began reading *The Hunt for Zero Point*, a nominally "mainstream" examination of secret technology, UFOs and antigravity. Are flying saucers of terrestrial invention? Is the entire "alien" conception an elaborate guise perpetrated by the military-industrial-mythological complex? I return to these questions obsessively, like Kafka's intrepid ice-skater practicing "where it is forbidden."

My best guess at this point is that scientists have indeed cracked the "gravity barrier," winning the attention of at least one otherworldly (although not necessarily extra-planetary) intelligence. Maybe there really is an alien "pact" of some sort – an interface probably defying trite political dynamics.

Who's in control? And how to reconcile "visible" events such as the Iraq conflict with this larger, veiled reality? Microcosmic gods vs. greedy bureaucrats: neither possibility is appealing.

28 MARCH

The entire Muslim world, not to mention Europe, knows the U.S.-led war for what it is: an invasion, not an altruistic "liberation" effort.

And by attacking (oops – I meant 'liberating') Baghdad we're setting the stage so Iraqi military scientists can eventually ply their trade as freelancers. Having them all under Saddam's iron-fisted regime was actually very convenient from a strategic point of view. Now they're going to be all over the world cooking up nukes and who knows what else for the highest bidder; there's more than enough "missing" plutonium with or without Iraq's proverbial (but strangely unseen) "weapons of mass destruction." The "hornet's nest" analogy is beginning to look uncomfortably apt. Duck and cover!

Strangely, for someone who doesn't watch TV (let alone stare into the maelstrom of CNN), this war has colored my thoughts lately, very much an unwanted invasion in its own right. I need to attain cool, cosmic detachment lest I disintegrate.

Chapter 4

April 2003

1 APRIL

It must be real fucking easy to condemn a bunch of teenage soldiers to possible death when you're a "born-again Christian" who thinks that people have immortal souls that go to Heaven when they die. Let's see what you've got, Bush. Suit up, parachute into Baghdad and give this country a lesson in patriotism. God's on your side, after all.

I think I finally realized what this insanity might be about. Rumsfeld may well be a complete bloody idiot, but my paranoid side says he's craftier than the Iraq "liberation" disaster would have us think. To maintain a "New World Order," one must have an equally pervasive New World Disorder. Hence a swiftly crumbling relationship with the Muslim world that will very likely keep us up to our necks "liberating" neighboring countries for years, if not decades. Oh, yeah – and it plays off America's most bigoted, xenophobic fears, too, ensuring that everyone's too busy "supporting our troops" to get a straight answer.

Perhaps grotesqueries like this are what our factory-like public "schools" are really all about: deprive a child access to critical and creative thought and you wind up with a malleable, broken excuse for a human being that's good for basically one thing: following orders. A lot of these drones are likely to join the armed forces – another plus; the New World Order will require a lot of meat if the festivities are to continue.

The US has launched probes to the planets, sent humans to the Moon, erected fantastic cities, and produced brilliant art.

A nation that can do these things can remove one sad, twisted fuck from an office he was never elected to in the first place.

3 APRIL

I'm typing this with a brand-new keyboard, purchased impulsively today while on a rare visit to my hometown of Independence, Missouri. I was tired of having to super-glue the spacebar on the last one. It was cheap and somehow obstinate, in the way that only electronic hardware can be.

The dental visit was a pleasure. Apparently I'm grinding my teeth at such a rate that they'll basically cease to exist by the time I'm 50 unless Expensive Dental Procedures are undertaken. Needless to say, I'm taking them, albeit with a little reluctance.

I was tempted to ask the hygienist if she could simply spray my teeth with a protective carbon monomolecular laminate but thought better of it.

4 APRIL

Remember 9-11?

You know, when Palestinians bombed the Empire State Building, or something like that?

Remember all of the tear-jerking iconography that infected our streets immediately thereafter?

It's back!

Clip-on flags fluttering from the cabs of pickup trucks whose drivers assail us with wit such as "Real Men Love Jesus." It's like a bloom of noxious toadstools. Shiny "American Pride" stickers: "These Colors Don't Run." You've seen 'em.

The one I like the most informs viewers that "We Will Never Forget" 9-11-01. Let me make something clear: as atrocious as the attacks were, in a million years the human race will have ceased to exist in any recognizable form, and I somehow doubt anyone's going to give a damn about them.

If humans are around in a mere few thousand years (in one mind-boggling posthuman incarnation or another), they will have necessarily made it past this "God and Country" fixation that presently engulfs the world like a grisly caul.

5 APRIL

I agree with the basic sentiment being voiced by the anti-war protests, but a somewhat more nagging portion of my brain is appalled at how big and dumb they are. Don't take this as "waffling" on the Iraq issue. I think the Dubbya administration's invasion of Iraq is monstrously wrong-headed. And I don't think that protests are necessarily anachronistic. But they need to mutate. I'm tired of the trite slogans and simplifications that fuel the wrath of the pro-war crowd.

In an earlier post, I suggested that Americans are unable to digest a concept that can't be reproduced on a bumper-sticker. But that holds true for the antiwar "movement" as well as for the Bush-loving God 'n' Country crowd.

Unfortunately, large gatherings of angry people are not amenable to subtlety. Doubly unfortunately, most people are immune to subtlety anyway. The Iraq war is a multilayered malignancy with a host of ugly and complicated geopolitical nuances and needs to be attacked as such. So we're left with the confounding problem of "wising up the marks." And quite honestly, I don't think we'll succeed.

Maybe after a few more civilians have been casually butchered and the forerunner of the U.S.'s quasi-occupational government is doing its thing, a few more people will have the nerve to address this atrocity sensibly. In the meantime, we'd be well served to abandon this idiotic fascination with "good" and "evil" that's predictably entered the wartime lexicon. Dubbya might inhabit a storybook universe governed by religious abstractions, but that doesn't mean you have to fall for his speeches.

In the cartoon language of placard-wielding street protesters, "Support Our Troops – Bring Them Home" makes a certain amount of sense. I've expressed the same sentiment in this blog. But these people weren't drafted. Even in a society that promotes xenophobia and the pragmatic fiction of absolute good vs. absolute evil, it doesn't take a whole lot of brains to realize that signing up with the armed forces just might mean being forced to kill people for reasons with which you may not personally agree. Ideally, by retooling the Orwellian machine that passes for "education" in this country, there will simply be no troops to order into battle.

And, one hopes, no soulless control-freaks to condemn them to slavish "patriotism" in the first place.

7 APRIL

I have an implacable nostalgia for urban decay, derelict architecture, ideas quick-frozen in bleached anonymous concrete, the echo of unheard fountains in emptied shopping malls, expanses of forbidden parking lots, rusted and unusable fire-escapes mounted to the sides of weathered, defeated buildings, solemn ranks of archaic grain silos and smoke stacks hovering like pale, listless fingers over forgotten horizons, paralyzed escalators, the demeaning glow of fluorescent lamps, institutional tile off-seat by time-beaten steel and peeling vinyl.

8 APRIL

I'm turning into a William Burroughs scholar of sorts. Rereading biographies, buying "restored" versions of his books — what next? If Burroughs was still alive I'd probably be pounding on his door in Lawrence: "Open up! You're the only sane person left on this planet! Please speak to me!"

Actually, I did exchange words with Burroughs once, at a symposium at the University of Kansas. Usually meeting authors is boring. It's their books we're interested in, after all. And while I didn't "meet" Burroughs, it was almost intolerably cool just to have him sitting nearby.

In other news: Boy, we sure "liberated" some Iraqis today, huh? A field correspondent on NPR said that the hospital in Baghdad had stopped keeping track of the bodies. Fifteen of them had been stuffed in a freezer to keep them from rotting prematurely.

The US blew Iraqi TV headquarters to smithereens, of course. Why? Most likely to seal a potentially nasty public relations breach: I doubt Dubbya is too keen on the idea of actual reality intruding on his crusade in the form of televised corpses. It's in bad taste. And it's unpatriotic.

We should all be buying Precious Moments "freedom fighter" figurines (yes, these infernal goddamned things actually exist) and tying yellow ribbons around trees and in general acting like the brainwashed numbskulls we're inexorably becoming.

Maybe I should stop reading Burroughs for a while. I've heard those *Left Behind* books are addictive!

9 APRIL

It appears as if the war has ended. Predictably, Saddam is missing in action, leaving a sequel of some kind as a possibility. CNN's already purchased the rights. And more worryingly, no sign of any weapons of mass destruction.

Not that Dubbya has to worry; I think the public has dutifully forgotten that they were the reason we invaded to begin with. Ostensibly, of course. Nothing about this war has been presented in a coherent manner by the administration. The White House has trotted out one of the most ridiculous parade of lies, distortions and omissions in modern American history.

Still, some of our estranged international neighbors might not take the Missing Weapons of Mass Destruction issue lightly. Even now questions are being asked, like: "If they had them, why the hell didn't they use them"? Allow a moment's paranoia: I think that if the pressure to come clean with evidence to "justify" this conflict is focused enough, the US will gladly "arrange" for some WMD to be found. But I'm getting ahead of myself.

While Iraqi looters throw shoes and overturn Saddam Hussein's statue (with the help of a photogenic US tank), the country's intellectuals – even the most ardent Saddam haters – are paralyzed with despair over the encroaching political melee. Meanwhile the rest of the Middle East is wondering who will be the next country lucky enough to get "liberated" (Iran? Syria? Maybe eventually Egypt?), and is gelling into something of a pro-jihad consortium.

This whole turn of affairs is curiously predictable. Has Dubbya read too many *Left Behind* books? Could the raison d'etre behind the last few months' geopolitical derring-do be to set the stage for an "Armageddon" conflict? Dubbya's minions loudly remind the public that the war has nothing to do with oil. But they're relatively quiet on the religion front, perhaps sensing a level of historical absurdity. After all, the crusades were a long time ago, and surely irrelevant. But not to Muslims.

We have disturbed the hive. We have shaken it, beaten it with sticks, poked it until its sides are dripping and buzzing with pure insect menace. When the next wave of terrorist strikes hits, there won't be enough paper for the "God Bless America" bumper stickers we'll be needing.

10 APRIL

I got a ticket for running a red light while driving home from work today. It was pretty iffy, and the police officer seemed reluctant to write me up. Actually, I don't think he was going to until he went back to his squad car and talked on the radio; evidently the city of Overland Park, Kansas is hard up for cash. What a wonderful way to end the day.

At least he wasn't an asshole. No tough-guy routine like you get with some cops.

11 APRIL

Started a new story today:

Anime stepped from the recessed bed, cool recycled air playing against her bare skin. She glanced down into the shallow contoured basin that held the gel mattress; the man's sleeping body had curled into a fetal position beneath the randomly flickering translucent sheets. She was reminded of insect pupae, snug in cocoons of dried slime while the world progressed around them as if in time-lapse.

The buoyant lunar gravity seemed to caress her as she navigated the darkened bedroom. She had never known the torturous pull of Earth or the chest-constricting push of take-off. Her bones, though augmented by supplements and periodically refreshed by nanomachines, were as temperamental as so many glass sticks.

The bedroom was cavernous: faceted walls, dormant flat-screens, polished lunar regolith that absorbed shadow like vampirish sponge. Silicates extracted from lunar soil had been turned into walls of opaque glass, inset with palm-sized newsfeeds and free-form holography. The screens bled light, illuminating transparent furniture, scattered components of virtuality workstations. A brain-link lay coiled on the floor between her feet, nasal studs encrusted with blood and mucus. The man she had slept with had used it before they had gone to bed, his eyes staring at nothing.

One side of the room featured a louvered window, shut to block the unfiltered glare of the Sun across the ash-gray plain. Invisible retinal scanners sensed the intent in her eyes and the louvers parted with a quick whispering sound. The man continued sleeping, chest heaving beneath the sheets. Mossy-green light played across his closed eyelids, synched to his brain rhythm by the room's mindful AI.

Standing naked in the dark, she wondered if she was something more than the AI, or possibly just a mere extension of its sensory embrace. She knew what she was; had seen her own skin lifted from a frothing vat like a pinkish wetsuit, hands like empty gloves, facial features deflated into a thoroughly demeaning caricature. The techs had installed her sense of body-identity before adding the actual body; her abrupt adolescence had been spent in a grueling immersive dialogue with Turing auditors.

Her first vision of the world – the real world, as opposed to the auditors' cybernetic fictions – had come when her body had achieved a semblance of womanhood. She remembered awakening in a scalding foam of nano-machines, gloved hands drawing her up into a haze of disembodied eyes and fluorescent strips that left rungs of purple light on her newborn retinas. She knew intuitively why the techs were wearing rebreather masks: rogue nano. She was an infestation in the form of a woman, to be handled with obsessive care.

Shortly thereafter, the first of her implanted memories had risen to the surface, silent and impersonal as newsfeeds. She knew they weren't true memories – her designers hadn't wanted to deceive her into adopting some phantom past. Not for her convenience, but for theirs; her sudden emergence on the Moon would have taxed any fictitious past, breaking its own narrative stability and quite likely her psyche in the process.

The Moon appeared behind the polarized glass: a tortured yet somehow peaceful surface of petrified dunes and hulking rocks that gleamed near-silver in the light from the landing beacons. The Earth was an anonymous crescent, defining features veiled by cloud. Memories: episodic flashes of oceans overgrown with a gray, fibrous substrate, hordes of metal insects dripping their armored eggs over quarantined cities. A mushroom cloud seen from a great distance: as insubstantial as a cheap hologram – not the incandescent orange she would have expected had the memory actually been hers, but a sickly luminous gray-brown, the unassuming color of a camouflaged moth.

She walked away from the window, a chill creeping up her legs as she headed for the bathroom and donned a thin white robe that adjusted itself to her contours with a flourish of piezoelectric trumpets. Above the toilet – little more than a streamlined bulge emerging from the yielding dun-colored tile – was a mirror. She looked into it, wincingly, bothered by the quizzical stare, lank black hair, pursed lips.

13 APRIL

I tried to take a nap yesterday but some guy with a megaphone was standing over by the Horse Fountain shouting out some masturbatory tirade against the Iraq war. And this was Saturday – the big antiwar protest is today, so the Plaza's probably really in for some incendiary amplified rants. I suppose I should be glad the war is being opposed – and I am – but I've become horribly cynical about the protest scene, with its limp slogans and quaint simplifications. I still don't know exactly what's going on. The war and the administration that spawned it is a diabolical hall of mirrors. The best I can do is make educated guesses and try not to become a drooling conspiracy-monger.

14 APRIL

In a strip a few days ago, cartoonist Bill Griffith noted that Dubbya doesn't pronounce "terrorist" correctly. He contracts it into two syllables: "terrist." To say nothing of his persistent mangling of "nuclear."

The United States is spiraling into a fetid vortex of unbridled stupidity. Blind faith, unquestioning adoration of authority and indefinite suspension of creative/constructive thought have become fixtures of the new American Dream, powered by an out-of-control government, soulless yet nonetheless sinister corporations, and an obliging mass media. I'm tired of this crap.

I demand a world free of opportunistic, pathological politicians, arrogant underhanded agendas, and the ever-present threat of convulsive violence. I demand an immediate end to all cottage industries and retailers who are profiting from ignorance in the form of "heartwarming" gaudy figurines and omnipresent flags. I demand an end to shitty, mass-produced music and the spineless drones who listen to it.

I've had more than enough of pop stars, post-modern media spectacles, infotainment, edutainment, civilian casualties, pretentious novels, professional athletics, gun-happy policemen, religion in any shape or form, with the possible exception of Buddhism, spurious medications for nonexistent psychopathologies, obnoxious holidays, SUVs, "What Would Jesus Do?", the abortion "debate," NASCAR, genetically modified foods, viral epidemics, depleted uranium, "Shock and Awe," hunting, pub-crawls, Starbucks, "poetry slams," vanity presses, et cetera.

You know, I thought the 21st century might be cool. It had promise. But unfortunately it's just a lot more of the same old tired shit.

15 APRIL

The 1980s and 1990s spawned once of the most satisfying mythologies of the 21st century. In essence, it goes like this:

The U.S. government has known that UFOs are alien craft since the late 1940s (actually, not totally impossible). Formal contact with the aliens was established in the 1950s. Shortly thereafter a deal was struck between the government and the extraterrestrials: the aliens would be allowed to abduct citizens for research and experiments in exchange for technological information.

Here the line of reasoning suffers a critical fracture: why would a star-faring — or dimension-hopping, depending on who you ask — alien species need our government's permission to do anything? One would think it could do as it wished with impunity, much how we tag and research ants without bothering to "negotiate" with their representatives. While I don't necessarily preclude the idea of some form of official human-alien contact, the human-alien "deal" recounted in the Silent Invasion Myth strikes me as very questionable — unless, of course, the ETs were simply staging the whole thing.

It was supposed to work like this: the aliens would furnish the government with a list of their human abductees, never going over "quota." But soon the horrible truth became apparent: the aliens were abducting more than their legal share of unwitting humans! And to top it off, they were performing grotesque biological experiments with cattle and leaving their handiwork in plain view! How insolent! Moreover, some of the abductees weren't coming back.

One naturally wonders if the government knew exactly what kind of "research" the aliens were up to when it signed its Faustian pact. Apparently the aliens duped the humans into thinking they were nothing more than benign interstellar anthropologists, free of ulterior motives.

The brass panic. Although armed with some ET-derived technology (possibly including crashed alien vehicles such as the one allegedly discovered at Roswell, New Mexico), they realize they're no match for the aliens (or, as they are now known, the "Grays"). Pandora's Box has been unleashed.

But that's not all. You know those experiments the Grays have been up to? They're secretly creating a hybrid alien-human species adapted to terrestrial conditions. In other words: pod people! They're going to take over the goddamned planet!

But the Grays are a sympathetic bunch, in a way. They've destroyed their home planet through environmental abuse and direly need a fresh source of DNA to invigorate their gene-pool. That's where we come in.

The basic idea here (i.e., impoverished aliens seeking to better their condition by invading another planet) is much the same as H.G. Wells' in *The War of the Worlds*. Some say the issue is deeper than this, and suggest that the Grays are actually interested in the human spirit, as opposed to our genome. Many writers and close encounter "experiencers" have postulated that the Grays can transfer and manipulate souls about as easily as people change the oil in their cars. Some embrace this quasi-religious interpretation while others vehemently denounce it as "New Age" babble.

In the meantime, UFOs continue to be seen. Some are human-piloted alien vehicles while others are ET. Abductions continue, as do cattle mutilations (or "mutes"): evidence that the Grays are still perfecting their "master race" of hybrids.

Where is this happening? According to a variety of leaked documents and insider testimony, the Grays have either built or taken over underground bases in the American Southwest, colonized the ocean floor, and constructed bases on the lunar far-side in which to further their goals for planetary conquest. Invasion is imminent.

Further complicating things, an unknown government agency appears to be actively assisting the Grays (or is it the other way around?) during horrific kidnappings known as "MILABs" (for "military abductions"). Military personnel – apparently the same crowd that tools around in unmarked black helicopters – have supposedly been seen working with Grays in an unknown context.

Is there an ultimate common agenda on behalf of the "hidden government" and our ET visitors?

This is, of course, the "downer" version of the Gray mythos. Other variations exist, and in some of these the Gray aliens are seen as Christly figures helping to prepare the human race for impending ecological catastrophe.

16 APRIL

I'm going to lay off the Iraq issue. It's being covered ad nauseum by others. I will remain vigilant, but I don't want to become redundant. So unless I have a profound or original insight, I'll spare you my kvetching. I'm not apologizing, by the way. I just don't want to run this blog into the ground dwelling on trends that should be apparent to any thinking person.

My central stance, for readers who don't feel like slogging through the archives, is that the US administration has been dishonest in its portrayal of Iraq as a threat. I think the "War on Terror," as it is being waged right now, is a politically prudent fiction whose primary goal is to reinvent the world political stage for reasons that, on close inspection, appear to be less than noble and certainly not worth the huge loss of life witnessed in the last few weeks.

But enough about that for now.

I began reading Colin Wilson's *Alien Dawn* last night. So far I'm very impressed. Wilson realizes that the concept of alien contact is thoroughly interconnected with other mysteries. UFOs and abductions, whatever these things turn out to be, are not discrete phenomena that can be plucked from the experiential world with a pair of tweezers and examined in isolation; they're components of something bigger, more confounding, yet possibly more coherent than we typically expect.

Wilson thinks in the same basic vein as Philip K. Dick, R.A. Wilson and Jacques Vallee: postmodern, quantum-era intellectuals who realize that "reality" is being orchestrated, manipulated and consequently hidden. Existence is a juxtaposition of cosmic conspiracies and battling memes. "Nothing is true; everything is permitted."

Our species has taken the easy way out. We've forfeited the achingly weird and beautiful realm of expanded consciousness in favor of trite information management and "politics of the imagination." Reality is a much more complex place than we've allowed ourselves to acknowledge. We're committed to a stupor of denial and politically correct "skepticism," believing in outlandish religious fictions but denying laboratory evidence that quietly but forcibly expels our assumed rule over a "material" world. We like reality spoon-fed to us in Platonic blocks because our cognitive digestive system has atrophied almost beyond repair.

If close encounters mean anything at all, my guess is that they're deliberate shocks to our ontological framework. Nothing is more unnerving than something "alien," even if the special effects are dredged up from our Jungian unconscious. But our visitors go a step farther: they're often absurd, mocking, unbelievable caricatures of what we suppose aliens "should" be like. Close encounters are innately psychedelic experiences that challenge the senses as well as the intellect, all the while ducking the radar of our fact management priesthood.

New Agers talk about saintly extraterrestrials who are here to rescue us from ourselves, or to hasten the transition to a new form of being divorced from workaday materialism. They may be close to the truth, although I personally doubt that the "aliens" (if that is indeed what they are) are altruists in the conventional sense. I also doubt that there is an impending change in global consciousness. Our visitors have always been here to whisper strange warnings in our collective ear. The goal, ironically, might not be change so much as homeostasis.

17 APRIL

SARS is an unknown disease. We don't know where it came from; the possibility exists that it came from space or was cooked up by a terrestrial lab. Already, the virus is mutating. Just beneath the calm surface of newspaper headlines, a viral storm is brewing. We'll probably weather this one out. But what about the next one? And the one after that?

A barrage of mutations, new vectors, failed quarantines. A choking silence engulfs the planet.

19 APRIL

I mentioned that SARS might be extraterrestrial. I wasn't joking. Noted astronomer Fred Hoyle pioneered the concept of panspermia, and concluded that life on Earth almost certainly originated not on the planet's surface, but in the warm, watery interiors of passing comets. I read his book *Diseases from Space* a couple years ago and was very interested in his study of flu outbreaks. Strong circumstantial evidence indicates that new flu strains arrive from above, evidently from space.

In 2001 a research team detected unknown organisms thriving in the upper atmosphere: they very well could have been ET microbes that had taken up temporary residence. The prospect is totally plausible, but "experts" seem to have an ingrained aversion to things dealing with space; consequently, the necessary research isn't being done.

I'm reading a new science fiction book called *Slave Trade*, by Susan Wright. I'd read Wright's book about Area 51, which held my interest (although it wasn't nearly as well-executed as David Darlington's *Area 51: The Dreamland Chronicles*). *Slave Trade* – the first in a projected trilogy – is a disconcerting *Star Trek* rip-off in which aliens kidnap humans, who are horrified (and sometimes thrilled) to discover that they are prized as sexual delicacies.

I immediately e-mailed Wright about the biological implausibility of an alien species finding Earthlings sexually desirable. Her response was sincere yet somehow flippant, and totally unconvincing. I pointed out that I tended to doubt the "real life" alien abduction theories of Budd Hopkins and David Jacobs, who think that the "Grays" are manufacturing a hybrid species using alien and human DNA. This is roughly as likely as a human mating with a grasshopper and producing viable offspring. Hopkins and company would insist that either:

1. the Grays are related to us, allowing genetic compatibility; *or*
2. the Grays are extremely talented genetic engineers.

But if "2" is the case, why the fascination with human DNA? Why don't the aliens just synthesize it? Surely the supposed "abduction program" is inefficient and redundant. Unless, of course, the extraction of reproductive material is a metaphor for something else. This is Dr. John Mack's take. I personally think it makes more sense than Hopkins' doomsday scenario. If we're interacting with a muilti-dimensional intelligence as opposed to interstellar visitors, then this might have a strange limiting effect on the human mind and the mechanics of perception. The aliens' methods might seem primitive or nonsensical to us simply because our three-dimensional minds are incapable of grasping the big picture. There's actually a field of quantum physics that deals with this sort of thing.

21 APRIL

Maybe it's infantile or escapist, but I'd like to live a thoroughly wired existence. Brain implants. Cognitive enhancements. "Bionic" senses. Media players and cameras embedded in my eyes. Unlimited memory. 24-hour Internet access at the speed of thought. All on my own terms, of course.

While we're at it, let's eradicate the need for sleep. Sure, the dreaming part is neat, but life is just too damned short.

Last night I started Ken MacLeod's *Dark Light*, the sequel to *Cosmonaut Keep*. MacLeod is formidably intelligent and one of the top ten speculative writers working today. His stuff is sharp, surreal and very rewarding.

Sorry this is short; it's been a tiring Monday and I'll probably end up taking a nap. How pathetic. I've got things I want to do!

22 APRIL

This is a truly embarrassing thing to admit, but packing a laptop computer makes me feel "cool." I feel "with it," man. The reasons for this are probably science fiction-induced; if you read William Gibson's first three novels, you find his characters inhabiting an unspecified near-future where "cyberspace decks" are all-but-ubiquitous. Cyberspace decks are decidedly unlike most real computers, such as the Compaq Presario I'm writing this on. For one thing, they're sleek and very portable – kind of like a laptop.

My laptop has Gibson-esque potential. It's a token from the world of *Neuromancer* and *Count Zero*; its ideological lineage can be traced to nonexistent rain-slicked streets and the inescapable pallor of brooding outdoor holography.

Gibson made computers sound sexy. Of course, he didn't own one when he wrote *Neuromancer*, so he didn't know any better. J.G. Ballard intentionally reinvented the subtext of the automobile for his novel *Crash*. *Crash* is satire, although elusively so – *Neuromancer* was written with consummate punk naivete.

I have an apparent heightened sensitivity to the mass media. I can't tolerate radio or TV; both make me acutely uneasy. I'm not implying that it's a physical response, although sometimes the intensity of my reaction rivals a literal allergy. The single exception is NPR, which I can take in small doses before rewarding myself with a week or so of "media sabbatical."

My idea of ultimate stress relief is to be set loose in a room full of TVs with a baseball bat. Or maybe a gun, like Elvis. Not having fired a gun in my life, I don't know if this would have the same satisfying effect that bashing a screen with a bat would certainly produce. I'm guessing it would be OK.

Interestingly, I'm immune to the Internet. I hate spam and pop-up ads as much as anyone, but they don't piss me off the way TV commercials do. And while I really can't stand pervasive and unnecessary public cell-phone use, I think I'm getting used to it; I don't have to like it, but it doesn't bother me as much as it used to.

Other things I don't like:

1. Driving. I have a vague fear about driving. Nothing terrible or disabling, but I secretly wish for matter-transmitter pods, or at least ubiquitous mass transit.

2. Elevator buttons. Why do they make them so difficult to press? You really have to mash your finger against them at the proper angle. This is a very minor but potential annoyance.

3. Magazines about music. What's the point? They all look and read the same and they're all about the same bands/entertainers/whatever. Yes, there are exceptions. But not many.

4. Maya Angelou. I have a deep-rooted, largely unspecified hatred of Maya Angelou.

5. Trendy young "literary" authors. There's never a shortage of these. Their books are praised as unparalleled genius, prominently displayed in bookstores, and inevitably compared to Thomas Pynchon and/or William Burroughs. And they're all about the same thing: befuddled neo-Bohemians taking drugs and getting into confused relationships.

This list could go on forever.

23 APRIL

In most science fiction dealing with space exploration, space colonists leave Earth to find reasonably Earth-like planets to settle. In actuality, I think this will be quite rare: what do planets offer settlers? They're subject to extinction level events, nasty plate tectonics, uncontrolled mutation, and the caprices of climate.

It's more likely that future colonists will construct space stations. In space, construction is infinitely easier since nothing weighs anything. Tweaking our genes to support a space-borne existence is likely to be easier than "terra-forming" an alien world. Want gravity? A space station can be rotated to produce whatever amount of gravity you want (or, of course, none at all). Planets might be fun places to visit, but only eccentrics will choose to live there for any length of time.

Of course, while writing this, I realized I could argue persuasively for the other side of the argument. The important thing to remember is that futurism is less prediction than stream-of-consciousness. Who's to say with authority that we won't perfect gravity control (i.e., "antigravity")?

Who says we already haven't?

The scenario above seems to make sense from our perspective right now. But "right now" has an interesting way of going away really quickly. Colonists might prefer to use antigravity selectively while living on a planetary surface, or use an artificial gravity field while in a microgravity environment. It's simply not a matter of one or the other. Attempts to pin down the future will invariably fail – but hopefully in intriguing ways.

Antigravity totally upsets quaint ideas of rotating space stations. A few hundred years from now, film enthusiasts might watch the revolving, spoked space station in *2001* with the same kind of mirth we experience when watching cheesy movies of astronauts fending off giant spiders on Mars.

The multiverse continues to branch into alternate incarnations, all equally valid.

Meanwhile, I think it's profoundly disappointing that so many people can only "express" themselves through clip-on "designer" cell phone faceplates, bumper stickers, and obnoxious clothes. Compulsory corporate schooling has churned out a plague of mentally deficient cogs with no other means of self-expression. Of course, the trends they latch onto aren't "expressive" at all. It's just the best they can do given limited resources.

24 APRIL

It really struck me the other day how absurd our collective disinterest in nonhuman intelligence really is. To me, the possibility of nonhuman intelligence is absolutely pivotal. One could argue that I have a natural inclination toward "weird" things because of my literary interests. But are the things we deem "weird" really weird? Could our smugness be hindering our intellectual / psycho-spiritual / cognitive progress?

As planetary citizens, we're a dreadfully solipsistic lot. The mind-numbing holy trinity of Western civilization – religion, patriotism and professional sports – keeps us from asking basic questions. It's no surprise that answers are in short supply. We have entrusted the idea of extraterrestrial intelligence to a small and rigid priesthood of self-proclaimed skeptics (however sincere their intentions). The "alien" as a meme has been quarantined under the most stringent protocol. Occasionally we glimpse it retooled for the big screen in the form of *Independence Day* or *Contact*. Advertisers seem to have an inexhaustible penchant for using the alien meme as kitschy media fodder.

The consequences of this are intellectually devastating. Americans, in particular, have taken the "alien" inquiry and turned it into a ridiculously binary issue of "belief" in flesh-and-bone extraterrestrial visitors. But the possibilities are so much more fascinating, as Dr. Jacques Vallee and John Keel point out in *Passport to Magonia* and *The Eighth Tower*. We have allowed our imaginations to dim like so many cheap light bulbs.

My research has led me to the conclusion that the human race is indeed interfacing with some sort of nonhuman intelligence. I don't know what it is, where it comes from, or what it looks like (although if pressed I'd suggest that it could look like whatever it wants).

Whatever this intelligence is, it is unimaginably potent. If technological in origin – as it seems it must be, at least in some abstruse sense – then we're dealing with something very different than anything yet contemplated by humans. The evidence indicates it may desire to remain unknown (assuming it's knowable in the first place.)

By refusing to entertain "weird," potentially heretical ideas, we've disarmed ourselves against a universe bristling with epistemological weaponry.

26 APRIL

Synchronicity!

"Alien" encounters!

Paranormal activity!

I was enjoying a cinnamon latte and reading Colin Wilson's *Alien Dawn*, which contains some fascinating material on bizarre "coincidences." Then I walked home, turned on the computer, and the first message in my email box was a recounting of a minor weird coincidence from Steve Melling. Another layer to the the Jungian onion, or too much dopamine? Maybe the universe is constructed like a hypertext filing system (i.e., a "cosmic computer" like the one Peter Gersten talks about). Events with no apparent causal connection may be intersecting points in a multidimensional database or archive.

28 APRIL

Thinking is not an innate human skill. We're born capable of stimulus response, which we refine to varying degrees during the course of adolescence and adulthood. Thinking is an acquired skill, like learning to ride a bike. But unlike riding a bike, it's not a skill that can be conquered over a single afternoon. The distinction between blind stimulus response and actual thinking is crucial and almost entirely overlooked.

Everyone seems to be under the illusion that they can think, just as everyone with a political ax to grind "knows" that their cause is the "right" one.

In my experience, this couldn't be farther from the truth.

Chapter 5
May 2003

1 MAY

The following text appears in the current issue of my employer's online magazine. It's accompanied by a picture of a silhouetted soldier with a machine gun slung over his shoulder and a praying figure superimposed on the American flag:

> Thursday, May 1, 2003 is the 52nd annual National Day of Prayer. This is a wonderful opportunity to unite together, as one nation under God, to collectively ask for God's mercy and blessing on our country. We urge you to join us in Training Room at 11:05 A.M. as members of the ****** family come together to observe this special occasion and thank the Lord for His goodness to our nation.

It should be noted that my employer claims it doesn't discriminate based on religion, in which case the presence of this piece of emphatically Christian propaganda is rather difficult to justify. As a non-Christian, I'm bothered and very disappointed. Why does corporate America assume its constituents share the same faith? Perhaps more pressingly, why does it feel the need to tout religion in the first place?

If the "Day of Prayer" announcement is an attempt to create a sense of solidarity among employees, my employer is in blatant violation of its own supposedly non-discriminatory policy. Consequently it alienates those who don't happen to share in the belief than an omnipotent deity chooses to dish out "mercy and blessing" to the United States. Those who don't believe in the theocratic fiction that the US is somehow protected by divine will are implicitly told that they do not belong, that their input is inherently without value and that their belief system (or lack thereof) is starkly invalid.

My company's Christian rallying call (with its obvious "patriotic" connotation) is nothing especially new, and as much as I'd like to be able to blame it on the Bush regime's apocalyptic Christian rhetoric, I know its roots run deeper. Religion is about control. An administration (governmental or corporate) that can appeal to religious inclinations has an immediate monopoly on sentimentality. Americans, citizens of an ostensibly "godless" society, are victimized daily by self-righteous "authorities" who peddle hope, fear and pride in the form of religion. The ultimate goal is the destruction of self-worth and independent thought, two variables that pose toxic threats to conformist ideology.

Religion is virulently persistent. Any effort to excise it from our lives must first be able to detect its presence. Ironically, the theocratic drivel churned out by the post-9-11 Bush regime may be the administration's Achilles' heel. Now that its Christian hype and Fundamentalist leanings are flaunted as part of its Nazi-like program of coerced patriotism, the government can be more easily seen as the unconstitutional mutation that it is.

No more "One Nation, Under God." No more "In God We Trust." No more "God," period.

"Belief" is an illness. It almost makes me wonder if we were genetically engineered by beings who wanted to maintain a means of controlling our psyche. After all, computer programmers install "backdoors" through which they can covertly enter a machine's system architecture. Our willingness to believe in higher intelligence – when faced with the option of critical thought – is frightening indeed.

Arthur C. Clarke has called religion a "disease of infancy." My concern is that we will remain a stillborn species, failing to migrate into space because of the obsolete chips embedded in our brains.

Curiously enough, we don't hesitate to upgrade our computers to keep them up to speed. But we ignore the software in our own brains, never installing new components, not even scanning for the occasional virus. Humans are deficient by definition; we must mutate or we will fall silent, a genetic failure, a curiosity in the fossil record. As George Carlin has remarked about politicians, "Garbage in, garbage out." Are these mangled excuses for human beings the best we can do? Or are we caught up in a retroactive feedback loop? And this is assuming for the sake of argument that we live in a true democracy, which we certainly don't.

This planet is stifling. I feel trapped, glued to the ground by dogma and short-sightedness. My grumblings about Bush and his cohorts are actually aimed at a much larger spectrum of human failures, as if I'm single-handedly staving off the ideological detritus of an entire species.

And yet there is compelling evidence that we're not the only so-called intelligence around. Something vast and wonderfully cryptic is interacting with us, possibly extraterrestrial but more than likely multidimensional. We're so used to its presence that we're essentially blind to it, which is exactly what the "other" intelligence wants. Quantum physics offers a useful analogy: a quantum-level event cannot be accurately measured because of an apparent limiting mechanism in human perception. We can choose to observe the momentum or position of a subatomic particle, but never both at the same time. The alien intelligence in our midst seems curiously similar: it observes but fails to interact in a way that would fundamentally disturb the world at large. Perhaps it is simply incapable of doing so, just as particle physicists cannot defy the Uncertainty Principle. Or so it seems to us, trapped in three dimensions.

Scientists sympathetic to the UFO problem have wondered if there is something like a cosmic "hands-off" policy keeping alien visitors from making the explicit contact we've been trained to expect from science fiction. There is almost certainly some truth in this; the last thing a technologically or mentally superior intelligence would want to do is reveal itself in all its novel splendor unless it specifically wanted to exploit our predisposition for belief. There may very well be egomaniacal "gods" lurking in hyperspace, but it seems as if we're dealing with something more akin to an infestation of goblins. I suspect they (if it's a "they," which is far from certain) are using our collective unconscious as a means to propel us forward along unseen psycho-evolutionary rails. So in a sense we're being exploited – but not for the alien intelligence's short-term ego-glorification. Whitley Strieber might have said it best when he wrote, simply, "It seeks communion."

Hence my interest in the alien-human hybrid phenomenon, whether real or fiction. Dr. John Mack interprets encounters with nonhuman intelligence as "reified metaphor": the visitors' intentions manifested symbolically. There may be no flesh-and-blood hybrid fetuses sulking in vials of synthesized amniotic fluid. But the implications they conjure – the joining of two worlds, the intimate juxtaposition of the alien and the familiar – achieve the desired end nonetheless.

2 MAY

I see several of the same cars while driving to and from work, which I recognize from their bumper-stickers. I feel like the drivers (myself included) comprise some sort of secret club, and often wonder if they recognize my car, a thoroughly hideous white '86 Caprice that looks like it's survived several bomb explosions.

I think the first of these recurring vehicles I noticed was a white car with a so-hip-it's-lame Darwin fish and two bumper-stickers reading "Goddess Worshipper" and "Pagan and Proud." I've never gotten a good look at the driver, but I have the impression she's mousy and embittered. And I can't help but roll my eyes at this cleverly marketed "pagan" thing. Adherents of "Wicca" think they're rebelling against the status quo; instead, they're dutifully lining corporate pockets. "Rebellion" is totally commodified, just like everything else. I find the Darwin fish particularly insulting. $100 says this self-infatuated "goddess worshipper" doesn't even know who Richard Dawkins is.

Then there's this blue car with an upward-tilting Jesus fish. Seriously, how hard is it to glue one of these stupid things on the back of a car correctly? Does the tilted fish have some esoteric meaning I don't know about? Interestingly, the driver's a black guy – the only black person I've ever seen with a Jesus fish on his car. I thought the Jesus fish was the official icon of white trash. Apparently I was mistaken.

There's another car that I see occasionally while driving home. It boasts a glittery bumper-sticker that instructs me to "Expect a Miracle." Oh, really? Could you be more specific? From the shape the car itself is in, I'm guessing the driver's been "expecting a miracle" for a very long time now.

3 MAY

I've noticed that we're experiencing an outbreak of futurism.

A British astrophysicist thinks the human race may have reached its final century. The author of *Our Posthuman Future* anticipates humans becoming something substantially different. Meanwhile, the likes of Billy Graham and Tim LaHaye believe we have entered the dreaded "End Times" of biblical revelation.

Maybe both camps are somehow touching on a central truth, even if the latter relies on psychological terrorism to spread its memes. "Apocalypse" means "to unveil." This isn't a bad thing; there is no shortage of veils that need to be lifted. Perhaps when we finally do, we will have become avatars of the posthuman future.

6 MAY

Have you noticed how most people conform to a recognizable "template" or "operating system"? I meet people who are, in all respects except physical appearance, identical to countless others. I'm not saying they're subhuman zombies or selfless drones. But there's definitely something sobering about it. Are people really this easily conditioned? Or is it all just an act we play when interacting with each other, a kind of dehumanized neutrality?

Lastly but by no means least, why my smug conviction that I'm immune to it? It's more likely that I try quite desperately to blend in and just happen to fail. Or do I? It's unsettling: I have very little clue how I'm perceived. My intuition tells me this is a good thing.

It's probably a pointless exercise, but I can name a few famous people I feel I certain kinship with. Don't laugh.

1. William Burroughs. I'm really nothing like Burroughs. No bizarre life story, no consuming addictions (that I'm consciously aware of). I suppose I relate to Burroughs because he was iconoclastic; I've always had a problem with established "experts."

2. David Bowie/Michael Stipe. Here I'm probably just flattering myself. Both are consummately creative, which is certainly something I strive for. And I have a weird respect for the way they handle their celebrity – "weird" because I don't happen to be a celebrity. I never claimed this made any sense.

3. Franz Kafka. But then again, anyone who's read and understood his books must feel precisely as I do.

Oh yeah – and Robert Crumb. I'm self-obsessed and misanthropic, although probably more accessible (and slightly less neurotic) than Crumb.

Meanwhile, the "blogging" phenomenon was on NPR this morning. It's interesting how weblogs are routinely presented as a novel, subversive medium. I suppose they are, in a sense, but are they really the forerunners of the next communications revolution? I think the potential is there. It's too early to tell whether blogs will evolve into a social/cultural force to be reckoned with.

Audio-blogging is presently in vogue. I can imagine the info-sphere forty years from now, when bloggers have wireless devices grafted directly into their brains. Instead of sharing sound clips, imagine sharing dreams or flashes of dizzy intuition.

I don't think the concept of an electronic "hive-mind" is necessarily Marxist or depersonalizing. In fact, effortless access to consenting minds (human and otherwise) just might be the catalyst we need to shrug off our current geocentric consciousness. The larger the brain, the vaster the frontier. And new frontiers will spawn new and different varieties of minds.

7 MAY

I never see my neighbors. A couple guys moved in next door to me several months ago. I saw them in the process of moving their stuff in, but that was it. Sometimes I think I hear a muffled noise coming from my kitchen wall, but for all I know they're long gone. I certainly wouldn't recognize either of them if I saw them.

A week ago two more guys moved into an apartment on my floor. I haven't seen them since and really don't expect to. It's like once you've moved in, you become somehow incorporeal. Maybe all the apartments come pre-tuned to different dimensional frequencies; we could be passing right through each other in the hallway and in the laundry room without realizing it. A building full of quantum semi-persons, a hive of perfectly invisible bees.

8 MAY

The hype surrounding the new *Matrix* movie is interesting. Does some of the original film's appeal come from the premise that "reality" is a fraud used to control human beings, and not merely the great special effects and combat scenes? If what I think I know about the UFO intelligence – Philip K. Dick called it "VALIS" (for "Vast Active Living Intelligence System," which is about all he ventured as to its actual nature) – is correct, then we are indeed living in a simulation of sorts. No wires running out of our skulls, mind you; when you believe in something thoroughly enough, virtual reality pales in comparison.

We generally think we inhabit an unremarkable planet in a lonely universe spawned by an anthropomorphic Creator. I'm inclined to disagree with this. I think we inhabit a universe flooded with life and intelligence, some so exotic we simply don't recognize it as such from our provincial vantage-point. At least one of these intelligences appears to have seized on our capacity for belief to control us for ends that may be for our ultimate benefit but unquestionably cause untold suffering now. All of this is disquietingly *Matrix*-like.

I don't think our universe is merely a computer. More likely it's an intelligence itself, artificial or otherwise – possibly one of trillions that swarm through hyperspace.

12 MAY

Today was a quintessential Monday: labored, tiring and much too soon.

I have a fantasy of building a soulless android duplicate of myself and sending it to work in my stead, leaving me free to surf the Web, read and drink coffee. But with my luck the duplicate would start getting huge book deals and going on dates with beautiful women.

One of us would have to die.

13 MAY

If you're like me, you probably get a lot of email that goes something like this:

Due to my careful search for an honest, reliable and sincere business partner, i ask if you can be trusted not to break an agreement? Still, it took me time to make up my mind to contact you and to offer you this proposal of mine of which my whole life depends on.

Entertaining the idea that this isn't a crude rip-off (just for the fun of it), the logic and sentimentality here are interesting. Apparently this person, who introduces himself below, has been scouring the Internet for a potential business ally. Of his admission, his whole life depends on my trustworthiness. Isn't that an empowering idea!

Dear, my name is BANGOURA F.KABILA the son of the late president DR.LAURENT KABILA,the former president of ZAIRE (DEMOCRATIC REPUBLIC OF CONGO). I am 24 years old and presently residing in DAKAR-SENEGAL in West Africa under political asylum.

The plot thickens. This isn't some hopeless nerd; it's none other than the son of the late Dr. Laurent Kabila, former president of Zaire! And he's contacting me! What can I do for you, Bangoura?

My mother happens to be a nurse whom the late president had an affair with during his life style as a play boy,

Wait. This is suddenly taking on the flavor of a half-baked soap-opera…

and the affair resulted to my birth,but it was unfortunate that the late president did not marry my mother legaly and as a kind of settlement, for my mother and i,my father deposited the sum of Eight Million one Hundred thousand $US cash($ 8.1 million US.dollars cash) to my mother for my life inheritance.

Sorry for my interrupting. Did you say $8.1 million? Keep talking, Bangoura…

my father stashed these sum of money and deposited it in a financial house in DAKAR-SENEGAL and my name appears as the next of kin. After my father was killed by his body guard ealier last year 2001, and my mother died also ealier this year just two months after my father's death, and at the age of 24 years old,i am left with this huge sum of money ,and i need a partner who will help me transfer this money oversea for immediate investment as i have made up my mind to invest in your country.

"Invest in your country." Sounds like it could be Bush's campaign slogan in '04, doesn't it?

Your compensation for your immediate assistance is 5% of the total money as soon as it arrives your country while 2% will be for any local and international expences that will occure during the transfer.

Hmmm. 5% of $8.1 million is quite a bit – considerably more than I'm getting paid for my book about Mars, come to think of it. Maybe I should give Bangoura the benefit of the doubt. After all, he trusts me. And I feel a strange sort of kinship with him, almost like I've known him my entire life.

I will like truth and honesty to be our watchword in this business.

That's the spirit! For a second there I thought this might be a scam involving sharing my bank account with a total stranger!

You can contact me through my personal e mail address: bangorafk24@yahoo.co.uk Yours sincerely, BANGOURA.

Hang in there, Bangoura! Together we'll work this out! And sorry to hear about your mom!

14 MAY

The "end of the world as we know it" meme has achieved something eerily close to escape velocity.

Christian and Islamic Fundamentalists are fanning the flames of "end times" speculation, complete with high-budget special effects. The tech-geek core of the trans-humanist movement awaits the singularity, a nodal point when artificial intelligence and nanotechnology redefine the human condition in a single sweeping flourish. On the UFO front, true believers in a large-scale government cover-up anticipate official disclosure of an extraterrestrial presence on Earth, via government sources or from the aliens themselves.

This sense of anticipation has gelled into an almost palpable fog of incipience, a ubiquitous postmillennial funk, the raw psychic effervescence of which zeitgeists are made. But who's forging this emerging zeitgeist, with its curious emphasis on apocalypse? A collusion of advertisers, military strategists and New Age writers? Godlike alien intelligences?

I propose that we're dealing with a meme that has mutated in order to colonize different sectors of the collective unconscious. A meme is a life-form, no different than a virus (physically "real" or encoded as data and set loose to prowl the embryonic planetary brain we casually call "the Internet"). Our evolution has been hijacked by an automated intelligence concerned only for its own survival. Fortunately for the apocalypse-meme, we're willing and gracious hosts.

We must track down the origin of this meme. In doing so we will subvert its agenda and make the first tentative step toward the creation of something very new: a viral intelligence, shocked from its neural slumber and forced (at gunpoint, perhaps) to sprout an intellect to match its tenacity.

Somewhere in space-time, or perhaps encased in its Escher-esque folds, is our eternally abiding Patient Zero.

16 MAY

I think I might take in *The Matrix Reloaded* tonight. Then again, I might end up reading. I generally always enjoy movies but for some reason I have a massive reluctance to make the pilgrimage to the theater down the street and cough up $7. It always feels like a massive commitment. Maybe this explains my vacuous love-life.

Speaking of which, I took out a singles ad on Yahoo Personals. Why not? To my amazement, I received a reply today. I have no illusions about the overall effectiveness of online mingling but this was at least encouraging.

17 MAY

I'm reading Francis Fukuyama's *Our Posthuman Future*. To my dismay, he interprets "posthuman" as a thoroughly negative word, whereas I find it an extremely hopeful term: after all, it implies that there will be some form of presumably superior intelligence after merely human intelligence has vanished from the evolutionary stage. Scientists like Hans Moravec and Marvin Minsky grasp this. But Fukuyama, a philosophical polemicist, is more comfortable embracing "human nature" as is.

"Humanity" is a dead end. "Human nature" can be whatever we want it to be. Needless to say, these sorts of grandiose statements carry a great deal of ethical and philosophical ramifications, and I'm not suggesting for one moment that we ignore them. But I don't think Fukuyama's breed of conservatism is the answer we need if we're to escape the next millennium.

25 MAY

Isn't it weird how any mention of Iraq's dreaded weapons of mass destruction seems to have vanished from the mainstream media? Supposedly, the "WMD" issue was the reason the United States launched its hasty pre-emptive invasion. If the WMD ever truly existed in the quantities implied by the Bush administration, they now appear to be strangely missing (not to mention curiously unused during the actual conflict, which has left something like 6,000 civilians murdered).

My question: Why is the "missing WMD" issue being ignored? One would naturally assume that it would be the central political issue right now, a threat ranking with the Cuban Missile Crisis. After all, if these weapons existed, then they must have been spirited away by would-be terrorists, posing a grossly greater threat to US security than if they were confined within Iraq's borders.

The people who choose to believe that our invasion of Iraq was to relieve Saddam Hussein of weapons of mass destruction should team up with the Flat Earth Society. They're natural allies. The Iraq war, already fading from American consciousness with the rapidity of a particularly lukewarm TV commercial, was an atrocity, an evil fiction, a geopolitical fever-dream, and a rude glimpse of a future when the American public can be utterly and astoundingly duped in wholesale quantity. All it takes, it seems, is some bumper stickers, presidential "tough talk," and a complete disregard for human life and intelligence.

26 MAY

Apparently there's a new article in *Scientific American* about the multiverse; I tried to find it but couldn't. But undoubtedly many trillions of alternate Macs in other universes found it and are writing about it as I type this: a disquieting realization.

I call the world we think we inhabit the "ontosphere." It's rather like *The Matrix* in that it's basically synthetic and hallucinatory; control and power over "reality" is a carefully orchestrated feat of fact management overseen by self-appointed experts. Their weapons are religion and belief, drummed into our skulls by an omniscient media.

But the multiverse is like some monstrously potent secret weapon, an upwelling in the fabric of consciousness that, if exposed, promises to shatter normality.

Jacques Vallee, one of my favorite thinkers, thinks that we're interacting with denizens of the multiverse in the guise of flying saucers and absurd humanoids. Just as time, space and energy are different ways of addressing the same fundamental mystery (existence itself), sentience overshadows all three. The multiverse is intelligent, self-reflective, inscrutable, abiding.

William Burroughs, with characteristic prescience, urged the masses to "storm the reality studio."

Are we up to the task?

28 MAY

Yesterday was tiring after 3 days of idle productivity. I managed to read instead of falling asleep early. I think my apartment's pool is open now. It's between two high-rises so it's basically always in the shade and extremely cold, but agreeably so.

I'm getting a new cat on Friday. She's 8 weeks old. Not having more than one pet at a time before, I'm not sure how she'll get along with Spook (whom I've had since October and who feels imminently comfortable with my comings and goings). Ebe, the new cat, is an unforeseen variable. I hope they get along; I don't think I could handle waking up in the middle of the night to break up a fight.

While I'm on the subject of animals, I have a minor confession to make. Although I'm a vegetarian, I developed this uncanny hunger for cold fried chicken yesterday. Someone had left a tray of it in the office lunchroom, and I greedily ate a couple pieces. I don't feel particularly guilty, but I did break my meatless streak. Then again, I eat anchovy pizza regularly.

Celebrity watch: Ted Nugent is appearing at a local Borders to promote his new cookbook called – get this – *Kill It and Grill It*. I never really knew who this guy was until I started leafing through his

first book called – again, get this – *God, Guns and Rock and Roll.*
Charlton Heston, gun-nut extraordinaire, is on record claiming
Nugent as "one of the good guys" due to his tireless promotion of
what Heston somewhat cryptically terms "outdoor sports." I suppose
what he actually means is "hunting."

I wish to make something clear. "Hunting" – whatever one thinks
of it – is not a "sport." The deer, elk, bears and god-knows-what-else
that hunters go out to kill aren't on an opposing "team." Far from it;
they just want you to get back in your pick-up and go the hell away.

If hunting is a sport, why do the humans always win?

And why do the humans always get to decide the rules?

Just once, I'd like to see some suburbs laid to waste by murderous
bears with AK-47s.

29 MAY

The Matrix Reloaded has taken its share of heat from fans of the
first movie. I liked the movie quite a bit but I also found room for
complaint. Here's a quick list of problems – many of which, sadly,
could have been effectively remedied if the film-makers had given a
fraction of their attention to actual screenwriting as opposed to lavish
CGI effects.

1. The movie suffers from "superman syndrome." Neo is the One.
We know he is, for all intents and purposes, invincible. So while the
fight scenes are a scream to watch, there's really not much point. Why
doesn't Neo simply fly away from impending danger?

2. The movie suffers from too many "plot coupons," a trait
familiar to anyone who's ever played a video role-playing game or
read a sophomoric fantasy novel. It goes like this: "Find Mr. A. and
he'll tell you where to find Mr. B. After doing whatever you have to
do with Mr. B., you'll discover a map that leads you to Mr. C." *The
Matrix Reloaded* could have opted for a subtle, film-noir approach to
the revelations sought by Neo and his friends, but instead it adheres
fairly rigidly to adolescent plotting.

3. Persephone and The Merovingian. Potentially cool characters,

but what exactly is the point?

4. Likewise with the albino, shape-changing twins. This movie has literally hundreds of one-dimensional bad guys (i.e., the cloned Agent Smiths). The twins seem to be have been inserted merely for novelty's sake. And maybe to make the video game a bit more colorful.

Having said that, I think this film deserves some leniency. Some reviewers found Zion a gratuitous distraction; I thought it was convincingly rendered and becomingly gritty.

I unabashedly liked the chase scenes and kung-fu brawls; for what's essentially a sci-fi action film, *The Matrix Reloaded* does an impressive job of toting its share of Philip K. Dick-like paranoid philosophy.

The Architect's admission that Neo is not the first, but the sixth, generation of digital messiahs to have hacked into the Matrix's system core was a great touch. I would have preferred that Neo discover this for himself rather than glean it from the Architect's rapid-fire monologue, but even so it shows the writers reveling in fresh ideas that will hopefully infuse the final film.

30 MAY

Blogs are the text-based equivalent to "reality" TV: ubiquitous, candid and fueled by the same sort of once avant-garde aesthetic. If a future artificial intelligence wants to really know what's going on in the outside world, it may choose to peruse the entirety of the world's ever-growing infestation of blogs - in which case bloggers' innermost thoughts and day-to-day meanderings will be assimilated into a vast living snapshot of humanity.

Fifteen nanoseconds of fame – if you're lucky.

31 MAY

I ran into my high-school algebra teacher today. She just turned 40 and she has cancer. She's survived a sustained onslaught of chemical and radioactive therapies as well as surgery, and shrugs this off like an annoyance. She still runs, for god's sake.

If I were religious, I suppose I would have said something condescending and greeting card-sappy like "My prayers are with you." I had the feeling she's endured enough of that shit.

If I ran this planet, people facing unfair, life-threatening illnesses who had to listen to pretentious religious-sympathetic drivel from their blissfully cancer-less peers would have the right to blow such people away with a firearm of their choosing. No questions asked. Move on; nothing to see here.

But life isn't fair.

If life was fair Howard Zinn would be President. [6]

---

[6] Howard Zinn (1922 – 2010) was an American historian, author, playwright, and social activist. He wrote more than 20 books, which included his best-selling and influential *A People's History of the United States*. He wrote extensively about the civil rights and anti-war movements, as well as of the labor history of the United States. Zinn described himself as "something of an anarchist, something of a socialist. Maybe a democratic socialist." His website is: www.howardzinn.org.

Chapter 6

June

1 JUNE

The motorcyclists outside the coffee shop like would-be cyborgs, decked out in midnight polymer, bikes like craftily contorted insects. Matte-black Space Age fabric, ergonomic cushions and helmets like bulbous gleaming skulls.

3 JUNE

I read somewhere that the word "posthuman" is becoming increasingly mainstream as a response to heightened awareness of biotechnology (i.e., cloning). While this is encouraging as an example of meme-dispersal, it's also sort of sad. The term is bound to get cheapened and watered down for easy public consumption. How long until McDonald's starts selling Posthuman Happy Meals? How long until Honda's Insight hybrid car is advertised as "ideal for today's posthuman lifestyle"? I'm sorry, but we're not there yet. Barring cataclysm, we might get there in the not-unforeseeable future, in which case I think the last things on our minds will be fast food and cars. Not to mention "monster trucks."

8 JUNE

I went on a date last night and braved the crowds at The Cheesecake Factory, one of the biggest attractions on the Plaza. This was only the second time I've been there, despite the fact that my apartment overlooks the restaurant. The tower is now lit red, white and blue at night in honor of "Operation Where the Hell Are Those Weapons of Mass Destruction?"

The Cheesecake Factory is one of those places that excels at serving industrial-size helpings of just about anything you can think of. The service has the efficiency of an assembly line, and it's impossible to get in without a fairly lengthy wait outside. So I sat around and watched the Hare Krishnas do their stomping 'n' swaying routine.

9 JUNE

Work was frustrating today. The basic situation is this: in theory, overtime isn't mandatory, but – and here is where it gets Kafkaesque – there's an implicit threat that I might lose my job if I don't work overtime (ideally, large chunks of my weekend).

The part that makes me the angriest is that the corpses don't – or more probably can't – understand the concept of wanting to do something other than work.

Frankly, I put in my 40-hour week and I don't want to even think about going back until Monday morning. Yes, I can appreciate that we're understaffed and behind schedule. But is this my fault? Might it conceivably be the fault of the corpses making bad hiring decisions? Oh, but we mustn't entertain such heretical notions.

I had a nice chat with one of the main corpses this morning. He/it demanded to know what I did on my weekends that was so valuable. I really fumbled for words on this one. I don't have to justify my desire for two days' peace out of the week. Even so, I mentioned my contract with Simon & Schuster, to which he/it replied "Well, why don't you do that full-time?" with a leer that made me want to rap his skull against his desk a few times.

For many people, "free time" equates to "watching TV." Faced with the option of staring into a computer screen seven days a week and making a few dollars or listening to the toxic silence of their own minds, they choose the former.

For better or worse, I'm plagued by the ability to actually enjoy and cherish my time off, away from work and away from the soulless corporate culture that would have me do nothing but toil. To the corpses, this is tantamount to a severe mental illness.

I routinely complain that I don't get enough done on my weekends, but I do more than most people: I read, write, correspond with friends, give interviews – I *think*, or at least enjoy pretending I do. To say nothing of cultivating some semblance of a social life, which is neither convenient nor exactly easy for a self-obsessed cyber-yuppie whose immediate interests include extraterrestrial archaeology and reading the complete works of Philip K. Dick.

My livelihood is being threatened, presumably because I'm not a consummate "team player." But I don't recall joining a fucking "team." I remember getting a job, which I happen to be good at. I've been at my present place of employment for a year. I have broken no rules.

Occasionally, I've even been congratulated for doing a good job and told to expect a welcome raise, although this is never forthcoming (or, I must presume, even seriously considered).

Final word?

My weekends are *mine*.

10 JUNE

Yesterday's spiel was decent therapy. I think one of the central reasons why Americans typically work longer hours than their counterparts in other developed countries is that most Americans simply don't know how to have a good time. They may think they do: a trip to Disney World (really nothing but an extravagant walk-through infomercial) suffices as a vacation and getting drunk at a smoky, dimly lit bar constitutes "letting loose."

Give me a break. I'm tired of having to circumvent the lame, mindless reality tunnels so abundantly emplaced by our so-called "culture."

I'm reminded of my comparison between people and computer operating systems. In the software world, contending systems include Windows, Macintosh and Linux. In "meatspace," contending systems include Talks About Cars All the Damned Time, Pseudo-intellectual Snob, Inane Gossip and Aren't My Kids Cute? – among others, most of them distasteful. Sometimes you meet someone and you want to say, "You know, I've met you before – hundreds of times, actually. There's nothing even vaguely authentic about you. You're like an extra for some mercifully nonexistent film."

The Earth is teeming with the human equivalent of spam email. Read/met one, read/met them all. Click "delete." Move on. There's so much to see and do, so many landscapes to explore.

11 JUNE

"Emoticons." Do I use 'em?

A year ago, my answer would have been an emphatic "no." Now I find myself using a couple every once in a while, specifically

:-)

and

;-)

and occasionally even

:-0

to denote mock horror. My problem with communication-via-smiley-face is that some people essentially replace the written word with them. Ready-made animated icons have their place, but they're not a replacement for text.

Yet.

In some of my science fiction stories, characters communicate with "e-glyphics": animated, interactive hieroglyphs that inhabit ultra-thin flat-screens, turning the urban landscape into something like an enormous animated billboard as conceived by Bosch and Gibson. Some e-glyphics are digital wildlife. Some can even change substrates and cling to human flesh in the form of cunning ornaments.

For some cool examples of e-glyphic-like technology in action, see *Minority Report*. I can't claim that Spielberg cribbed my ideas since the basic motif has been alive and well since at least the early 1980s, i.e. *Blade Runner* with its ubiquitous electronic screens and television monitors urging Earthlings to relocate to off-world colonies. And that smiling Asian woman, like Orwell's "Big Brother" transmogrified into a pill-popping geisha.

Will a thoroughly "cyber" culture eventually devise a high-tech pictographic language? William Burroughs was keen on the idea. Making the switch from linear text to visual association blocks will likely require a fundamental shift in the way we think. We might alter our brains to facilitate information intake or have our brains retooled by the very process of absorbing association blocks.

Is technologically assisted meditation any better than the "real" thing? Does the brain care whether its user spends decades practicing or if s/he simply has access to the motherboard?

Information itself, arriving in unmatched density and increasing complexity, might be a no-kidding evolutionary catalyst.

Sink or swim.

14 JUNE

He pauses under the awning and breathes in aerosolized rain, fresh despite the taint of fossil fuel. The storm turns the skyline into a strobing silhouette; cars pass like oversized insects nearing the end of meandering lives, dimly recognizing their futility.

Flesh bursting along unlikely seams. A glimpse of muscle and tendon before laces are nonchalantly tightened, buttons fastened in a series of quiet metallic clicks. Octopi sulking in tepid bathwater, feasting on doughy wads of bloodless human skin. Teeth sprout from fingertips. Crockery levitates, shatters, falls to floors littered with anonymous feces and delicately severed limbs.

Vinyl apocalypse.

Prophetic fluorescent night.

A landscape of entwined skin and rubber faces, enormous worms writhing in a parody of genetically cultivated sentience.

Holograms, mirrors, ranks of spotlights and the ruby-needle stab of elusive lasers.

Skulls made of rudely compacted sand.

A liquid crystal dragon courts its own flaming fractal breath before vanishing.

15 JUNE

I've written a great deal about "weird" subjects such as alien contact, so it's ironic that I've barely even mentioned the crop circle enigma. The subject is dauntingly strange, but it's also rife with fraud, and inundated with even more brainless New Age thinking and professional debunking than the UFO phenomenon, if such a thing is possible.

If I had to guess, I'd posit that there is an actual mystery behind crop formations. And I don't think it has anything to do with atmospheric plasma vortexes or black-budget defence projects, although the latter may play a peripheral role. I think there's a nonhuman intelligence involved and that hoaxers and disinformationists have exploited the prevailing mythos to their own ends.

The prospect of hard evidence of nonhuman intelligence scattered throughout the crops and frozen lakes of the world is almost insidiously intimidating. Given the large numbers of known human circle-makers, it's little surprise that this enigma hasn't received the attention it deserves. Perhaps a strange sort of dialogue is unfolding, with feints and subterfuge from both participants.

Some close encounter researchers have noted that the so-called "abduction" epidemic seems explicitly personal, even intimate. The crop formation controversy shares this same "grassroots" sensibility, sometimes even literally. It's as if something is bypassing established lines of communication in order to:

1. avoid contaminating the recipient culture; and
2. remain hidden behind a screen of "plausible deniability."

The implications are dizzying. We may not understand the formations' message until we develop an actual physics of consciousness. I predict that this may arise, at least in part, from artificial intelligence research. If we can construct a sentient mind, we may inadvertently crack the code that renders crop formations and close encounters so maddeningly absurd. The "parasphere" – that liminal realm of subjective anomaly and official duplicity – may suddenly begin to make sense, even if we have to learn a new cognitive syntax.

Like learning to process visual association blocks, crop formations may catalyze the very way we think.

But how?

And why?

17 JUNE

Science fiction writer and mathematician Rudy Rucker has proposed a low-cost alternative to biological immortality: an interactive, portable neural net-based computer capable of imitating its owner's personality and artificially duplicating his or her memories. Rucker describes the device as a sort of attentive Palm Pilot that asks its user questions about every conceivable topic, establishing a rudimentary neural "map" as the interview progresses, a process that may last years. In essence, the device acts as an autobiographical ghost-writer and companion.

But as fun – or annoying – as working with such a device may be, its purpose is far from trivial. Its ultimate job is to replace you. When you die, the device will have gathered a massive cross-referenced database that can be used to conjure up an ersatz version of your deceased self. Presumably your ancestors may enjoy "your" company, or future historians might use your duplicate to conduct research. Copies of the quasi-intelligent replica could be made as easily as we now duplicate images and sound files.

A collector's market may arise, with the best and brightest recorded personalities achieving virtual superstardom. Entirely fictional personalities could be culled from promising recordings. Or a virgin device might be tutored by two or more recordings, resulting in an interesting "splice." Bandwidth is the only limit; unlike a device absorbing a human's persona, "imprinted" devices could communicate among themselves digitally, spared cumbersome, time-consuming human speech.

Most would agree that this isn't true immortality, but a novel imitation. But Rucker sees such technology as a stepping stone to an actual uploaded human psyche. If humans choose to upload themselves into a computer substrate prior to biological death ("de-animation"), a few years of vigorous dialogue with a "personality recorder" would help simulate the user's own neural "system architecture." This map, as crude as it may be compared to the complexity of an actual human brain, could serve as the basic scaffolding for an authentic human upload, ensuring that the final product is as indistinguishable from the original as technically possible.

So where are these things now? Interactive, infinitely customizable electronic devices are ubiquitous in the form of PDAs, cell-phones, laptops, digital cameras, and combinations thereof. Rucker's fictional invention would likely be a sure seller, but two factors keep it from becoming viable: memory and intelligence. The first problem, constructing a device with the staggering amount of RAM needed to soak up its owners' personality, is probably surmountable. But enabling the device with the conversational savvy to allow for competent "interrogation" is another matter.

But perhaps we're getting closer than we know to realizing Rucker's speculative stab at immortality. DARPA (the folks who brought us the Internet) recently unveiled a project called "Lifelog," which diligently tracks human respiration, brain rhythm, speech, and movement, allowing future scientists (in theory) to create consummately life-like simulations of day-to-day activity.

And the blogging phenomenon shouldn't be discounted either. If a Net-based artificial intelligence is spawned in the next 20-30 years, it may elect to trawl the Web, greedily digesting any written material in its path. Blogs, from the explicitly personal to the more technically oriented, may provide a newborn AI with a broad-spectrum glimpse of the human ordeal. A globally networked AI might be a kind of amorphous, innately schizophrenic entity, adopting and modifying personality elements to suit its whim.

19 JUNE

Every day I get "spam" email: generic ads for Viagra-like products, career-building software, come-ons from nonexistent women who urge me to view their private webcams, etc.

Spam is possible because of digital media's ability to reproduce at a staggering rate. It follows that if people eventually colonize a computerized substrate in the form of sentient software uploads, people themselves can be copied at will, resulting in a deluge of (post-) human spam.

Today's overpopulation is a crude but useful analogy. The Earth is spared complete destruction because food and energy are finite. It takes time to produce a human child. Not so with digital "wildlife."

If we decide to live an uploaded existence, will we succumb to the urge to multiply unnecessarily, perhaps out of sheer hubristic fanaticism?

Will we inundate the Cosmos with copies of ourselves?

20 JUNE

National Public Radio has been doing their annual funding drive, which is so whorishly self-congratulatory it's actually painful to listen to.

If I attempted the same sort of campaign for my website or this blog, it might go something like this:

Spokesperson 1: "And where else but PHB can one find such stimulating essays on misunderstood scientific phenomena?"

Spokesperson 2: "And that's saying nothing about the great book reviews! This is definitely a site that that deserves a hearty financial contribution!"

Spokesperson 3: "I'll say, Spokesperson 2! I think it's time for all the people who have enjoyed Mac's online material to team up and give him a large sum of money so he can continue to bring us the absolute best in oddball commentary, eclectic links and utterly selfless truth-seeking!"

Ad nauseum.

21 JUNE

Chinese for lunch; Mexican for dinner. Listening to Radiohead's *Hail to the Thief* (finally). Possible review forthcoming. Doing laundry. Need to work on Mars book. There's a cat asleep on my leg.

22 JUNE

I'm convinced some crop circles are the real thing. I wouldn't be at all surprised if the "Close Encounters of the Third Kind" phenomenon shares roots with crop circles. Both seem to function as ecological/environmental warnings; "abductees" almost always emerge with some sort of heightened environmental sensitivity, and reports of (presumably) predictive simulations of the End of the World are rampant. Perhaps it's no coincidence that crop circles appear in consumable grain crops; the substrate medium is part of the message. In this case, we're offered an implicit metaphor for life/death/renewal.

Somehow, it's easier for me to accept a "New Age" collective unconscious explanation for crop glyphs, i.e. messages from a distressed planetary overmind, than grasp at altruistic extraterrestrial visitors. See Carl Jung's *Flying Saucers: A Modern Myth of Things Seen in the Skies*.

Authentic crop circles certainly represent some form of intelligence, but I feel it's a human intelligence at work. In *Neuromancer*, William Gibson describes cybernetically augmented performers who use holograms to "dream real." Crop circles and "alien" abductions might be what happens when an entire sleeping species "dreams real"; few would argue that the phenomenon, whatever it is, lacks in absurdity or surrealism.

23 JUNE

I had my eyes checked today because I'm picking up a new pair of glasses. Instead of dilating my eyes the optometrist's assistant used a digital camera to take full-color pictures of the inside of my eyeballs.

This involved staring into a device that flashed about as brightly as a nuclear explosion. But the photos were worth it: my eyeballs' interiors look uncannily like the cracked surface of Jupiter's moon Europa (blood vessels and nerves substituted for Europa's icy fractures).

Meanwhile, here's a poem…

Caffeine laughter
Julia sets
(anomalous magnetism)
Captured on film
(we study reports)
Acres of glass,
Imitation marble
Raw squid
and infomercials
Hyper-oxygenated blood:
more durable memory
Rorschach calligraphy /
Thinking machines
No, truly thinking
(aware of quantum manifestations)
Why don't we all meditate
on the singularity
Or
Small Gray men
(suits of reptile flesh,
cardboard and cinnamon)
?

26 JUNE

Evolution is fact, not theory, but that doesn't mean that it's without its share of mysteries. For example, the transitional forms expected by Darwinian natural selection simply don't seem to exist in the expected quantity. It's as if evolutionary leaps from one species to another occur in fitful bursts, a phenomenon that to some implies an intelligent designer.

While I don't think that life on Earth has been steered by an omnipotent deity (although extraterrestrial intervention shouldn't be discounted), the lack of transitional specimens in the fossil record may be an important window into the mechanics of evolution. Rather than laboriously searching for "missing" links, perhaps scientists should concede, if only as an exercise in thought, that there are no transitional specimens; perhaps life has found a way to circumvent awkward transitional forms, hastening the evolutionary process. It's possible that DNA possesses its own collective intelligence, perhaps only loosely allied with its host species, resulting in morphological "quantum jumps."

The human lineage is by no means exempt. While contemporary humans share a common ancestry with apes, we have yet to find a transitional proto-human that would end the "missing link" controversy. Of course, no amount of evidence will ever placate "Creation scientists" possessed by the idea that we were somehow created by divine will, but that's another matter. But just maybe there wasn't a "missing" link. Maybe proto-human genes, sensing some incipient change in the biospheric zeitgeist, launched a new version of humanity to increase their chances of survival.

This sounds like an act of intelligence, but is it really? Temporarily setting aside the paradigm-smashing concept that living things are endowed with sentient or semi-sentient "morphogenetic fields" (a term coined by Rupert Sheldrake), an evolutionary "leap" might be purely reflexive. Ants and wasps construct elaborate "architecture," yet no one accuses them of intelligence. Similarly, viruses capably hijack cell nuclei, yet biologists hesitate to even consider them "alive" in anything but a rudimentary technical sense.

The implications of evolutionary quantum jumps are far-reaching, and disturbingly relevant. Humans have reworked the Earth's biosphere in countless ways in just the last few hundred years, exceeding the influence of our ancestors at a rate that promises to exponentiate. We have added new ingredients to the fabric of our planetary chemistry, saturated the skies with electronic transmissions, shaken the earth with nuclear explosions, and unleashed a veritable zoo of psychoactive substances. We live in an environment increasingly besieged by information of all conceivable forms; consequently, we suffer from new maladies and addictions.

Will these trends spur an abrupt genetic "upgrade"? Will homo sapiens cease to exist within a handful of generations? Fossil-hunters of the distant future, still seeking the worryingly absent links in the human continuum, may find the skeletons of "Starbucks Man" suddenly superseded by a new, improved version.

None of this is to say we shouldn't take measures to deliberately hasten our evolution. We may be unique in being the first humans capable of making the transition to a higher form of our own volition – not an opportunity to be taken lightly.

27 JUNE

When I'm writing/thinking/drawing in top form, messing around with ideas is like jazz music: very spontaneous, loopy, packed with riffs and digressions, yet ultimately with some sort of meaning. Linear, sequential thought is antithetical to creativity. Thinking should be fluid, energetic, volatile. The alternative is atrophy, stasis and eventual extinction.

My website and blog are preoccupied with hidden realities: aliens, other-dimensional intelligences and ideological agendas. Thus far I haven't had much to say about the "God" question other than my periodically revised case for agnosticism.

To clarify: I think words like "spiritual" are crude masks for possibly real phenomena. I shun "belief" but I'm not without ideas. I suggest that reality is knowable, that all is one, and that consciousness is an unrecognized but integral aspect of space-time. Physicist David Bohm reasoned that the universe has an "implicate order" that's barred from unaided perception. I think that as we interface with machines – which, like microscopes and particle accelerators, provide us with surrogate senses – we will begin the process of grasping the implicate in a more meaningful way. Conversely, the explicate order that comprises "normal" human reality will change, perhaps drastically.

29 JUNE

Next weekend I'm heading for St. Louis, which should be fun. I'm so habitual, almost neurotically so sometimes; I need to take more trips and take in more scenery. The alternative is what William Burroughs called "stasis horror" – the logical result of spending too much time in the same place. The true "horror" is the inability to see what's happening and inadvertently feigning sanity or, even worse, worldliness. You see this most readily in small towns.

30 JUNE

Becoming posthuman may not be enough. We must become post-biological. From a sheer computational perspective, meat-brains are inefficient and decidedly user-unfriendly. They cling to faulty reality constructs and suffer from hardwired glitches that we've mistakenly labeled "normal" and "virtuous." Superstition is glorified while the reptilian urge to seek out leaders, real or hallucinatory, is condoned under a blanket of "patriotism."

Biological, meat-based life might be a necessary larval form of intelligence, the mentational equivalent to the Industrial Revolution's reliance on environmentally debilitating fossil fuel. But permanence is an illusion; we are a species in transit. The prospect of moving on can seem so devastatingly soulless. What happens to emotions – neuro-chemical ephemera – when we control our minds instead of the other way around? Will post-biological humanity (an oxymoron, to be sure) cling to emotions when they're no longer needed? They may be viewed as charming cognitive mementos or they may be systematically erased.

Philip K. Dick's androids could be revealed by their incapacity for empathy. Yet they remained eerily human, like peripheral reflections of ourselves.

Mathematician Roger Penrose thinks that artificial intelligence is impossible because the human brain relies on quantum-level structures that, in his view, can't be duplicated artificially. Conceivably, uploads that fail to take quantum effects into account will be unable to collapse the quantum mechanical wave state, leaving reality unwritten. A universe without consciousness becomes a blur of raw probability, a realm antithetical to life as we know it. We might have to take some meat with us after all, or at least a convincing simulation. But will we choose to bring along the capacity for fear, self-loathing, love, despair?

If aliens are contacting us, what do they possibly want from us? Interestingly, many "abductees" claim that extraterrestrials have evolved past the need for emotion and now seek human assistance to revitalize their genetic stock. Are we dealing with a post-biological species that uses visual symbolism? The "aliens" might actually be our descendants, a tragically posthuman race on the razor's edge of extinction, unable to summon empathy without a mediating intelligence. They may be posing a question: Do we take our emotions with us or leave them on the evolutionary scrap-heap?

There's something chilling about abandoning emotion. Emotion is at the very core of our heritage as a species, just as a water-bound existence was to early life forms. Posthumans may elect to become emotional amphibians, deliberately savoring pangs of jealousy and wonder one moment and becoming "vast, cool and unsympathetic" the next.

To say nothing of creating altogether new emotions.

Chapter 7
July 2003

1 JULY

Conspiracy theories are the folklore of the 21st century. Almost invariably, a conspiracy theory, no matter how lame or implausible, casts the American Dream in a cynically revealing light.

Here's one I came up with a while back, during the beginning of "Operation Iraqi Freedom." Remember that wild dust storm that brought troop carriers to a virtual standstill? U.S. personnel and Iraqis alike were quite specific about just how awful it was. Keep in mind that Iraq gets its share of dust storms; they're far from unknown. Nonetheless, longtime residents appeared on NPR commenting on this particular storm's singular ferocity. Some felt that there was something forbiddingly different about it.

Such bad vibes may be chalked up to the imminent siege of Baghdad, and as far as I know there is no official weather report to show us quantifiably how "different" this particular dust storm was. But the storm's timing is interesting. It happened right as U.S. and British troops headed for their protracted confrontation. Allied forces were hit where the storm's effects were most crippling: in the middle of the harsh Iraqi desert.

The conspiracy I'm proposing hinges on a few postulates:

1. The United States military has an interest in the strategic use of ground vehicles in desert warfare. A reasonable assumption.

2. The military-industrial complex is interested in weather modification. This pill's admittedly tougher to swallow. Then again, what technological advantage isn't the military interested in? As possible "hard" evidence, I offer the HAARP atmospheric research

installation.[7]

3. If the U.S. military has weather modification technology at its disposal, then this is undoubtedly a "black ops" project, unknown to Congress. Again, a reasonable guess.

The theory itself:

Military insiders used the trek to Baghdad to experiment with the effectiveness of weather modification in desert combat conditions. The "dust storm" was manufactured event.

There you have it, folks – a "respectable" conspiracy theory. Tell your friends!

2 JULY

I've been noticing a new trend in "literary" book publishing lately: the covers of a large number of new books feature close-up photos of cheap plastic toys, dolls, action figures or marzipan figurines.

Doubt it? Take a look around the new releases at Barnes & Noble. It's bizarre. Apparently the "close up figurine photograph" meme has infected the graphic design departments of a great many publishers. I personally suspect that, while we're collectively oblivious to this trend today, it will become obvious in retrospect. Twenty years from now, the few scattered people who still buy and read books will pick up hardbacks minted in 2003 and chuckle to themselves.

What's the agenda behind this meme? I'm not exactly sure. And I'm frustrated that I wasn't able to catch it when it first appeared; pinpointing its first emergence into the consumer ecology is going to be a daunting task now that the shelves are stacked with trendy clones.

Fortunately, you can help fund this research initiative by sending

---

[7] The High Frequency Active Auroral Research Program (HAARP) is an ionospheric research program jointly funded by the U.S. Air Force, the U.S. Navy, the University of Alaska, and the Defense Advanced Research Projects Agency (DARPA). See: www.haarp.alaska.edu. The program is a frequent target of conspiracists, who usually claim it is a weather-modification weapons system.

me money. Or, barring that, keeping your eyes open and letting me know the titles and publication dates of the books in question.

Believe me, you'll know the ones I'm talking about.

Meanwhile, a correspondent has posed a logical question to my proposed conspiracy scenario: Why conduct the weather modification experiment when it could actually hinder the war effort? Why not conduct a mock-up in, say, Arizona (my correspondent's home state)?

Here's my slick, imminently paranoid retort:

"Operation Iraqi Freedom" (man, I hate that name) involved an enormous number of ground vehicles. If the object of the hypothetical experiment was to test the effects of dangerous weather during wartime conditions, then a "mock-up" based in the U.S. would simply be too big to hide. People would notice the huge build-up of vehicles in the American southwest and wonder what was up. And if given a vague dismissal from the military brass, the ensuing artificial storm would be certain to get their attention. Better that the experiment be conducted overseas, where sandstorms are known to occur anyway.

It can also be argued that conditions in Arizona or Nevada (home of Area 51) are simply too unlike conditions in the Mideast, precluding a meaningful study. The Bush regime's foreign policy indicates that the United States intends on maintaining a presence in the Mideast for some time to come, in which case only an "on location" test would suffice.

4 JULY

Sweltering weather; the air is laden with smoke from impending pyrotechnics. I'm over half-done with Rucker's *Spaceland*.

I just saw a bloom of fireworks in the distance – either that or a most convincing hallucination, like the metallic bubbles I sometimes see when I'm exhausted and don't consciously realize it. I, for one, am not especially in the mood to celebrate the U.S.'s so-called "freedom." America is in a state of decline that cannot be remedied by a mere change of administration, which won't happen anyway.

It's getting darker by the moment.

5 JULY

I'm not exactly a winter person, but I'm most emphatically not a summer person. Every cell in my body is rebelling against this heat. I want to crawl into a cryogenic escape pod and wait 'til October.

6 JULY

Free sample of chai latte at LatteLand: great stuff. Bought a book from the Hare Krishnas. Tipped street musician. Man in coffee shop absorbed in do-it-yourself cryptography.

"Have you read *Cryptonomicon*?"

Concrete heads silhouetted against the evening sky as I sipped espresso and read from *Spaceland*. Slight undercurrent of synchronicity; the dialogue in *Spaceland* seemed to mirror the previous hour's events. I yearned for a notebook.

Human refuse congregates outside the movie theater, a Sargasso Sea of thwarted human ambition.

Vapid blond woman cursing into her cell phone.

I watched *28 Days Later* tonight, although I missed the opening sequence. A terrifying and beautiful film, definitely one to get on DVD. I haven't seen an apocalypse so convincingly rendered since *12 Monkeys*.

And so my three-day weekend comes to an unremarkable end. Frothy chai and peppermint. Blistering heat and conspicuously empty sidewalks. On the way back from the ATM across the street, I thought I heard fanatical screaming from the general direction of the Horse Fountain. The hallway outside my apartment is sauna-like.

I feel like one of Abbott's Flatlanders, missing out on a whole spectrum of reality. I'm a node of awareness encapsulated in a ridiculous frame of temperamental meat. Maddening sweat; omnipresent limbic urges like the taut strings of a sadistic puppeteer. "Hungry? Sick? Strung up by the wrists?"

The acid sting of unwanted endorphins. Dreams of conversation and conversations like fragments of dreams, latching onto the lining of my skull until I'm dizzy with their weight.

My head sags to one side and splits open, oozing steam and sparks. I gather cracked silicon in disbelieving palms and see my universe reiterated in delicate copper whorls.

7 JULY

This evening I introduced my cats to a palm-sized canvas bag full of "Cosmic Country Catnip." They love it. No, "love" doesn't quite convey it. "Frantic infatuation" is probably more accurate.

I have, on my hard drive, the next-to-final version of my Mars book. Essentially all I have to do is correct some line edits, split/combine a couple chapters and add a bit more introductory material and we're laughin'.

I just got back from the coffee shop, where I almost finished *Spaceland*. Expect my review tomorrow or possibly the day after. Prediction: It will be favorable. Like some other books by Rucker, it starts slowly but gets satisfyingly weird.

The sink-repair guy hasn't been back. I'm glad – I don't like the idea of strangers in my apartment while I'm away -- but at the same time I'm afraid to drink the water from my kitchen. While filling ice-cube trays, I noticed that it's worryingly effervescent, like some sort of science-fair experiment.

Whatever. I suppose if I start mutating I might get free rent. Perhaps I'll awake from uneasy dreams and find myself transformed into a giant insect. This would have its advantages. No more waiting for the elevator, for example. I could scale nine floors by crawling down the outside of my building.

And at night I could keep cool by keeping low to the floor.

9 JULY

I completely crashed last night after getting home. Really pathetic. I was all psyched to finish *Spaceland*. My "day job" has been sort of exhausting lately and I typically fall asleep early once a week – usually Monday, but it's unpredictable. I'm wishing I'd gone for a swim instead.

I'm eager to start *The Sirius Mystery*, which I picked up in hardback. The "ancient astronaut" meme exerts a noticeable pull on me, and *The Sirius Mystery* is probably the most "sirius" treatment of the idea I'm likely to find. Zechariah Sitchin is interesting – sometimes even compelling – but he's very technically limited, not to mention utterly committed to his interpretation. Reading his books can be a lot like reading religious propaganda.

10 JULY

I'm admiring the online ad campaign for *28 Days Later* – it doesn't tell you anything about what the film is about, only that it's "raw" and very much orthogonal to mainstream Hollywood cinema. I have to agree with both points.

I've started reading Jack Williamson's *Terraforming Earth*, about the aftermath of our planet after it's struck by the next global-killer asteroid that's inevitably heading our way as I write. It's compelling. Successive generations of clones, born millions of years apart as the Earth recovers from an asteroid collision, attempt to render the planet habitable to human life. But evolution on the "new" Earth has taken weird turns. Is "terraforming" it worth the effort? Is it even ethical? Author Jack Williamson poses worthwhile questions.

I missed work today and, quite honestly, have spent the entire day worrying about what's in store for me tomorrow. Worse still, I don't have the energy to throw myself into any worthwhile projects in the meantime.

11 JULY

Bad day at work. Blinding headache. Went for a swim when I got home. I'm working some overtime on Sunday. Will it be enough? Will it ever be enough?

The self-proclaimed skeptical elite delight in using the maxim

96

"extraordinary claims require extraordinary evidence," yet they're strangely adverse to admitting that consciousness/self-awareness could possibly be an epiphenomenon (that is, a by-product of brain function rather than its purpose). Surely the concept that consciousness is a patterning of information is less "extraordinary" than requiring some unspecified "ghost in the machine"?

Committed skeptics secretly hope that awareness lasts after the death of the physical brain. And who knows? Perhaps it does. Occam's Razor is flawed. We're not looking for the simplest answer; we're looking, one hopes, for the right answer.

12 JULY

Reading *Spaceland* has caused me to view some UFO reports in a new light. Apparent "vehicles" that seem to change shape while in the air may not be spacecraft at all, but cross-sections of four-dimensional objects that bisect familiar 3-D reality. For example, a 3-D cross section of a 4-D tube would appear spherical. And if the tube was irregular in shape, we would expect it to "change shape" in our three dimensions as it moved, much how a sphere passing through a two-dimensional plane would appear like a rapidly growing disk to any watching Flatlanders.

There's at least one good multiple-witness case on record that makes sense if the UFOs seen were 4-D objects (or a single 4-D object) occurring at right angles to our three spatial dimensions. The pilots involved described the shape-changing objects as "flying jellyfish," pretty much what one would expect a 4-D phenomenon to look like if it happened to move through three-dimensional space.

The slightly unnerving aspect to this theory is that it implies that we literally coexist with the UFO intelligence (if it is, in fact, intelligent). But we're unable to see it unless it happens to intersect with us. And even then we're limited to glimpsing tantalizing cross-sections; our 3-D minds must turn to mathematical esoterica to reconstruct what the invading object/s actually look like. In *Spaceland*, Rucker does an excellent job of showing us how bewildering a four-dimensional landscape would appear to a 3-D observer. In short: Gnarly!

Summing up: A hidden world with four spatial dimensions might account for some UFO sightings. The oft-reported lenticular shape may be a clue as to what these 4-D manifestations really look like. This theory also conveniently disposes of the supposed incredible distances extraterrestrial UFOs would presumably have to cross in order to reach us. It also resonates with Jacques Vallee's idea of a vast, intersecting "multiverse."

13 JULY

In William Gibson's *Pattern Recognition* the heroine suffers from intense psychosomatic allergies to certain consumer icons. Among these is the Michelin Man.

While I don't have any particular aversion to the Michelin Man, I do have an inexplicable fear of bobblehead figurines. So perhaps it was inevitable that they'd come out with a Michelin Man bobblehead figurine to commemorate Gibson's fictional neurosis and my own uneasy relationship with big-headed statuettes.

The first time I realized I was afraid of bobbleheads was when I was working in a department store tending a display of grotesque bobblehead caricatures of various Kansas City Chiefs. The listless way their heads moved reminded me of a weird dream I'd had about finding a dead alien in my closet. In the dream, the alien's body was extremely slight and the head was bulbous and slack, very much like a bobblehead. To make matters worse, the department store also stocked these hideous animatronic football players who would lip-sync to Hank William Jr.'s "Are You Ready for Some Football?" theme song. Like the Chiefs figurines, the lip-syncing robots had distorted oversized heads.

The whole situation was demonic. I didn't like the way the football robots would wriggle their squat plastic bodies and move their semi-articulated jaws. It was fucking creepy. And people were buying these things. They thought they were cute! There was a sickening dreamlike quality to the whole situation: the same kind of feeling Gibson's protagonist must have felt toward the Michelin Man.

Anyway, it's very good to get that memory off my conscience. Thank you for listening.

16 JULY

Look at any galactic spiral. Forget for the moment that you're looking at an alien galaxy. Pretend it's home.

Each mote of light is a star, as transient in its own magnificent way as the blinking of fireflies. Nothing is permanent, yet billions of the stars embedded in this cosmic swirl have lasted long enough to accrete planets: ponderous, striped gas giants to which Jupiter is but a comma; hot, rocky worlds that mirror Mars, Venus and – quite probably – our own Earth.

A "billion" can be a difficult number to truly appreciate, except maybe as an abstract sum of money. Our minds never evolved to deal with such celestial arithmetic. Our rational left-brains, good enough for drafting spreadsheets and tallying the month's bills, are left in embarrassed stupor. I don't know how many stars this galaxy has, but let's say 100 billion. Again: a challenging number. No wonder people made fun of Carl Sagan – speaking of such immensity in merely human language is discomfiting to the point of being comical.

The known universe has over 100 billion galaxies, each hosting its own retinue of stars. Most of these stars have planets; it's statistically inevitable that some of these cradle life. And of these, a fraction almost certainly harbor intelligent life: thinking beings following un-guessable agendas. As much as we pretend otherwise, the Earth is not central or even significant in this dizzying sprawl of suns and planets. No anthropocentric deities watch over us or offer assistance.

Sagan encapsulated our predicament by comparing our planet to a pale blue dot, a speck of dust adrift in a sunbeam. But we're not the only speck of dust, and the sunbeams are so numerous that they interpenetrate until all is a rich, uniform white.

The human species, unique and vulnerable, has perhaps a few hundred years left unless radical measures are taken. If we fall silent, our broadcasts will outlive us, phantom emissaries slicing through the interstellar dark, growing steadily weaker as they're pummeled by clouds of dust and drowned by the electromagnetic wailing of rival stars. Eventually our presence will be reduced to the abstruse realm of quantum fluctuation.

The maddening stammer of "current events," a trite and forgettable dream.

The sky is alive with light.

17 JULY

The vapid corporate environment is a perfect example of a pseudo-reality. If Philip K. Dick wrote a book about a cubicle farm, I imagine it would be elaborately paranoid. Like his androids, PKD's "fake humans" don't know they're fake. That's what makes the onrush of media/profit-dictated realities so inescapable.

Corporate "culture" is one of the 21st century's biggest threats to human well-being. Sterile hallways. Ranks of identical cubicles. The same limp attempts at "office humor" repeated day after day after day under the unforgiving glow of fluorescent strip lighting. Predictable efforts to boost morale, overblown Christmas parties, omniscient supervisors – how horribly condescending and creatively bereft.

In the mood for a real-life zombie movie?

Take a camcorder to an office park.

18 JULY

I'm burstingly happy it's Friday. As the last few posts indicate, I'm sick of work and eager to do something interesting.

I suffer from what can be best described as sensory deprivation when working in a sterile office environment. The worst symptom is of somehow changing positions within the building. This creepy feeling of displacement usually comes on after an abrupt change of schedule (i.e., an unscheduled staff meeting).

After the unscheduled event has ended, I return to my cubicle only to find that my body can't convince my brain where exactly I am – or is it the other way around? It's a strange feeling of being somehow adrift or unanchored. I can look at my surroundings and know, intellectually, that my cubicle is in the same damned place it used to be. But my intuitive sense will have none of it.

20 JULY

Something I like about pre-Space Age science fiction book covers: The Earth is always depicted without clouds, like a cartographic globe. Not one cloud. The oceans are an unimpeded, uniform blue and the continents are masses of untroubled green.

Last night I slept badly because my bedroom doesn't get enough cool air from the AC box in my living room/office. I slept part of the night on the futon and stumbled into the bedroom sometime in the early morning, although my memory of this is hazy. After working online for a while, I collapsed for a few hours. Fearing a wasted day, I spent the rest of my time reading and drinking caffeinated beverages. I started Norman Spinrad's *Agent of Chaos*, which I quite like, and returned from the coffee shop with a stabbing pain in my head. The heat is pretty bad, although I noticed a cool breeze tonight.

I've had a buried preoccupation with death the last couple days, judging from the content of my dreams. I think it's the temperature; I have to be perfectly comfortable in order to get a good night's sleep. The slightest disturbance can make me feel drugged or feverish. Variations in air pressure give me headaches.

Sometimes I feel a little bit like "Newton" from Walter Tevis' *The Man Who Fell to Earth*. Newton, a human-looking alien, was on a mission to transport water to his dying home planet. I don't have a mission. No extraterrestrial imperatives to appease that I know of. I think this is why spy movies are so popular; the romanticized spy lives a life with a defined purpose, whereas those of us unlucky enough not to be James Bond suffer from a sort of amnesia, as if awaiting instructions that will never come.

21 JULY

I found a *Chick* tract in the men's room at Borders today.[8] It's been a long time since I've encountered any of these; several months ago I found *Chick* tracts veritably littering the store, evidently the work of one dedicated crusader. Anyway, I pocketed the gospel tract and made for the "New Age" section, although they don't call it "New Age" at Borders; books on UFOs and nasty conspiracies are labeled, somewhat condescendingly, "Speculation." My reasoning was that the crusader – call him the Chickster – would have planted tracts at strategic points throughout the store. Books on such blasphemous subjects as cosmology, homosexuality, feminism, evolution, UFOs, and non-Christian world cultures doubtlessly make tempting targets for the Chickster and his fellow idiots.

No luck. I came back from my lunch break with one damned tract that I've seen a million times. It's about how teenagers everywhere are really into rock and roll and killing themselves. It goes without saying that the main character, a misfit in a "No Fear" T-shirt, finds himself burning in Hell after hanging himself in his bedroom. The truly hilarious part is how Jack Chick, the artist and founder of Chick Publications, is able to (inadvertently) make eternal damnation seem hysterically funny. Hell is filled with big-nosed goblins that say things like "When you get the big picture, you'll be absolutely... TERRIFIED!" and "I tricked you! And now you're mine... FOREVER! Haw Haw Haw [sic]" (actual examples).

22 JULY

I was in a car wreck on the way to work this morning. It was a traffic accident and happened so fast that I honestly don't know how it happened. But it was real enough. I suddenly found myself clutching the wheel and unable to breathe, the car inexplicably no longer moving. The hood of my car was creased and folded. Large

---

[8] *Chick Publications*, www.chick.com. Their website banner sums them up: "Publishing cartoon gospel tracts and equipping Christians for evangelism for 50 years."

portions of my dashboard were conspicuously absent. A turn signal blinked meaninglessly. Numb, I stared out the driver's-side door and watched a milling crowd of medics and onlookers.

Everyone was very nice. The medics pried my door open and I more or less slouched out, now breathing rapidly. My car was a disaster. You've seen ugly car accidents before; embarrassingly, I was now the focus of one. Thankfully no one else was hurt.

I was driven to the emergency room in an ambulance, where a medic told me my pupils had dilated widely from sheer adrenalin. From the hospital, I managed to phone work. The next few hours were a blur of muscle relaxer-induced fatigue, psychic exhaustion, X-rays, and more than a little existential confusion. What now? What next?

Diagnosis: multiple contusions and severe muscle strain. Nothing broken. I had been wearing a seatbelt – and have a red welt across my chest to prove it – so I was spared having the steering wheel crack through my sternum.

The next few days (weeks?) are going to be rather painful. I have little strength in my upper body and my chest feels like it's been whacked with a bowling ball a few times. I can feel my muscles continuing to stiffen as I type.

Enough of that for now.

I'm OK.

Time to get a new car.

On with the show.

23 JULY

Well aware that this could be much, much worse, I'm nevertheless in a fairly high degree of pain from yesterday's crash. I spent today sleeping and trying to limber up. I can walk fine, but every bone in my upper body feels fused into a single, inflexible mass. My neck's not nearly as bad as I feared it might be; most of the pain is concentrated around my breastbone.

I'm going to work tomorrow armed with a fresh bottle of Advil.

24 JULY

My "new" car will probably be a '95 Chrysler LHS. I haven't seen it yet but I'm told it's pretty nice. This will be the first car I've owned with powered locks and windows; I'm actually kind of excited about this.

Eventually people will purchase new and "refurbished" artificial bodies much how we presently shop for new cars. Coming to a showroom near you circa 2200.

25 JULY

A friend in England has taken a picture of what looks like an alien. In his kitchen, no less.

The drama started when he noticed that a pile of change had inexplicably formed into a graceful semi-spiral of the kind often seen in fractal-based crop formations. He immediately picked up his digital camera and documented the strange configuration of coins. The first photo looks directly down at the table and the coins. For the second, he stepped back slightly for context. The third image is taken from a different angle and shows a small portion of the kitchen.

By this time my friend was experiencing a sense of being watched, and clicked a fourth image from the same vantage as the third. To his bewilderment, this one shows his kitchen bathed in a weird, orange-brown glow. The overall impression is murky, and I suspect something fouled up his camera. Nevertheless, a diminutive humanoid figure is visible.

Having looked at the image, I don't think it's a fortuitous juxtaposition of furniture; the "alien" figure is symmetrical and very much like the classic "Gray," albeit with what looks like an elongated chin and no visible hands or feet. It's mostly in silhouette, making analysis difficult.

Although small, England has a long, perplexing history of unexplained phenomena, from UFO sightings to "hauntings." Monuments such as Stonehenge were likely built, in part, to take advantage of electromagnetic "window areas" in which normal objective consciousness is altered by the Earth's own geomagnetic synapses. My friend's unexplained visitor, like UFOs and crop circles, may be an oblique manifestation of hidden forces.

27 JULY

One of the "tacky figurines" I purchased today (at a dollar store) is a nicely packaged female "Nordic" alien. For the uninitiated, the Nordics – tall, blond quasi-humans often reported by alien abductees – have become part of the contemporary UFO folklore. My "Nordic" figurine basically looks like a female crew member of the starship Enterprise. She wears a blue jumpsuit complete with a cryptic emblem near the breast.

The presence of "Nordics" aboard UFOs is unsettling from a "politically correct" perspective. They're creepily Aryan, like denizens of an alternate post-WWII Germany. Note to self: I'm surprised this meme hasn't caught on among paranormal conspiracy theorists. After all, the Third Reich was busy designing disc-shaped aircraft up until the end of the war, and the book *Hitler's Flying Saucers* attempts to make sense of the fact that Barney Hill recalled the "leader" of his "alien" abductors wearing a Nazi-like uniform. I suppose that if you really wanted to go "out there," you could suggest that a clutch of technologically inclined Nazis escaped Germany and is presently scheming to take over the world using flying saucer mythology as a smokescreen. I don't buy it, but I'm sure some people would.

I really don't want to go to work tomorrow. I'm emailing the polished version of my manuscript to my publisher this week and I want it to be perfect.

I'm still doting over my car. Compared to the other cars I've driven, this one is like a spaceship. I drove it through the ATM a while ago just for the hell of it. It has a great sound system but, alas, only a tape deck. I'll have to make copies of favorite CDs on cassette, or maybe buy an adapter for the DiscMan knock-off I won at the office Christmas party last year. It's still unwrapped, awaiting a good excuse for me to use it.

28 JULY

I'm in an unexpected amount of pain from the crash I wrote about a few days ago. Apparently I have a deep contusion that's just now making itself known. The entire right side of my body is in agony, and when no one's looking I walk sort of like Jeff Goldblum did in *The Fly* after he starts mutating: a kind of stooped shuffle. I feel like lying down in the bucket seat of my new car and staying that way for approximately two months. I'm popping Advil to no avail. This calls for heavier stuff, but at the same time I don't want to drug myself to the point where I can't drive to work. This whole situation is absurd.

I was thinking about getting my hair cut after work or stopping by Best Buy to pick up blank cassettes, but instead I think I'll crash. No pun intended.

29 JULY

I stayed home from work today to give my "deep tissue" wound some time to heal. It still hurts, but I like to think that I've experienced the worst of it. It's not as if I'm old and feeble; I can only suffer so many aftershocks before the pain starts receding.

I was walking along the sidewalk near Restoration Hardware when totally out of nowhere I was accosted by this tall, slutty looking girl and a silent, dark-haired guy who must have been her boyfriend. She immediately launched into an aimless spiel about restaurants and cars, prefacing her monologue with "I don't mean to be rude."

I didn't know where this was leading. At one point she played with her top as if considering removing it. I suppose this was supposed to be wildly endearing. Finally she concluded with a lame request for money so she could buy gasoline for her car.

I reluctantly gave her a quarter for her effort.

31 JULY

I'm dating a girl from China who's given me an assortment of interesting Chinese prepackaged meals. Opening the refrigerator is suddenly a somewhat alienating experience: I can't read the labels, and everything has an elusive soy aftertaste. One thing that's incredibly cool: the lids come with self-assembling plastic spoons. This is accomplished by means of clever hinges, which remind me of the joints in insect legs. Unfold the spoon and, in theory, you're ready to eat, although I advise disposing of the fold-up utensil after relishing its novelty and using real silverware.

Meanwhile, bumper-sticker ideas:

PREGANCY is a DISEASE…

It's not ILLEGAL to be a WEIRDO…

KILL the AMISH (just joking).

Chapter 8
August 2003

1 AUGUST

I got a letter from the Kansas City Public Library today. It seems I've had some books of theirs for over a year, and they're prepared to get tough (if a library can be said to "get tough") if I don't give them a rather large sum of money. Naturally, I called the library and feigned outraged indignation. I fully intend to give them their books back, but damned if I give them cash. The next logical step is to sneek into the library and put the books back on their respective shelves.

Wish me luck.

4 AUGUST

My concept of hell: being strapped to a chair in a room filled with Precious Moments figurines and forced to listen to Bette Midler's "From A Distance."[9]

Last night I dreamt that I was hanging around with William Burroughs. Only it wasn't William Burroughs; it was an impersonator of some kind, although at first I refused to accept it. Instead of books, the pseudo-Burroughs "wrote" ingeniously haphazard, ink-blackened pamphlets, possibly inspired by the underground press depicted in *Perdido Street Station*. Mental snapshots of nonexistent

---

9 The website for Precious Moments figurines describes them as follows: "Cherish the many happy memories of life with Precious Moments figurines. For years to come our angel, Disney character, Christmas, and birthday figurines will symbolize the dearest, most memorable moments of your life." See: www.preciousmoments.com.

locations, all tarred by dilapidation. I remember a particular rural mansion with crumbling walls and ugly green paint. Strange empty rooms.

I have a barely concealed interest in architectural entropy. It flavors my dreams and haunts my fiction.

Perhaps consciousness is holographic in nature, accessible to humans and non-humans alike. In a holographic model, past and present are meaningless; they're products of our meat-based brains, which evolved in a harsh and mercilessly causal environment.

I'd like to shed my body, if only to taste a moment's raw, unobstructed experience. In my dream of the abandoned hotel, I was surrounded by frolicking humanoid forms. There was something beautifully insubstantial about them. They were somehow diaphanous, child-like, otherworldly – yet paradoxically perfectly at home among the ruins. I'm not suggesting this was anything other than a dream. But it was a uniquely affecting one, possibly laden with subjective meaning.

5 AUGUST

The "world situation" has become so overwhelmingly repugnant, thanks in major part to World Leader Pretend Bush, Jr., that I can almost sympathize with the growing hordes of masturbatory "end times" junkies.[10] The United States has spawned an ever-escalating Orwellian drama that will only end in catastrophe. It's nastily ironic: we make it through the Cold War and breathe a furtive sigh of relief at the prospect of not disintegrating into radioactive ash at any given moment, and then Dubbya gets his hands on the control panel. That good old Cold War sense of imminent apocalypse is back, this time with a walloping dose of postmillennial paranoia just to make things interesting.

And that's merely the political end of the spectrum. While we try

---

[10] Tonnies was specifically referring to American evangelist Tim LaHaye, the author of the apocalyptic *Left Behind* book series. See: www.timlahaye.com.

to ignore the near-daily headlines about dead Americans in the anarchic wasteland that used to be Iraq, the climate's going fucking crazy. Europe is burning as I write.[11] I bet you didn't know that, but I'm not making it up. Our polar icecaps are actively melting, like the prelude to a particularly lame Kevin Costner movie. Yet somehow we're still enamored of patriotically themed cell phone faceplates and macho bumper-stickers.

The United States is in the throes of a profound disorder, dutifully obliging every attack on decency and human freedom doled out by the insane asylum formerly known as the White House. We have lost our capacity for wonder; we are pragmatic, gutless drones in a windowless neo-con hive. We die and we are replaced. Some of us may kick and scream, but in the end it's futile. So we stand on the beach and await the fallout from overseas, readying our syringes behind the wheels of our SUVs and fume-belching pick-ups.

Scientists have begun predicting our species' extinction with a certain morbid glee. Stephen Hawking gives us a thousand years, tops. Others, no less informed, offer us 100 years. Or even 50. The unsettling truth of the matter is that we deserve to perish. Not because of Bush, but because our capacity to tolerate Bush and so many others like him is, apparently, inexhaustible. The only hope left to us is that we can turn the tide of obsolescence in our favor, so our post-biological descendants can, in some sense, take us with them. Otherwise the human experiment, so profound from ground-level, will have been as quaint as a bloom of mold in a petri dish.

The level of sheer terror infecting every waking moment of our lives, as evidenced by the news media's increasingly idiotic and obvious evasion tactics, is stunningly revealed in the film *28 Days Later*, in which a virus dubbed "rage" obliterates an entire country in a month. Most of the survivors, if that is the proper term, are savage zombies who feed on the virus' human aftermath. I cannot think of a

[11] Michael McCarthy, "Britain bakes, Europe burns. Is this proof of global warming?" 4 August 2003. www.viridiandesign.org/notes/351-400/00376_europe_burns.html.

more relevant analogy for the Bush Regime's treatment of human life in the gut-wrenching wake of its invasion of Iraq.

For whatever it's worth, I add my voice to the small fugue of horrified onlookers: the current administration must be stopped. Our government's casual approach to wholesale murder and environmental abuse is not an ethical abstraction. Maybe once it could have been, and we could have afforded to view the world political stage as a reassuringly nebulous entity. But times have changed. Time itself is accelerating. The shadow of climatic plunder and bio-warfare hovers over our cities like the malignant mother-ships in *Independence Day*. Only the aliens aren't monstrous amalgams of insect and reptile flesh; they're smiling politicians and aspiring technocrats. They run our corporations, our medical care system and our schools. They profess to fervent religiosity, yet they nurture war and relish destruction. The takeover isn't imminent; it's done. Decency has never been much of a contender, and the invasion spearheaded by our unelected "President" stifled even the mildest show of dissent within seconds.

We are approaching the end of history in recognizable form. The new world will require its own ontology, its own schematics. We must bravely face the fact that we may or may not be included in its plans.

8 AUGUST

I return to the notion that our evolution has been modified by a nonhuman intelligence. There is a node in our brains that exhibits spikes of electrical activity when the subject is experiencing religious ecstasy. An instant God-fix. As Burroughs would have said, "a man within." Darwinism explains our propensity for religion as a mechanism for maintaining solidarity among members of a tribe or group. It might be this simple, or the node studied by neuro-theologians might be a genetic graft designed to keep us Earth-bound. Our species' violent history is a reflection of our devotion to Belief and the power if wields over us.

Charles Fort wrote, "We are property." Religion is an invisible fence, trapping us on an increasingly hazardous planet. Perhaps the only way we can conquer it is by daring to modify the holy scripture of our own DNA.

9 AUGUST

Tomorrow" morning I take my kitten, Ebe, to the vet's for her third (and final) booster shot. That gives me just enough time to come home and talk to my editor about illustrations for my book.

I spent tonight reading *Perdido Street Station*. This is the best book I've read in memory. Outstanding on every level.

On the way to the coffee shop I saw another idiot shouldering an almost true-to-life-size cross. Fortunately for both of us he didn't attempt to engage me in conversation.

11 AUGUST

You thought 9-11-01 was shocking? Get some perspective: that was a couple airplanes slamming into a couple buildings. Wait until the world's oceans are so thick with excess CO_2 that they finally start out-gassing, leaving coastal cities as sprawling, biohazard graveyards. Vice President Cheney's undisclosed location better have plenty of oxygen tanks.

I keep seeing this great patriotic slogan on bumper-stickers: "9-11: We Will Never Forget." But that directly implies that we're going to be here forever, which we're plainly not. Ultimately, no one's going to care because there won't be anyone left.

Sheesh, you're thinking. This guy's overreacting! Am I? Look at the surface of Mars. There used to be oceans there. Not anymore. Something happened, something almost unthinkably bad.

I fear the 21st century is going to be one prolonged atrocity. The hideously backfired spectacle of "Operation Iraqi Freedom" will be less than a footnote compared to the eco-disasters we'll be contending with in the next few decades. Take a deep breath.

Meanwhile, I visited a grocery store a couple weeks ago, and over the weekend I spent some time in a Wal-Mart "supercenter." I'd forgotten what depressing places these are. Is it just me or does Hy-Vee cater to would-be circus freaks? I saw some real specimens. The book selection at Wal-Mart is especially intriguing; there's a vast selection of Tim LaHaye titles, including my personal favorite, *Are We Living In the End Times?,* a companion volume to the sickeningly popular *Left Behind* series.

The *Left Behind* thing is primarily disturbing because of the blurring definitions between reality and entertainment. In the post-September 11 zeitgeist, isolating truth is just too difficult and confusing for most people. The military-industrial-entertainment complex's answer is to bind politically expedient myth and pre-digested "facts" into an unenlightening but market-friendly chimera. It's cheap, vulgar candy. But man, does it sell.

Physicist Bernard Haisch is working on a series of science fiction novels specifically designed to counter the appalling idiocy that fuels the "end times" craze: a seemingly workable exercise in meme-warfare. The trouble is that Haisch's premise is basically intelligent. As such, his fiction is effectively satire, and satire's main demographic is the already-convinced. The "masses" (in this case, the drooling savants toting wooden crosses across town and handing out *Chick* tracts) will be bypassed completely. One glance at an intentional subversion of the cosmology cooked up by the likes of Bush, Robertson, Falwell and LaHaye and they'll scream "blasphemy." Fundamentalists hate scientists anyway, unless they're the sort who cite "Piltdown Man" as "proof" that evolution is false.

12 AUGUST

I found yet another *Chick* tract in the men's room at Borders. This one's not nearly as funny as most. It's less of a story and more of a thinly veiled threat that if you don't believe the Bible literally you're going straight to hell, where I assume dumb-looking goblins with cucumber-noses say things like "Gotcha, sucker!"

The company I work for has this truly hilarious Web filtering software. It's supposed to keep prurient cubicle-drones from looking at *Victoria's Secret* catalogues and living it up in chat rooms, but all it does is get in the way. For example, I tried accessing a site that lampoons Republicans and the "Religious Right" and was denied access because the content was "tasteless." Curiously, I seem to have no problem at all viewing authentically offensive sites praising Bush and advocating prayer as a method of keeping "evil-doers" at bay; my company's own online newsletter is slavishly sympathetic to dirtball "God and guns" ideology. And it goes without saying that many sites dealing with esoteric science are labeled "cult."

I think it would be a great hack if someone could lock out access to business-related sites with a screen that says "Forbidden: Mind-Numbing Bullshit."

14 AUGUST

A giant insect that inhabits its own liminal imaginative reality, uncoiling only to eat or copulate (which it does seldom and unknowingly). It feeds off the ectoplasmic potential of human flesh, using gnarled, bladed limbs to eviscerate its victim while glands near the thorax emit an odorless, paralyzing gas. The minds of its infrequent meals find themselves uploaded into the insect's cognitive matrix, trapped in a web-like dream of harshly illuminated corridors, bland corporate art and unfathomable appliances. The laws of physics are routinely bent or violated, filtered into abstractions in the insect's un-sensing mind. Time is made malleable. The insect sleeps and dreams endless dreams, its captives actors in unscripted Kafkaesque dramas.

15 AUGUST

Here's an idea: Why not make it a law that a former U.S. President's child cannot be elected to the same office? It sounds kind of silly until one remembers that the official reason the United States was formed was to break away from the tyranny that typically accompanies a monarchy. If you argue that such a law is "un-

American" and an insult to individual freedom, remember that persons born in countries other than the United States are not allowed to be President. If that's not an insult to individual freedom in a so-called "land of opportunity" in which "all men are created equal" I don't know what is. So at least there's a similarly contradictory precedent for my proposed law. Of course, this presupposes a fair, valid voting system.

I just realized that for all of my political diatribes, I've never commented on my own voting preference. I'll be honest: I didn't vote in the 2000 election. Partly because it was intuitively clear to me that Bush would be appointed President regardless of the actual outcome, and partly because Al Gore, certainly the lesser of two evils, struck me as a worryingly bizarre and uniquely pathetic person. I thought Gore's campaign antics were whorish; Dubbya talks religion, so Gore proclaims on *60 Minutes* that he, too, is a "born-again Christian."

Give me a break.

And his infamous Internet and "Love Story" statements were disconcerting as well. I think it takes a generally misguided ego to enter the political arena in the first place; Gore seemed not only starved for votes, but possessed by an inflated, fictional counterpart a la Walter Mitty.

Will I vote in '04?

Somehow I really doubt it.

17 AUGUST

I live on the top floor of an apartment high-rise originally built in 1928. If you look carefully, the flowered decorations of the original masonry can be seen protruding through multiple layers of paint, a fading veneer of elegance. Last night when I exited the elevator I saw what I originally thought was some sort of massive insect clinging to the Victorian trim above the door to my apartment. I took a closer look. It wasn't a bug; it was a roosting bat. How's that for Gothic?

I called a friend with experience caring for wild animals and she referred me to a bat expert. I attempted to catch the bat in a bath-towel, but it took off and flew soundlessly up and down the short hallway, grazing my head. I gave up trying to herd the bat into my towel and took some pictures of it in flight, then phoned the apartment's front desk. I left the number of the bat expert on the answering machine.

Anyway, I was on my computer tonight, waiting for a pizza to arrive, when I noticed that Spook, my oldest cat, was unusually interested in the window above my air conditioner. I followed her gaze. The bat from the previous night was hanging from the blinds! Inexplicably inside my apartment!

It immediately started flying all over the place, coming perilously close to the ceiling fan. I ran to the phone and called my apartment's emergency maintenance number and was told that a loose bat in my apartment didn't constitute an emergency. I told them it fucking well did and that they better send someone to help me trap it. None of this was the bat's fault. I actually like bats; I just don't like sharing my living room with them.

By this time both my cats were chasing the bat with gleeful abandon. The phone rang. It was the pizza guy calling from the lobby nine floors down. I grabbed my checkbook and met him at the door just as a maintenance guy and my building's new manager began conferring about the Loose Bat Situation.

The bat, probably exhausted and starving, flew into the kitchen as we walked into my apartment, and the maintenance guy was able to trap it in a towel. It made angry buzzing noises through tiny fangs as he escorted it into the hall. Fortunately, he had every intention of setting the bat free outside. Now my cats are listless and forlorn. At first, Spook diligently kept looking for it and meowing plaintively. I think the realization that the bat is gone is finally hitting home. But it was certainly fun while it lasted.

18 AUGUST

Appalling greenhouse heat. Brush Creek is almost completely

overrun with vomit-colored algae.

Typical Monday.

19 AUGUST

Today my Yahoo! Mail account was pounded by a deluge of virus-ridden spam, so if you sent me a message and it was returned to you, that's why. My in-box was 117% full; I'm not even sure how that's possible.

It occurred to me this morning that the argument over the nature of consciousness (whether it's an epiphenomenal by-product or the reason for our existence) is basically a dumb, binary way of approaching the subject. Consciousness might be both a side-effect of cognition and a pivotal evolutionary development.

20 AUGUST

A democratic government has one defining function: to protect the rights of its citizens. The President is the human extension of this philosophy and nothing more. For all of the grandeur attached to the position, the President is, ultimately, a public servant.

But look at the god-like power we entrust to our Presidents. They're enamored of special interest groups to whom the "public good" is a laughable fantasy. They think nothing of committing the lives of men and women younger and smarter than they are to pointless death in the service of thinly concealed corporate machinations. And we let them get away with it.

Short of replacing the President with an impartial artificial intelligence (which, in the long run, seems eminently sensible), there are ways to counteract the petty dictatorship the office of President has become.

Consider locating a doctor. Communications technology has made it relatively easy for prospective patients to choose a doctor best equipped to their needs. Careful searching can locate the most qualified physicians for the malady in question. This freedom to choose has saved the lives of discerning patients who would otherwise find themselves at the mercy of incompetents.

This is in striking contrast to electing a worthy President. A typical election presents us with two ideologues who both reassure us that they want only the best for the country they've chosen to represent. Most of the time voters vote for a particular candidate not because they think he's particularly savvy or competent, but because he is simply the lesser of two evils.

Our current President has committed the U.S. and its reluctant allies to an Armageddon-style shoot-out with the Islamic world, as witnessed by the social, political and intellectual grievances precipitated by "Operation Iraqi Freedom." Thousands of the Iraqi citizens he sought to "liberate" died within the first weeks of conflict. Now, months after the obligatory "victory" photo-op in the ruins of Baghdad, casualties are escalating. Yesterday the United Nations embassy in Iraq was bombed. A few days before that a gas-line line was bombed, resulting in $7 million a day in lost revenue. Iraq's cities, patrolled by an occupation force with a curious penchant for opening fire on unarmed protesters, are waterless and without electricity.

Even a good President can miscalculate. But our current President acted both aggressively and mulishly against the best advice of the world community, of which the U.S. is an inextricably entrenched participant. The decision to "liberate" Iraq, founded on the "threat" posed by nonexistent weapons of mass destruction, had nothing to do with the U.S.'s offensive against "terror" or with deposing Saddam Hussein from power. It most certainly had nothing to do with the best interests of the American people. We're left to confront a President whose ties to industrial interests and Christian Fundamentalist ideology are blindingly obvious. His actions are not remotely consistent with the public service role epitomized by his station.

How do we prevent future Presidential debacles? Simple: subject candidates to the same psychological screening processes enforced in the private sector. If a would-be President plans to use you or your children as human fodder in a spurious war, shouldn't you at least have the right to gauge his/her mental profile sans the boorish spin-doctoring that typifies election year politics? If contenders for the role of President are the altruists they expect us to believe, they should have no qualms about publicly submitting to lie-detector tests and stringent personality profiling.

This isn't to condemn the prospect of genuine leadership; a President need not be selfless. Ego and ambition are healthy traits that can be harnessed by a strong administration to institute change for the better. But, overwhelmingly, Presidential wannabes share the same tepid, myopic outlook. They offer more of the same and deliver the worst. Autographing flags and delivering speeches in military raiment may rouse some twisted variant of "patriotism" among the "Love It or Leave It" contingent, but it solves nothing. It doesn't absolve atrocity.

If we're to maintain a pretense of democracy, the office of President demands mutation. America cannot withstand an endless procession of frauds.

22 AUGUST

My email account was spammed beyond capacity again last night. I've been macbot@yahoo.com so long now that I really don't want to change. For one thing, it would require manually changing the HTML code in every one of my Web pages. And it's logical to assume I'd get the same damned junk mail even if I switched user-names. Hopefully Yahoo is aware of the problem and can put an end to it. If not, spam tends to come in waves; it's the online equivalent to a short-lived but tenacious predatory insect. In this case the insects are locusts.

A more unsettling possibility is that Yahoo! has deliberately reduced my email storage capacity so that I'll buy more disk-space from them. That's basically what they did when they realized that their free website hosting was too good to pass up — they decreased the data transmittal so that anyone with any effort invested in a GeoCities site pretty much felt compelled to upgrade. For nine dollars a month, it's not a bad deal. But still…

My birthday was Wednesday.

I'm 28.

I think tonight I'm meeting my parents for dinner. Also, I'm going to return my year-late library books and cough up a check. My plan to sneak the books back into the library never materialized, which is probably a good thing.

The weather is outrageous. My car's thermometer registered 112 F last evening.

Last night I dreamed about a five-star restaurant that served "gourmet breakfast cereal." Everyone raved about it. My curiosity piqued, I dropped by one morning for breakfast. The inside was cathedral-like, with lots of gold trim. Well-dressed waiters carried glass carates of chilled milk.

Although I had been assured the place was incredibly popular, I seemed to be the only customer. I stood at the counter near the foyer and tried to read a tiny menu attached to the opposite wall.

I hesitated, then asked, "Do you serve Cap'n Crunch?"

The man behind the counter nodded indulgently.

23 AUGUST

Along with the "Sobig" virus scourge that threatens to flood my in-box, there are also some interesting anonymous political messages circulating (under hijacked email addresses). I just got this one, seemingly from a proprietor of a website devoted to weird Mars images:

Personal Message:
Terrorist sympathizer, you are being watched.
With Regards,
saudi_4u.

One theory about "Sobig" and related plagues is that they're permitted to roam free so that Bush Regime cohorts like John Ashcroft will have a ready-made excuse to advocate increased

Internet monitoring. The "terrorist sympathizer" message now making the rounds is just menacing enough to accelerate plans to crack down on Net traffic. Ultimately, of course, the Department of Homeland Security will be satisfied with nothing less than hidden webcams in the homes of computer-users everywhere.

On the way out the coffee shop tonight I saw the *Kansas City Star*'s front page: this week's squalid heat was – surprise! – a new record. Of course, in twenty years people will look back on 110+ degree weather with utter, consummate longing. This is nothing.

24 AUGUST

I've been immersed in *The Communion Letters*, which is unexpectedly fascinating. I'm skeptical but very much sympathetic to the notion of contact with nonhuman beings, whether they're "extraterrestrial" in the popular sense or, more likely, something much stranger. Many of the first-person accounts in *The Communion Letters* describe trance-like sleep-states that could easily be sleep paralysis if not for the attendant weirdness. If "bedroom encounters" are neurological aberrations, then the definition of sleep paralysis needs to be expanded to include some truly bizarre special effects.

I've experienced sleep paralysis once or twice, fleetingly. It was very much as it's described in the popular literature: my mind was fully cognizant but my body was so much useless baggage. Accompanied by hallucinations or lingering nightmares, such an episode could be easily attributed to paranormal forces. Fortunately, I knew what I was experiencing as I experienced it, due in large part to my familiarity with "abduction" research.

Accounts of childhood encounters are uniquely interesting. If consciousness is as strange as modern physics suggests, then it seems weirdly reasonable to expect communication with nonhumans at a young age. Ever since encountering Strieber's books, I've idly fished for anomalous memories that might reflect a "buried" close-encounter episode but haven't surfaced with anything remotely conclusive. I recall some seemingly weird phenomena from a very young age, but the chances of any of it being other than memorable dreams or waking fantasies are preposterously slim.

I have a vague "memory" of playing with a diminutive helmeted figure in the woods. But as far as I know, I was never in a place where this could have happened. Some die-hard theorists would insist that my memories were intentionally scrambled. But it's far more likely that an early childhood dream took on a life of its own, escaping my neurological filing system. After all, memory is not a reliable filmstrip; it's amorphic, malleable and, for all of its assistance, remarkably unreliable (hence my extreme skepticism toward "hypnotic regression" as a method of uncovering distant events).

Then again, the mostly unrecognized universal nature of the "visitor" experience makes me question the barrier Western ontology has set up between "dream" and "reality." My subconscious insists this delineation is too binary, like most intellectual constructs. Like David Bohm, I think reality is holographic in nature.[12] Our brains are limited to peering at the universe's outermost skin. When we finally tunnel deeper, I predict we'll discovery a riot of nonhuman consciousness.

26 AUGUST

It rained briefly this evening after weeks of record-setting greenhouse heat. My aunt from Chicago is in town; I'll see her Friday. Work has been, for lack of a better term, a drag. I'm really tired of having to effectively split my psyche in two in order to keep up with creative projects. I'm like some pathetic super-hero trying his hardest to keep his two alter-egos as far apart as possible.

---

[12] David Bohm (1917 – 1992) was an American physicist who contributed to theoretical physics, philosophy of mind, and neuropsychology. Bohm is widely considered to be one of the most significant theoretical physicists of the 20th century. He propounded the theory that the brain operates in a manner similar to a hologram, in accordance with quantum mathematical principles and the characteristics of wave patterns. See: www.david-bohm.net.

If you're wondering what I do, don't bother. It's unspeakably dull. It involves files; I'll leave it at that. There are only so many things you can do with files, and none of them are exceptionally rousing or interesting, except possibly setting fire to them.

I better stop while I'm ahead or the Karma Police are going to come for me.

27 AUGUST

Today at work I looked up from a mass of file work to see my supervisor standing next to my desk. "Here," she said. "I thought I'd give you this." Her tone was friendly and I assumed the sheet of paper in her hand might be a brief "thank you" for the punishing amount of work I've been doing this week.

Not so.

The sheet was a prayer guide with all sorts of helpful advice for submitting to Our Lord Jesus before beginning a day at work. I wanted to shoot myself. This wasn't the first time I'd fielded religious drivel from co-workers. If it had been, maybe I would have let it go. But I'd already been through the no-religion-at-work issue; it had raised its head before with predictably ugly results. I had even emailed my supervisor, privately requesting that religion and work be kept distinct. Is she dense?

I promptly photocopied the "inspiring" prayer and gave a copy to our human resources manager.

"If she wants to hand out gospel tracts, let her do it outside the Palace Theater on the Plaza," I said, the Palace being a regular hang-out for brain-dead gospel crusaders and other human refuse.

I think it's notable that I work for a large corporation where rules and regulations are obsessively standardized and enforced. Loud signs in the break-room proclaim that all employees are entitled to equal treatment. Yet the assumption that all employees are rabid Christians seems strangely ubiquitous and goes conveniently unquestioned. I was perhaps the only employee to take offense at the hideous juxtaposition of Christian/military iconography that graced our online newsletter's obligatory page devoted to the National Day of Prayer.

"God Bless America."

"God Bless This."

"God Bless That."

Does "God" really want me to perform to the best of my abilities at a corporation that mocks the very notion of "time off" and threatens its employees with termination if they should fall sick? Am I the only one who sees something tragically and fundamentally warped about this?

Apparently so.

28 AUGUST

Sadly – and perhaps fatally – we marginalize outer space. There's an omnipresent "giggle factor" at work that keeps us from dealing with space as the vast, portentous reality that it is; references to spaceships and distant planets inevitably conjure adolescent comparisons to lame science fiction. We suffer from a profound need to keep our reality tidy and anthropomorphic: nothing less than a terminal addiction to a collectively mandated "normality." If experience can't be framed by a TV screen, we grow uneasy. So we spend our lives marinated in a vapid brew of professional sports, predigested "news" and trite "issues."

The media plays along, as usual. Perhaps if we took space seriously, as both a frontier and a potential threat (specifically, in the form of near-Earth astcroids), NASA wouldn't be the malformed, ineffectual entity witnessed by the *Columbia* crash.

There is another reason we marginalize space: exposure to outer space broadens consciousness. So long as conventional political regimes control access to launch facilities, there will be no manned Mars missions. Seeing the Earth from space shatters the timeless "us v. them" mentality that control systems on this planet rely on. Perhaps the Moon missions were abandoned, in part, because the astronauts who returned from the gray lunar desert returned irrevocably changed, unable to see Earth as anything but a seamless biocosm, unperturbed by humanity's petty agendas.

Right now, Mars is as close to Earth as it's been in 60,000 years. Go outside at night and look at it; imagine looking back at Earth, glowing a faint blue-green in a darkening salmon sky as shadows swallow the Martian surface and all is dark.

As William Burroughs said, "We are here to go."

I received evidential support for my space-marginalization theory while listening to NPR on the way to work today. A newscaster was declaiming the headlines in perfectly spoken English. Then he arrived at a story about NASA's continued failure to meet safety requirements. He started stammering, as if even speaking the words "space shuttle" was somehow beneath him or extraordinarily taxing. He paused, continued fumblingly, and stumbled over simple words for the rest of the the monologue in a pained "let's get this over with" voice. He was barely understandable.

Apparently the media is so divorced from anything remotely "futurist" that it has a latent fear of its very vernacular. This is most apparent with the word "alien." Three simple syllables – you'd think there's no room for error. Yet professional speakers manage to mispronounce "alien" as "ellian." Have you noticed this? Pay attention the next time you're watching a cheesy news clip on extraterrestrial life.

Along with "ellian," there's a depressingly large crowd that calls NASA "Nasaw." Where the hell is the "W" coming from?

Which brings me to another point: groups of letters such as "FBI" and "CIA" are not, contrary to popular belief, acronyms. An acronym is an abbreviation that's pronounced as a word, like NASA or SCUBA or OSHA.

I always thought this was pretty basic stuff until I started working corporate jobs, in which any combination of letters is passed off as an "acronym."

And let's not forget the contingent that insists on saying "ideal" when it means "idea." I personally don't think a society that literally can't pronounce "idea" will ever come up with any genuinely good ones.

29 AUGUST

Withering insect-reality. Eyes with no luster, brains fastidiously purged of neurons.

30 AUGUST

It's been raining continuously all day: an unremitting *Blade Runner*-like deluge. Running home from the coffee shop through the rain, cars like luminous undersea fish. I'm brimming with images for new stories.

Chapter 9
September 2003

3 SEPTEMBER

This afternoon I started reading Francis Fukuyama's *Our Posthuman Future* in earnest. I had read the first chapter while standing in line to see *The Matrix Reloaded* but had moved on to other things. I appreciate Fukuyama's concerns – any sane citizen of the biotech century should – but I can't help but take issue with his philosophical argument. Whereas I think that "human nature" is mutable and subject to redefinition, Fukuyama sees attempts to subvert the status quo via neuroscience and genetic engineering as necessarily dystopian and wrong-headed. But at least he's concerned about the future, which is more than you can say for most people; I could probably have a fun conversation with him.

4 SEPTEMBER

I find Japanese pop-culture uniquely repugnant, yet fascinating as a postmodern spectacle. What on Earth is the appeal of "manga" comics? The artwork is bland and the plotting, from what I can tell after thumbing through a few representative titles, diffuse at best. The heroines of manga are big-eyed waifs that defy ethnicity, not to mention biomechanics. There's something obscurely prurient about this stuff; manga characters seem to embody the repressed libido of an entire subculture.

There's even a thriving population of real-life cartoon avatars (predominantly female, as far as I can tell) who adopt the personae of manga characters through a Web-fueled movement known as "cosplay" (short for "costume play"). I was alerted to this phenomenon when my Mars website started receiving tons of hits from a site in Italy. I checked out the site; it's managed by a girl infatuated with "cosplay" who lists Cydonia (home of the "Face on Mars") as a "favorite place" on her personal profile.

Japanese consumer culture is like some cross-cultural fever dream in which Hello Kitty figures as nothing less than a minimalist deity.

But a deity of what, exactly?

6 SEPTEMBER

Yesterday I received a review copy of Michael Cremo's massive *Human Devolution: A Vedic Alternative to Darwin's Theory*. With Richard Thompson, Cremo authored the underground classic *Forbidden Archeology*, a 900-page encyclopedia of "impossible" – but scientifically verified – archaeological finds that point to a human presence on Earth lasting millions of years.

As I read the introduction to *Human Devolution* last night, I realized I had read *Alien Identities*, one of Thompson's independent works, without realizing his affiliation with Cremo. *Alien Identities* is an impressive cultural study that seeks parallels between the modern UFO phenomenon and ancient Indian Vedic texts. Both Cremo and Thompson are consummate scholars. Cremo, in particular, has some impeccable "mainstream" scientific publications to his credit. So it was most interesting to find that not only is he essentially a loner in a field governed by a crippling, monolithic paradigm, but an adherent to the philosophy of A.C. Bhaktivedanta Swami Prabhupada.[13]

I promptly started reading *Quest for Enlightenment*, a hardcover compilation of Bhaktivedanta's teachings, to learn what Cremo's "Vedic alternative" might be. As the title of his new book makes clear, Cremo thinks Darwinian evolution is flawed. This isn't an easy claim to support in today's academic and scientific climate. But given the wealth of archaeological anomalies described in his former work,

---

[13] Abhay Charanaravinda Bhaktivedanta Swami Prabhupada (1896 – 1977) was the founder of the International Society for Krishna Consciousness, commonly known as the "Hare Krishna Movement." www.harekrishna.com.

it's clear that some explanation is in order, even if it merely compliments natural selection, as opposed to toppling it. As a fan of Darwin and evolutionists such as Richard Dawkins, I can appreciate the magnitude of what Cremo is trying to achieve.

The main reason I'm sympathetic to Cremo is because he's willing to introduce entirely new disciplines that deal with such "abstract" concepts as consciousness. Krishna cosmology views physical reality as a devolved plane of existence which we can occasionally break through via out-of-body experiences and "psychic" phenomena. Rather than subscribing to a "nuts and bolts" universe composed of matter, advocates of "Krishna Consciousness" believe that reality is fundamentally "spiritual," whatever that word means; I honestly don't think humans have a proper syntax for nonconventional states of being, let alone a practical understanding.

If my preview of *Human Devolution* is accurate, then Cremo thinks that we can transform ourselves into an entirely new, enlightened order of beings. Shades of the people in *The Matrix* shedding their subservience to enforced virtual reality; Vedic literature warns us that the world we think we inhabit is a flawless illusion.

Will Cremo succeed in dethroning Darwinism? I don't know, although I will concede that he's already made a dent. It's disturbing – no, terrifying – to consider that we really might not know who we are and that our "rational" questions, while well-intentioned, have been somehow perverted by the fact that our consciousness, acting on a physical level, lacks the requisite dexterity.

8 SEPTEMBER

Since I have yet to finish Cremo's book, I hope including his ideas on my website isn't construed as an "endorsement"; I'm giving his hypothesis a chance, but at the same time I'm naturally skeptical. Most people seem to operate on the quaint assumption that one is necessarily a "believer" or a "disbeliever." I prefer to keep my conclusions in a state of willful flux, as unforeseen new developments always threaten to challenge the prevailing paradigm.

9 SEPTEMBER

Dreams of transit. Japanese-style tube-train; subsequent amnesia. Improbable vehicles like Dali-esque cockroaches, utopian lakeside suburbs.

11 SEPTEMBER

I was browsing Barnes & Noble the other day and found the official US guide to resisting terrorist attacks. It's an overproduced mass-market paperback and goes for a cool $10. Is it just me, or shouldn't the government be falling all over itself to hand this information out for free? It can be argued that the same information contained in the book is available via the Internet, but there's the "digital divide" to consider; not everyone has easy Net access. Hell, I own a computer and live in more or less constant fear that it's going to crash just when I need it most. In the event of a nuclear attack, computers are going to be lobotomized by the EMP blast anyway.

This isn't to say that the hints contained in the book are all that useful, or even intelligible. For example, here's a sagely bit of Bush Administration advice in case of a terrorist nuclear attack: "Use available information to assess the situation."

Well, what else are you going to do? Use unavailable information? Isn't that logically impossible?

12 SEPTEMBER

Although I tend to reject the "nuts and bolts" hypothesis for UFOs as a general phenomenon, there are certainly exceptions. If alien craft occupy another dimension or parallel reality, as suggested by both eyewitness reports and world mythology, then perhaps materializing in our "ontosphere" is rather like deep-sea divers suiting up for an underwater safari. Physical reality, as we define it, might not be the ufonauts' native habitat. Or maybe their technology is advanced enough that they take little or no interest in differentiating between "their" reality and "ours." After all, the existence of two parallel worlds suggests there might be many, many more.

13 SEPTEMBER

I almost saw a UFO last night. I was in my ninth-floor kitchen really early in the morning when I noticed a large, dark shape hovering outside my east-facing window. At first I thought it was a helicopter, but it seemed unusual. I went closer to the window and the sense of mystery dissolved; an office high-rise is being constructed just down the street from my apartment and the "UFO" was an object suspended from one of the giant cranes being used to haul building components from ground-level. I didn't have time to put my glasses on; otherwise I would have seen the supporting cable right away.

Yeah, I know what you're thinking: "That really was a UFO, Mac. The aliens simply disguised their craft so they could make close approaches to highly populated areas without being noticed."

14 SEPTEMBER

I spent most of today reading *Human Devolution*. Cremo's thesis is that the universe is constructed from matter, mind and consciousness, the latter defined as a cosmic wellspring from which all else originates. Cremo notes that physical matter of the kind regularly experienced by human beings is the basest of the universe's three ingredients – hence "devolution."

Cremo's model can be read as a spiritual version of Extropian / transhuman philosophy.[14] Instead of upgrading humanity via cybernetics and genetic engineering, Vedic cosmology offers the idea of ascension through transmigration. A leap of faith, to be sure. But Cremo does a good job of putting his evidence on the table: fossil anomalies, the perils of using mitochondrial DNA as a tool for dating

---

[14] Extropians believe in continuously improving the human condition through advances in science and technology which will someday let people live indefinitely. Dr. Max Moore, a key Extropian philosopher and futurist, defined extropy as "the extent of a living or organizational system's intelligence, functional order, vitality, energy, life, experience, and capacity and drive for improvement and growth." See: www.maxmore.com.

the human species, "psychic" abilities, etc. There's even a chapter on UFOs which I haven't gotten to yet. Along with a few iconoclastic titles like Michael Talbot's *The Holographic Universe*, *Human Devolution* has made me reevaluate what I think I know. So even if Cremo's balancing act fails and his discussion "devolves" into pseudoscientific posturing, at least I will have learned something.

Of course, professional skeptics will have a field day with this book. Let them; they're missing the point. Even if one ignores the bulk of archaeological strangeness that forms the basis of Cremo's dissatisfaction with the mainstream evolutionary paradigm, one still has to find a consistently plausible prosaic explanation for various out-of-body states, psychokinesis, religious "miracles," and UFOs. Personally, I don't think this can be done. There's a real mystery here, every bit as existential as scientific. *Human Devolution* likely doesn't contain the whole story, but it's a sincere, informed attempt.

Whitley Strieber and other alien contactees/abductees have described their "visitors" as enlightened beings with an implicit interest in human consciousness. If consciousness is a distinct material capable of existing without matter or mind, as suggested by Vedic scholars, then it's very tempting to wonder if the "aliens" are constructed of pure consciousness. They may be forced to adopt a temporary material existence in order to interface with us in a meaningful way. But the fact that we ourselves are conscious as well as decidedly physical beings implies that the "visitors" (to use Strieber's designation) can control their material aspects in ways that would leave modern physics mystified. The UFO intelligence (or Philip K. Dick's VALIS, which is likely the same thing) probably employs a technology of consciousness.[15]

In *Transformation*, Strieber describes dormant alien bodies stacked like cordwood, awaiting future use. Strieber's visitors appear to have the ability to inhabit and discard gross material bodies at will. The

---

[15] *VALIS* is a 1981 science fiction novel by Philip K. Dick. The title is an acronym for "Vast Active Living Intelligence System." See: www.philipkdick.com/works_novels_valis.html.

craft they allegedly pilot are similarly dualistic, appearing alternately as amorphous, physics-defying masses of light and structured vehicles. Close encounter witnesses grasp for "nuts and bolts" explanations when they describe entities walking through walls. But for the visitors, there are no walls in the sense that we perceive them; in *The Matrix* a similar revelation allows Keanu Reeves' "Neo" to sever his connection with a seemingly omnipotent virtual cosmology once he understands its inherent unreality.

Supposedly, apparent aliens once told a witness that they "recycled souls," hardly the sort of task one would expect of beings as simple as extraterrestrial anthropologists. If true, then presumably human consciousness persists after biological death. The presence of so-called "aliens" intent on insinuating themselves into our collective technological mythology presents fascinating questions. As Strieber argues, it would be incredibly naive to dismiss close encounters in which the witnesses see deceased relatives working in tandem with "Grays" simply because the prospect clashes with the prevailing materialist interpretation of the UFO phenomenon. Perhaps a hidden "spiritual ecology" is at work, with "aliens" functioning in some vital – if unknown – capacity.

Recently, physicists presented a model of reality in which everything can be reduced to pure information. People, houses, quasars, galaxies – in theory, all can be reduced to a series of "yes" and "no" questions reminiscent of binary computer code. Maybe human affairs are as inconsequential as the antics of Rudy Rucker's Boppers, with the "aliens" possessing the equivalent to "system operator" status.[16] Interestingly, Rucker, a mathematician with extensive experience with the concept of infinity, envisions "God" as a sentient pure white light. It may be no coincidence that both UFO encounters and near-death experiences often begin with the awareness of an all-encompassing light or glow. Psychologist

---

[16] "Boppers" are self-reproducing robots in the *Ware Tetralogy* written by Rucker; they did not obey Asimov's laws for robots (or any other man-made rules). For Rucker, see: www.rudyrucker.com.

Kenneth Ring maintains that "alien abductions" and near-death experiences are essentially the same subjective experience, with only minor cosmetic differences.

Returning to Cremo's thesis, perhaps our goal as a (partially) conscious species is to become one with the Cosmic System Operator – an entity that may well be godlike in many respects, although I'm wary of any overtly religious definitions. It might be the "maddening simplicity of unattended clockwork" posited by astrophysicist and UFO researcher Jacques Vallee, or the artificial intelligence to whom psychic and showman Uri Geller attributes his abilities.

I'm reasonably certain that nonhuman forces are attempting to guide us closer to some un-guessed revelation. Assuming we indulge them in their playful dialogue, will their message ultimately assist us or deal us a shattering blow from which we can never recover?

16 SEPTEMBER

I went walking around 10:30 after a day of staring into my computer screen. The Plaza was virtually abandoned. I stopped by a coffee shop, bought an espresso, and wandered, really enjoying the cool air and the unmistakable red glow of Mars leering overhead. A fat woman, who I suspect might be homeless, was sitting on a white plastic milk crate outside Pottery Barn and Barnes & Noble playing a gratingly bad rendition of "New York, New York" on a saxophone. Apparently passersby were expected to give her money for performing this unsolicited service.

I actually like most of the street musicians here, but I always feel a vague pang of jealousy when I see the dollar bills heaped inside their guitar cases; why I can't I receive tips for, say, writing? Or reading a good book? I should buy a fold-up chair, park myself outside Starbucks, boot up my laptop and put a "tip jar" on the ground.

How bohemian.

17 SEPTEMBER

Last night I had two of the most vivid dreams in recent memory. The first was an engaging lucid dream that took place in what seemed to be a future society or an alternate present in which all human activity took place in massive enclosures lined with vertiginous buildings.

There's a common misconception that lucid dreaming allows the dreamer to consciously control every aspect of the dream experience. In my experience, I can only offer "suggestions," which are absorbed into the context of the dream and regurgitated with sometimes unexpected results. Even though I'm partially if not fully aware that I'm dreaming, the experience is terrifically weird.

My other dream had lucid elements, but contained so much detail that I was preoccupied with taking it all in and didn't "experiment" as I had in the previous dream. Very briefly, this was an "end of the world" dream, something to do with an impending comet impact. I remember looking at a satellite image of the continental United States and seeing it progressively covered with ice and snow, as might be expected in a "nuclear winter."

For some reason, trains play a recurring role in many of my dreams; I really have no idea why. In this case, a desperate parade of rail-mounted vehicles sought refuge from the increasingly dangerous weather. In retrospect, it's unclear if the comet (or whatever) had already hit, or if people were readying themselves for an inevitable demise as imagined in the asteroids-hit-Earth film *Deep Impact*. My clearest, most lingering impression was the stoicism demonstrated by Earth's population. No running wild in the streets, looting or mass suicides. For the most part, everyone seemed almost alarmingly calm and resigned.

I think this dream might have been inspired by the fringe-science speculation that the nuclear-powered Galileo spacecraft, doomed to crash into Jupiter as it finishes its mission, might explode, igniting the gas giant's hydrogen and filling our sky with the celestial equivalent to the Hindenburg catastrophe. "Oh, the humanity!"

Personally, I don't have any qualms about living in a binary star system, however short-lived. There would be some devastating environmental effects, of course, and there would cease to be such a thing as "night," but the overall effect of Jupiter undergoing fusion reactions might force the world to look up and contemplate our collective vulnerability.

This might be a naively utopian view, but so be it.

19 SEPTEMBER

Today and this weekend is the annual Plaza Art Fair. I can view this event as:

1. a stimulating cultural event complete with free music and readily available beverages, or;

2. an invasion of insolent tourists with poor driving skills trampling all over my home turf.

21 SEPTEMBER

I started Greg Egan's *Permutation City*, a novel about uploading minds into computer simulations. It's not unthinkable that mind-uploading will be available in the next 50-100 years; I think we need to seriously consider the existential and political ramifications of such technology now.

Should an uploaded human have rights?

Yes.

Would uploads be self-aware in the sense that carbon-based human brains presumably are?

That's certainly cause for debate, much of it semantic. The uncomfortable truth is that I can't even "prove" that my next-door neighbor is self-aware (a generally accepted prerequisite for "humanity"), but this doesn't justify my killing her on opaque philosophical grounds. What sort of political entity gets to decide if uploads (or "Copies," as Egan calls them) get to live or die? How does one justify digital genocide?

If mind-uploading actually happens, probably as an outgrowth of medical scanning technology and advances in computer storage capacity, the first Copies are likely to find themselves marginalized. Whether or not they interface with normal reality will depend on the processing speed of their computer hosts. In *Permutation City*, for example, Copies' thought processes run seventeen times slower than meat-based thoughts, resulting in a communications lag with the outside world. For this reason, Copies inhabit virtual environments in the hope that increased processor speed will allow them to return to the "real" world in animatronic bodies (or, farther in the future, organic clones).

It's just possible that aliens, if they are visiting us, are a machine-based intelligence. They might upload/download themselves into a variety of specialized mechanisms and bodies as casually as we change clothes or trade in old cars. When apparent aliens speak of "souls," are they necessarily alluding to something metaphysical or "spiritual"?

Maybe the "technology of consciousness" is closer to actuality than religious interpretations would have us believe. I suppose it might be demeaning for some to discover that awareness is something that can be plotted within the guts of some future diagnostic imaging machine, but I'll take it.

Permutation City refers obliquely to the hubris and failure of cryonic suspension. Apparently in Egan's imagined future it never panned out, and it's entirely possible that it won't. But I remain hopeful; as a prospective cryonics patient, I suppose I have to be. Cryonics just might flourish before mind-uploading, or maybe both technologies will enjoy a mutual coming of age.

Ultimately, it's a matter of dealing with a single, mind-stretching question: Given the opportunity to become virtually immortal, will we take it? Do we dare overrule the tyranny of our DNA or are we hardwired for death?

Meanwhile, not only do I have to contend with professional panhandlers, Hare Krishnas and self-important street performers, but I now have to field literature from Jews for Jesus. As if the American landscape really needs any more evangelical posturing.

By the way, I'm really fucking tired of limousines full of shouting preadolescents, overdressed high-schoolers spilling out of rented "party buses" and haughty ex-yuppies who think walking arm-in-arm somehow helps restore their irretrievable (and most likely squandered) youth.

22 SEPTEMBER

Human Devolution has me walking an intellectual tightrope. Cremo does a credible job of looking at nonlocal consciousness through the lens of Vedic creationism; I'm enjoying the ride.

I'm increasingly convinced that close encounters, near-death experiences and out-of-body experiences are aspects of a central overlooked phenomenon; deciphering one will in all probability cast light on the others. While I don't believe in "life after death" as typically envisioned by religion, I'm sympathetic to the concept that consciousness is more than a dance of molecules. William James thought that the brain acted as a receiver for consciousness, rather than actually producing it.[17] This idea is appealing. Consciousness may not be an effect, but an actual "stuff" or force, however intangible it may seem to us.

This is where New Age nomenclature fails utterly; how to address something as strange and vast as self-awareness when limited to pseudoscientific jargon? I roll my eyes at vague references to "essences" and "vibrations" – but is mainstream science really doing any better? Both camps are, to some degree, spinning their wheels. If a new paradigm is to emerge, we'll need a new syntax. And to make sense of a new syntax, we might need to purposefully mutate. Even if consciousness is eternal and omniscient, we still have to filter it through our carbon-based brains, with all of their neuronal

---

[17] William James (1846 - 1910) was a philosopher and psychologist . He was the first educator to offer a psychology course in the United States. His seminal words include *The Principles of Psychology* (1890) and *The Varieties of Religious Experience* (1902). See: www.plato.stanford.edu/entries/james.

shortcomings, at least for the time being.

Again, I wonder if the UFO phenomenon is attempting to demonstrate something along these lines. It seems virtually certain to me that the "aliens" are not literal extraterrestrials or manifestations of the psyche. They're likely real beings, some more "physical" than others – and yes, I'm aware this sounds disappointingly like Victorian spiritualism.

23 SEPTEMBER

I saw my first Segway today.[18] The "driver" was talking on his telephone as he crossed the street, for all the world like some crude automaton. I hope Segways don't proliferate like cell phones; I don't need another essentially pointless technology to add to my list of urban annoyances. Having said that, I wouldn't mind having one.

I was blasted out of sleep last night by more anomalous beeps from my phone. This happened over and over, punctuating my sleep and mildly freaking me out. The beeps came in sets of nine and, at least on one occasion, a set of three. The paranormal history of the "nine knocks" phenomenon, which I read about most recently in *The Communion Letters*, comes to mind.

If this is something paranormal – and I haven't totally eliminated the possibility, even though it sounds stupid on first blush – then it seems oddly appropriate that I'm receiving the "signal" via an electronic device rather than hearing old-fashioned "analogue" knocks. Also, the beeping, which is recorded on my answering system, only seems to happen at night.

I should check my alarm clock – maybe it happens at 3:33 or 9:00. That would be circumstantial evidence that it's caused by something other than faulty microchips.

Occam's Razor: All things being equal, the simplest answer tends to be the right one. So in this case I'm going to chalk the beeps up to bad electronics unless I get corroborating evidence that it's

---

[18] The Segway is a two-wheeled self-balancing battery-powered electric vehicle, first unveiled in 2001.

something else. If this is an attempt by aliens to contact me, they need to try a bit harder.

Then again, perhaps I should be more careful what I ask for. I don't especially relish having an implant shoved up my nose.

24 SEPTEMBER

I had an interesting encounter with a homeless woman outside the coffee shop this evening. Noting correctly that drivers on the Plaza tend to come unnervingly close to pedestrians before braking (I once fast-balled a cup of coffee at a car of these fun-loving incompetents), she went on to describe the startling hidden agenda behind this bothersome but otherwise inconspicuous phenomenon.

Apparently, doctors in the employ of the Mafia (or is it the other way around) are recruiting drivers with bad driving records to purposefully run people over. Not to kill them, mind you. Just to bash them up enough that they're forced to be hospitalized, thus bringing in lots of cash to hospitals and the doctors who work there. And you thought our health-care system was bad enough already!

It gets better. The goons employed by this Mafia/hospital scheme tend to drive unmarked cars with darkened windows so that they can't be identified by their victims. And anyone who gets too close to the Awful Truth is – you guessed it – run over.

I could go on, but you get the idea.

25 SEPTEMBER

I've been operating under the assumption that Bush's ("re")election is a foregone conclusion, but in the last few days I've subconsciously harbored the idea that maybe, just maybe, voters will see through his macho, can-do antics and put someone else in office. I'm not saying this will actually happen, or even that there's a decent chance of it. But I'm actually entertaining the concept, which is much more than I was willing to do a month or so ago.

Voters are driven by fads, right? And this "patriotism" thing is played out, if you ask me. Even the yellow "Support Our Troops" ribbons sullying the lawn of a house down the street have turned a most un-American gray. Dubbya might have to pull something new from his bag of Orwellian tricks to keep voters distracted. Or not. I'm probably giving voters far more credit than they deserve.

27 SEPTEMBER

Maintaining my website is quite a bit like nurturing a bonsai tree: I'm constantly fretting over it, trimming redundant links, tweaking the text, rearranging the layout, etc. Slaving over my site may be more therapeutic than harmful. I'm reminded of the uploaded denizens of Greg Egan's *Permutation City*, who can literally edit themselves to conscious specifications. Lacking that ability, modifying my online presence is the closest I can get: an illusion of self-control.

28 SEPTEMBER

I think of myself as a "writer," but I've always felt equally comfortable drawing; creatively, I fail to perceive a tangible distinction between the two. William Burroughs, with his shotgun paintings and collage notebooks, felt pretty much the same way. Burroughs' visual legacy was an extension of his prose. Critics who complained that his art was contrived or sophomoric totally missed the point. Just as all of his texts comprised one composite book, his paintings and cut-ups complimented and augmented his writing. Burroughs' goal was to extricate himself from tedious normality; the medium that he used to pursue this was completely irrelevant. Technical proficiency was likewise immaterial.

If someone has something to express, I don't think formal training is necessarily an advantage. For some it might be an active disadvantage – witness my aborted journals, which while perfectly readable and critically polished, were too linear to do more than suggest what was occurring in my brain at the time.

Writing fiction is different. For me, fiction is more revelatory and honest than the most unsparing diatribe. Rudy Rucker, an author I admire in many respects, dubs his personal technique "transrealism"

– he intentionally models characters after friends and family. It works for Rucker but it doesn't work for me, as much as I wish it did. My biggest failures are stories that try too hard to incorporate aspects of the real world. Coming from an ever-aspiring science fiction writer, this sounds dangerously like a confession of failure. Science fiction is, after all, a well-equipped vehicle for satire, and it's no accident that the most well-known SF titles – *Nineteen Eighty-Four* and *Brave New World* – are dystopian send-ups of real-life techno-social trends.

But the subconscious moves with its own surreal logic. In time, it can be trusted, or at least appreciated from a careful distance. A fiction writer's job is to develop a working relationship with the irrational.

30 SEPTEMBER

Blogs by famous authors are sort of like the gratuitous "behind the scenes" material included on DVDs; for example, I have the special edition two-disc version of *Close Encounters of the Third Kind* and I've never once even thought of popping in the "making of" DVD. Part of me doesn't want to know. Yes, I realize that the UFOs in the movie are merely special effects, but I still want to suspend my disbelief, thank you very much.

Too much "behind the scenes" commentary and the illusion loses some of its luster. I want to keep my literary/movie-watching life rich but uncluttered. It's a matter of deciding when to draw the line. How many streams-of-consciousness can I take in without falling to the ground and twitching from sheer information overload?

Ideally, I could link a version of myself to the Net, let it soak up as much information as I could possibly desire, and have it upload a full report to me on a daily basis. Technology along these lines is making headway in the form of "intelligent agents," which will effectively extend the human sensorium into cyberspace. Search engines are a crude analogy. Eventually, humans will require computer-enriched brains just to survive. Look at us now: Palm Pilots, cell phones, laptop computers, GPS tracking systems and MP3 players (and combinations thereof) litter the techno-sphere. If consciousness is an emergent property and not something "spiritual," then it seems likely that our brains are wired for it simply because it's the simplest, most efficient way of dealing with disparate sensory input.

There are two obvious alternatives for dealing with the increasingly massive amounts of information we'll be confronted with in coming decades. We can augment our minds to deal with the flood, or choose relative seclusion. Information may want to be free, but an awful lot of it seems to want to be dumb as well. How many ads for penis-enlargement medication have you deleted from your in-box in the last week?

Easy access to lots of information doesn't mean that we'll find much of interest; even the most discerning intelligent agents may balk at the prospect of excavating nuggets of value from cleverly disguised spam.

I think our collective fascination with electronic gadgets, as manifested by the current zeitgeist, will prove surprisingly short-lived. We will continue to use global networks and user-friendly electronics, of course; we may even merge with them in ways that challenge the present definition of "human." But there will come a point where the sheer novelty will dissolve, like so many discordant pixels on an aging computer monitor. Expecting Western culture to carry on its love affair with state-of-the art, imminently portable electronics is like people of the 1950s expecting their children to inherit a world of flying cars, cheap interplanetary travel and 3-D television. The technology will still be there, but it will have migrated into the background: invisible, ghostly, and unobtrusively omniscient. Its value as fashion will have expired.

And that's when things start getting really fun.

Chapter 10
October 2003

5 OCTOBER

Flocks of teenagers materializing like thought-forms borne on the cool night air. An edge of autumn, brisk but not cold. The Cancer Survivors' Park like an apocalyptic oracle, its touch-activated television screen locked against the encroaching chill, its statues frozen copper silhouettes.

A couple making out in the passenger side of a new Porsche; I glide by clutching my coffee, libido twitching sullenly somewhere in my skull. I find myself rediscovering a close-knit labyrinth of fountains and staircases and charming apartment buildings named after long-dead writers. The lights of Saturday traffic and gaudy horse-drawn carriages are mercifully eclipsed. The world is all shadowed architecture, suddenly shattered as I reenter the realm of the living, coffee cooling steadily. The usual anonymous hordes and casual lovers refracted through caffeinated synapses.

I buy a smoothie at a coffee shop (Depeche Mode playing in the background) and gradually lose myself in John Brunner's *The Shockwave Rider*. The immaculate sidewalks, sparkling as if pregnant with diamond, steer me home, past hotels, across the dark scabrous flow of Brush Creek. My apartment building has a new entry keypad, sans telephone handset. Made of reinforced stainless steel, it has the worrying appearance of something designed to survive an imminent nuclear attack.

Through the abandoned lobby with its fading pink carpet and neatly arranged couches.

Into the elevator.

I punch 9.

7 OCTOBER

I finished *The Shockwave Rider* by the late John Brunner. Great book, and not just for its cybernetic trappings. Curiously, portions of this proto-cyberpunk novel take place in Kansas City. The book is most famous for predicting computer viruses (or, as Brunner calls them, "tapeworms," which is a really good metaphor; indeed, many real-life computer viruses are known as "worms"). Brunner also appears to have anticipated "phreaking" and today's preoccupation with identity theft. And although his imagined future has something very much akin to the Internet, it's more Orwellian than the real thing – or so I'd like to think.

8 OCTOBER

This afternoon at the coffee shop: fat, balding man and his ugly wife throw a tantrum about the price of the coffee. I was dizzy with anger at these morons and I don't even work there. The male specimen was really getting into his role as Defender of the Common Consumer, yelling at the top of his lungs, requesting completely irrelevant biographical details from the manager and punching numbers into his cell phone. He wanted names, dates. He wanted to know who owned the place. He was consumed in a righteous frenzy of masculinity and totally fucking enjoying it. He even threatened to take his business to Starbucks. How original.

Displays like this are the last refuge of the ineffectual. How temptingly easy it is for these meat-headed bastards to play Hitler to some blameless, anonymous face behind a counter. I don't believe in "hell." But if such a thing happened to exist, I sincerely wish people like this would promptly go there, preferably to rot.

In other news, "Ah-nold" has predictably won the California election.[19] Here's a guy who openly expresses his admiration for

---

[19] Tonnies is referring to actor / politician Arnold Schwarzenegger, an Austrian-born box office superstar in the 1980s and 1990s (perhaps best known for the *Terminator* series of films), who was elected Governor of California in 2003 as a Republican, and served until 2011.

Adolf Hitler, and people vote for him. American democracy is an ugly farce. George Bush could spend his 2004 campaign promoting genocide and he'd still win so long as he's framed by the proper iconography. Americans pay lip-service to this love of "freedom" that we supposedly have, but most of them are as empty and fragile as the man in the coffee shop, ready to abandon any loyalty to principles at the drop of a hat if it means a quick ego-massage or the chance to make-believe they're somehow important or noteworthy in the depersonalized milieu that is the early 21st century.

We have more information than we know what to do with. We're all solipsistic tyrants thrashing and twitching in choreographed planetary death-throes and pretending we're having a good time. We can order pizza online, so who gives a damn if our armed forces are busy slaughtering an entire culture to prove the machismo of a single worthless, unelected politician?

9 OCTOBER

I've been mulling over the "Dust Hypothesis" advanced in Greg Egan's *Permutation City*. The DH suggests that innumerable alternate universes exist, flawlessly creating themselves from random "noise" to match pre-specified template patterns. This implies that our seeming existence could rapidly blink on and off, and we'd never be the wiser.

Are our physical "constants" being rewritten and introduced into "our" space-time by an external force?

I don't think there's a way to tell short of finding a blatant flaw (or deliberate message) in the universe's system architecture.

10 OCTOBER

If this is a virtual reality, as I suspect all realities must ultimately be, how does one unplug himself from the system?

I've got to get my circadian rhythms under control. I'm exhausted and on the brink of despair. The world is groaning at the seams like some haphazard structure losing an inevitable war with gravity.

System crash.

White noise.

A new pattern emerges from the chaos, the informational equivalent to a quick-growing vine.

Blindly we stumble into the pungent green embrace of sentient plants.

Going, going, gone.

11 OCTOBER

Inside Starbucks, embalmed in ersatz serenity. The furnishings and posters and sale items are dangerously immaculate: ranks of stainless steel thermos bottles and miniaturized espresso machines with sports-car curves. I admit to a strange longing for Starbucks' spurious sense of order, where the most difficult decision I have to make is whether to have my espresso topped with steamed milk.

12 OCTOBER

I begin a new job on Monday. And while I'm fairly certain it will be better than my last one, I'm finding it extremely difficult to get excited; I have an authentic horror of corporate America and everything associated with it. Working a job is very much like serving a prison sentence for me, and my only possibility of "parole" is to become self-sufficient through my writing.

I see George Carlin Sunday evening. Carlin is one of my heroes; stand-up comedy's answer to Kurt Vonnegut.

Meanwhile, this evening I paused in my reading of *Day of the Triffids* (one of the scariest books I've read, because it's oddly plausible and well-realized), in the midst of a chapter called "A Light in the Night." I then walked down the street to Barnes & Noble, where I went to the New Age section and opened a book whose first chapter was also called "A Light in the Night." Moreover, I've actually been thinking about nightlights recently; just the other day I was checking out the selection in a drug store and almost purchased one.

Things like this happen quite often to me. Is it all sheer coincidence or am I glimpsing some sort of underpinning beneath the veneer of normal consciousness?

13 OCTOBER

My new job is worse than I could have possibly expected. It's a fucking Kafkaesque nightmare. Brain-chilling monotony.

Carlin was damned funny last night. He has misanthropy down to an art.

16 OCTOBER

I just got the following spam message and couldn't resist posting some of it. You never know when stuff like this will come in handy.

Subject: Drink bitch
Need a fake id to get into the nude bar and see some pussy?
Too young to get your girl drunk and screw her?

Really – don't you just hate that?

Meanwhile, imagine a new Space Race with the ultimate goal of extraterrestrial contact. I think this is conceivable. No more Apollo-esque dramatic gestures; there may not be time. The first political entity to "claim" ETI just might inherit the universe.

Michael Moore famously declared that we are living in a fictional era. More accurately, we're living in a science fictional era.

17 OCTOBER

I've survived my first week at my new job. It's ended on a much better note than it started – not that that means terribly much. My plans for this weekend are to finish *Day of the Triffids* and sleep in late.

19 OCTOBER

Yesterday I woke up to find that my replica Mars Pathfinder lander was missing from its customary spot beneath my lava lamp. I found it behind my fridge where my smallest cat, Ebe, had deposited it, miraculously without breaking off the solar panels in the process. Along with the miniature Pathfinder, I discovered a veritable graveyard of abandoned fake mice. I hadn't realized that cats stockpiled things. In any case, they're not nearly as habitual about it as ferrets.

Outside my window a strange annual spectacle known as the Duck Derby is in progress. This involves dumping industrial quantities of floating toy ducks in the artificial creek that winds past my street and betting on the outcome. The winner gets a Volkswagen or something. We Kansas Citians really know how to live it up.

20 OCTOBER

I tried to trade in my old Dr. Martens today. A split had formed on the sole. Unfortunately, it had been over a year since my last trade-in, so I settled with 40% off a new pair. I'm not being a cheap-shot, either; contrary to their advertisements, Dr. Martens will disintegrate just like any other pair of shoes if you wear them regularly. That said, they're still good shoes.

Work was unexpectedly tolerable today.

21 OCTOBER

There appear to be two principal ways of approaching the alien abduction enigma, provided one doesn't brush it off as psychological aberration. One camp sees abductions as the workings of physical space visitors who are here to harvest genetic material, apparently for an obscure reproductive agenda. Think "hybrids." The other laments our Western fixation on materialism and addresses abductions as "imaginal" events – that is, real events that somehow don't fit into normal waking ontology.

But both outlooks are beginning to merge. In his latest online journal entry, Whitley Strieber reveals that when he was stuck with the infamous "rectal probe" in 1985, a jolt of electricity stimulated him to an unwanted and unpleasant orgasm. He now suspects the aliens wanted a sample of reproductive fluid. This is something of a revelation coming from Strieber, who has always dodged the question of what, exactly, his "visitors" are, for the admirable reason that he isn't sure. But now he describes an unmistakably physical scenario that wouldn't look out-of-place in Temple University professor/abduction researcher David Jacobs' *Secret Life*. Strieber makes no attempt to attach any metaphorical interpretation to his unsolicited sperm sample; he thinks his abductors sincerely wanted to get their hands on his DNA. In other words, the event was physical, and so were the beings orchestrating it.

Meanwhile, materialist Budd Hopkins (*Intruders*, *Sight Unseen*) is recounting bizarre case-files that read like episodes from Strieber's books. Strange figures in bizarre costumes walking the streets of contemporary America. "People" in outlandish garb who appear and disappear in unlikely places like John Keel's beloved Men In Black. Apparently if a researcher sets off to prove a nuts-and-bolts explanation for UFO abductions, he's eventually forced to acknowledge the weirdness factor that leads other, more spiritually inclined researchers (i.e., Harvard's John Mack) to think that aliens are far more challenging to empirical analysis than "mere" extraterrestrials.

The growing acceptance of multi-verse theory is welcome to both groups, and is possibly the single-most important factor leading to a "grand unified theory" of alien abduction. Who needs outer space when you have unlimited parallel universes? In a very real sense, beings from a coexisting universe would satisfy criteria for "nonphysical," since they're presumably able to duck back and forth at will, eluding our eyes and instruments. Our science isn't up to this challenge yet, but perhaps, if we keep doggedly pursuing our strange guests, it will be eventually.

22 OCTOBER

Today was an unnecessary, parodic waste of time. I take full blame.

23 OCTOBER

I took in "Tempus Fugit: Time Flies" at the Nelson-Atkins Museum of Art in 2001. One of my favorite pieces was a doll with a webcam in place of one eye. It was accompanied by a computer screen showing the artist's website, which displayed still-frames of gallery onlookers at ten-second intervals. I made sure I was plainly visible.

I think "interactive," Net-based art generally spooks people. Which is really anomalous for a society addicted to cell phones. Americans want to be global but they also want the illusion of anonymity.

24 OCTOBER

The decor at my place of work is a drab patchwork of beige and yellow, the color of nicotine-stained teeth. You can buy aspirin upstairs. Would you like your coffee strained through one or two filter packs? See that gray screen? We'd like you to stare at it, all day long.

25 OCTOBER

Late trip to the ATM across the street. Children's artwork, none of it interesting, adorns the cement flanking of the still-skeletal Plaza Colonnade. $60 in crisp, sticky twenties, watermarks like puddled oil under the bleak outdoor lights. White limousines glide past storefronts like metal sharks, cold and purposeful.

Sitting next to a pretty Latin medical student in the coffee shop, so close we're almost touching. Intermittent flashes of digital cameras. Thick espresso lodges in my cracked lips like tar. My reflection in an adjacent mirror is bloodlessly pale.

This week was almost entirely worthless, but I sort of made up for it by buying *The Essential Simon and Garfunkel* tonight while wandering around and catching up on reading *The Day of the Triffids*.

I wish I knew how to play the theremin. I harbor vague hopes of eventually getting one. The theremin is arguably the world's first "techno" instrument, which partially explains why it features so prominently in 1950s flying saucer movies. In *Eclipse*, John Shirley describes an ostensibly futuristic electronic instrument that actually sounds quite a bit like a theremin.[20]

26 OCTOBER

I ran into a pretty dark-haired girl on the way to the coffee shop and we ended up talking for quite a while. Unfortunately, a bitter, incoherent old man sitting on the outdoor table next to us persistently interrupted with loud meditations on religion and his personal medical history while flashing his pink-painted fingernails. Encounters like this are inevitable in an urban environment, but I was extremely bothered by it. I happen to strike up a spontaneous conversation with a girl and some delinquent just happens to make the scene in order to render our encounter as awkward as possible. What are the odds?

To make the day even more unpleasant, the Kansas City Chiefs are playing tonight. Evidently they're on a winning streak. This means that a disturbing percentage of adult males are strutting around decked out in fire-cone-red Chiefs attire. Not T-shirts – actual jerseys, like they're on the damned team. The last I checked Halloween was on the 31st.

I could really do without these imbeciles and their decorated vehicles. The other night I walked by some forgettable truck with a prominent sticker on the back window: "Official Vehicle of the Kansas City Chiefs." Oh, really? Strange, seeming how members of

---

[20] The theremin is an electronic musical instrument controlled without discernible physical contact from the player. It is named after its Russian inventor, Léon Theremin (1896 – 1993), who patented the device in 1928. Dmitri Shostakovich was one of the first composers to include parts for the theremin in orchestral pieces, including a use in his score for the 1931 film *Odna*. Perhaps the best known use of the instrument occurred in 1945 as part of the soundtrack by Hungarian composer Miklós Rózsa in the classic Alfred Hitchcock film *Spellbound*.

the actual Chiefs franchise are probably driving Porsches and Jaguars that they can afford because our society's collective self-esteem is so low that its members regularly cough up hundreds of dollars for season tickets and stadium parking and overpriced beer. All so they can "root" for a bunch of mentally deficient strangers in make-believe gladiator outfits who wouldn't bother speaking to their self-proclaimed "fans" unless it involved a photo-op.

I hope the Chiefs fucking lose. Badly. Better yet, I hope the Midwest is plunged in a blackout that forces hoards of befuddled suburbanites in Chiefs sticker-emblazoned SUVs to find something to do with their time other than staring dimly at televised corporate iconography and trying their hardest to transplant their egos to some fictional "team" that they've been trained to entrust with their emotional lives.

But, of course, if these poor sods didn't exist, the machine would fail to function. People might be less inclined to purchase needlessly elaborate cell phones and long-distance packages because corporate sponsors wouldn't bother wasting advertising money on the "big game." People might start kindling sparks of unsuspected creativity instead of leading their usual precarious media-addled existence. Then maybe I could find a job that's actually rewarding instead of slaving in a harshly lit prefab cubicle so I can afford to buy an occasional book.

"Right," you're thinking. "Like Mr. Posthuman here doesn't have a TV." I don't. I can't stand the sight of them. I'd be overjoyed if all the televisions in the United States spontaneously exploded, taking their ostensible owners with them in big orgasmic blossoms of flame and broken glass.

It's very fashionable right now to worry about Iraq. And we should worry. But we're looking down the stainless steel barrel of a cultural apocalypse every bit as life-destroying as a rocket-propelled grenade. Idiots in little-boy costumes parade through our streets like shock troops for some malign invasion while the Nelson-Atkins Museum of Art fires eight employees because of budget cuts.

Sports nuts bitch and moan about spending a patently ludicrous $6 on a cup of watered beer at Arrowhead Stadium, yet someone's still coughing up the cash for it. And Kansas Citians continue to kvetch about the price-gouged parking that's heaped on top of the price of tickets.

To me, the solution to this problem is absurdly simple: stop going. Stop "supporting the team." Not just until the price of beer goes down, but for good.

Burn sports arenas to the ground.

Even better, use them as ready-made landfills for the televisions you won't be needing anymore.

28 OCTOBER

There's an enormous solar flare wafting toward Earth. Unfortunately, it's not expected to be terribly impressive viewed from the ground. Maybe some heightened auroral activity. I think it would be fantastic if it would turn the midnight sky beet-red or something like that. I'd love for the "end times" morons who dote on Tim LaHaye to get all excited about the impending "rapture" only to have their hopes dashed.

Chapter 11
November 2003

1 NOVEMBER

Halloween was uneventful. No costume. I did, however, wear my hat backwards, not because I thought it made me look particularly "cool," but because it's the only way it will fit. I've come to terms with the fact that I have a big head. It's measurably larger than other people's. You know those "one size fits all" fasteners with the little plastic pegs? I can unclasp the fastener completely and the hat won't even begin to fit; it just sort of balances on top of my oversized skull. To date, I've found two hats that I can actually wear: the R.E.M. cap I wore tonight, and another I picked up in a department store. The former has an elastic band inside instead of a fastener, and I suspect the latter is defective.

I should make it clear that I don't look like I have a big head. It doesn't appear disproportionate to casual observers. Nevertheless, my cranium is an anomaly. Maybe I'm an extraterrestrial-human hybrid; that would put my mind at ease.

Meanwhile, by cat Ebe has discovered that she can keep warm by dozing off on top of my computer monitor. I've decided to tolerate it; in a few months she'll be too big to curl up there anyway. Let her enjoy it while she's still a kitten.

2 NOVEMBER

I finally toted my laptop to the coffee shop to make some headway on my novel. I bought a double espresso, sat down, flipped the screen up, and discovered I hadn't charged the goddamned battery. So I sat there for a while, sipping idly and occasionally tapping the "ON" button as if that might make some sort of difference. It's charging as I type this. I have no idea how long it takes. Hopefully no more than 30 minutes.

4 NOVEMBER

I've made an appointment for Ebe, my "kitten," to be spayed on Friday. Her kitty hormones kicked in the other night and now she spends most of her time yowling and screeching and driving me absolutely insane. Evidently cats are amazingly horny; I don't think they have any sexual "down-time." I'm not sure why I'm surprised, given the thousands of strays that are "put to sleep" every year.

I was pleased to see R.E.M. on the cover of a music magazine, accompanied by a CD of music selected by band members. I'm exasperated with critics who downplay R.E.M.'s last few records because of (relatively) low sales in the U.S. As if songs about the mass media and mortality are supposed to compete with the likes of Britney Spears.

It was bitingly cold today. I almost didn't leave my apartment. But Ebe's theatrics forced me out into the night and for that I'm grateful to her. I picked up a $4.95 hardback of *Dracula*, which I've never read, and began Jacques Vallee's *Anatomy of a Phenomenon*.

There's a new homeless guy in town. At least I think he's new. He stands right in front of Barnes & Noble like some sort of installation piece, which means I have to circumvent him at least once a day. For some reason, panhandlers flock to Barnes & Noble like moths to candlelight.

The Plaza has begun the sad process of shutting off its fountains for the winter. I'm bracing myself for another impossibly annoying Christmas shopping season.

I've been marveling at newspaper headlines recently. Can the Iraq situation possibly be any worse, short of all-out thermonuclear conflagration? How the hell will this end, if at all? Will someone, in some future administration, get it through his head that we're not wanted?

Meanwhile, there's a very real possibility that the Bush

administration is going to announce a human return to the Moon. The Chinese military is quite serious about setting up a lunar base by 2008.

As I write, you can be damned sure the Chinese government is cheering the U.S.'s predicament in Iraq and toasting to the demise of *Columbia*. So if we go – and at this point I think we should – it will be the result of yet another "Space Race," to keep the Chinese from undermining our own military presence in space. I can only hope that while we're there we'll begin to appreciate the vast potential economic benefit.

With any luck, a militarized U.S. Moon mission might seed a legitimate off-planet migration. Because if we go, we'll go to stay. Or until we nuke it out in the Sea of Tranquility in an attempt to "liberate" Chinese astronauts.

6 NOVEMBER

The Matrix Revolutions is the sort of movie that DVD was invented for; it elicits the urge to jump back and forth between various scenes so you're sure you're on the right wavelength. With that disclaimer aside, I liked this movie. It's a much more coherent adventure than the second installment. This time around the hand-to-hand action scenes are quick and effective, not the distended pageants of the first two (however much superficial fun they might have provided).

Revolutions features some of the best art direction and visual effects yet, including a convincingly sinister glimpse of one of the sprawling, AI-dominated cities. Viewers may be surprised to find that Keanu Reeves' Neo is almost a minor character, with the bulk of the plot centered around the subterranean city of Zion, which is under siege by tentacled cybernetic vermin.

With Zion's inhabitants in the throes of a Giger-esque fever-dream, the philosophical threads that surfaced in *The Matrix Reloaded* become part of the narrative background. This is probably a good thing; one of the perils of a movie like this is existential overkill. In *Reloaded*, the storyline jumped helter-skelter from metaphysics to car chases to kung-fu brawls and back again at a seizure-inducing speed that utterly prohibited getting to know any of the characters, let alone caring about their plight. *Revolutions* remedies this somewhat.

We discover that Agent Smith, in an orgy of digital cloning, now threatens the continued existence of the Matrix; hence, he poses a threat to the malign AI that constructed the Matrix in the first place to keep its human livestock placated. This is the movie's most promising premise. It's also the most perplexing ("Wait – hand me that remote…").

Even though his appearances are few and far between, Smith is the rightful star of *Revolutions*. Hugo Weaving exudes a mechanically child-like wrath that captures the exponentiating insanity of his world; if a computer virus could speak, I imagine it would sound something like Weaving at the film's climax, when Smith faces up to his own unheeding autism.

Revolutions is replete with cool camera work, a few rewarding eyeball kicks (a subway billboard advertises "Tasty Wheat," for example, the product that inspired a memorable philosophical monologue in the first film), and at least one new idea: that informational goods can be illegally trafficked within the Matrix's pragmatic boundaries, provided you have the right connections.

The ending is ambiguous (what did you expect?) and possibly a shade too sunny for a trilogy that's repeatedly taken its visual cues from the grit and shadows of *Blade Runner* and *Neuromancer*. Regardless, *Revolutions* left me with a desire to see the first two films again, which is perhaps exactly what it was supposed to do.

8 NOVEMBER

Most of us think of existence as basically linear: to get to point C from point A, you must first traverse point B. I think it's more likely (and much more fun) to consider that we're recreated moment to moment out of raw information, and that points A, B and C don't exist except in our endlessly reconstituted minds.

Imagine the reels for every movie ever made – and, more pertinently, every movie never made. Now imagine cutting this infinity of footage into single frames. Thirdly, picture putting every single one of these isolated frames in a blender, chopping them into microscopic oblivion, and stirring them with the aerosolized remains of every other frame.

This endless deluge of celluloid confetti is emptied into space, where it forms a randomized nebula, a pixelated collage of all possible "sequences." Now suppose we want to view a "movie" of someone's life, knowing full well that sequentiality is a cognitive construct with no objective validity. We shine a laser through the glittering mist of would-have-been films, thus isolating a single "sequence" of particulated states. If we keep doing this, we'll quickly find that most of our laser-lit "sequences" don't make any sense. After all, they're composed of completely random bits of data, ultimately at the level of simple "yeses" and "nos", or, if you're into computer metaphors, ones and zeroes.

But since we're dealing with an infinity of this "powdered reality," we also recognize that some of the laser beams are illuminating coherent "storylines." They might break up and dissolve at some point, but the endless quantity of possibilities waiting to be realized ensures that they will resume at some point. In this sense, a given observer's "reality" is an elaborate, self-maintaining juxtaposition. Random patterns (read: "sequences") in our hypothetical embryonic cloud are able to link up with similar, equally random patterns, very much like a crystal impregnating a vial of solution with its own molecular structure. A sort of binary Darwinism takes hold. Meaningful "sequences" thrive; the rest is just existential static.

Time needn't be relevant in the cosmic screening room. Whether a particular pattern emerged in the past or future is irrelevant. Information from the "past" and "future" (mere cognitive constructs) freely integrate. This is a realm without spatial or temporal boundaries. It's something like the "implicate order" suggested by physicist David Bohm. The "explicate order," of course, is the intricate sensory illusion that we inhabit.

Or think we do.

The ever-changing patterns in the protean cloud dictate the nature of whatever universe happens to be illuminated by our imaginary laser. Since our perceived reality is constantly modeled by the myriad ones and zeroes in the timeless cloud, we find ourselves diced into informational slivers. From this perspective, "continuity" is meaningless. The "I" writing this sentence could be hundreds of billions of "I"s removed from the one that wrote the last sentence. More disturbingly, "I" might not have existed at all until right… *now*.

The newly formed "I" happens to have "memories" of composing this essay, but memories, like everything else, are simply advantageous fluctuations in the filmic cloud, subject to constant revision. And since I'm ostensibly a component in day-to-day reality, it's inevitable that the randomly constructed parameters that define my world – all of it, from my living room to the coffee shop down the street to the structure of galaxies – is every bit as flimsy and malleable. Reincarnation is quite real. It's happening all the time, invisibly.

Several months ago I was in an automobile crash. My memories contain the adrenalized moment of impact, the literally breathless aftermath as I pondered the crushed metal and broken glass, and a trip to a hospital inside an ambulance. It would appear I survived, albeit bruised and aching. But who am I to tell the story of what "really" happened? Perhaps the arc of my life, as defined by the fluctuating patterns (and bits of would-be patterns) in the cosmic screening room bifurcated shortly before I collided with the other car. In one variation I came to a bloody end. In yet another there was never an accident at all.

I pick the crash incident not because of any intrinsic importance – at the most fundamental level, the blind dance of possibilities doesn't care if I live or die – but because it illustrates how flawlessly one or two frames can be altered (or randomly inserted or deleted) to potentially catastrophic effect in the observable world. So long as a pattern remains intact – and it will, since it has infinite space and time to organize itself – so will some permutation of "I."

Which begs the question: What happens when someone dies? It's possible that informational death is impossible and that the person who "dies" in the "explicate order" is expediently recycled, living his or her life again and again in a state of total amnesia. Or maybe something like my crash incident applies and observers who die in the directly perceivable world are shuffled into a future in which they "miraculously" survive their own crashes (or cancer treatments or heart transplants).

There's nothing concrete or absolute about our so-called universe. It is an alluring, insidiously clever simulation. The Many Worlds Interpretation of quantum physics implies that the universe is constantly "branching" into parallel, exclusive states. A better term, in light of the scenario described above, might be "flowing."

9 NOVEMBER

The American body-count in Iraq has officially eclipsed that of Bush, Sr.'s Gulf War.

On a more hopeful note, I've noticed fewer "God Bless America" bumper-stickers lately. I think the proles are actually – *maybe* – beginning to get sick of being jerked around.

13 NOVEMBER

I first read about the mystery of the number 23 in R.A. Wilson's *Cosmic Trigger*. If I remember accurately, Wilson first heard of it from William S. Burroughs. The "mystery," if that's indeed the word for it, is this: 23 seems to crop up again and again in cases of apparent synchronicity, i.e., an athlete whose uniform number is 23 scores 23 points on the 23rd of a given month. Or 23 cars wind up in a pile-up on 23rd Street, resulting in exactly 23 deaths. That sort of thing.

As a reader of UFO books, I've noticed that a large number of sightings take place on the 23rd of their respective months. Maybe this is because I've been sensitized to the "23 mystery," and my subconscious brings candidate incidents to my attention when there's no statistical significance whatsoever. But after finishing Vallee's *Anatomy of a Phenomenon*, I really have to wonder. Page after page describes credible sightings on the 23rd – one account even describes a UFO descending over a "23 highway" somewhere.

So, is the UFO phenomenon attempting to draw our attention to the number 23 for unknown (and perhaps unknowable) reasons? Or is 23 somehow integral to the UFO experience, as pi is to a circle? Beats me.

Perhaps now that I've introduced you to the "23 mystery," you'll start noticing 23 cropping up everywhere. And maybe you'll be nagged by a simple but maddening question: was the 23 phenomenon always present, unnoticed in your life, or did it somehow "activate" upon my telling you about it?

15 NOVEMBER

I came home from the coffee shop racked by a headache and ate left-over Vietnamese food. I have a mild, senseless crush on one of the baristas. It's so much easier for me to be attracted to women I don't know. And since I really don't know any women, I find myself speculating on a near-constant basis. I realize this portrait isn't flattering; it makes me sound like some skittish, socially impoverished creature living on the margins of human existence, which isn't true. I'm actually pretty amiable and emotionally articulate. I suppose I'm simply a "work in progress," a postmodern installation piece.

Is it mere coincidence that I'm entranced by simulacra and the idea of the "alien"?

16 NOVEMBER

"Soft targets." "Combat fatigue." The modern battlefield is littered with condescending euphemisms designed for a population of armchair savants who can't stand the sight of blood unless it's conjured up by Industrial Light and Magic.[21]

---

[21] Industrial Light and Magic is an Academy Award-winning motion

The United States has become spineless, ineffectual, and nastily autistic. So we invent a new lexicon to protect us from the stark nightmare reality of mangled bodies arriving en masse from a war that never should have been.

We might as well get it over with. U.S. soldiers should be stripped of their human citizenship and rechristened "organic combat modules." Then we wouldn't feel nearly as bad when the next batch gets splattered all over the desert by a rocket-propelled grenade. And maybe we won't feel that pang of un-patriotic shame when another one of our troops puts a gun to his head or wanders off into the middle of nowhere to die.

18 NOVEMBER

It rained intermittently all day.

I finished reading *Night* by Elie Wiesel over a double-shot of espresso. Suddenly I was very tired. I browsed at Barnes & Noble for a while – *Filter* magazine has a good cover story on Michael Stipe. I'm fascinated by his face; every time I see it I want to pull out a sketchbook.

Last night was largely sleepless. I'm fighting a sense of emptiness that seems to have attached itself to me and inundated my cells. Too often, the people I encounter seem like little more than mass-produced animatronics. Memories seem more substantial, and certainly more exquisite, than reality.

Lingering dreams of transit. Solace in anonymity. Circadian ritual. Rain-slicked rooftop parking lots. The universe bursting into fragments.

Everything is under control.

19 NOVEMBER

I really wish I could relate some meaningful and/or interesting anecdote about my day, but I can't. I slept badly again, and resigned

---

picture visual effects company that was founded in May 1975 by filmmaker George Lucas. See: www.ilm.com.

myself to methodically eating canned goods, doing laundry and drinking the obligatory coffee (a new blend called – no kidding – "The Meaning of Life." Not bad for $1.47).

You know what? I'm really sick of the Midwest. I'm not putting it down; I'm just tired of it. I'd like to find myself suddenly wandering the streets of Cairo or Bangkok or Paris. Tokyo, Prague, Mars – just give me the ticket and I'm there.

20 NOVEMBER

I finally dined at the new Panera down the street. It's surprisingly spacious. Fortunately it was pretty empty except for a handful of yuppie hipsters with laptop computers and the usual residue of medical students from the University of Missouri – Kansas City.

I scheduled an overdue (and over-priced) haircut this morning. The stylist's name is Mac, or at least he claims it is. There was much generic bonhomie as the rest of the staff clued into the fact that there were two Macs on the premises.

This evening I took in a nature photography gallery, vaguely enjoying the role of thoughtful customer while the manager demonstrated the merits of anti-glare framing and chromatic printing.

Excellent weather, by the way.

21 NOVEMBER

My circadian rhythms are shot to hell.

23 NOVEMBER

So this is what I'm doing: sitting in a too-cold apartment glancing warily at the wintry urban landscape nine floors down and pondering the unread books on my shelves. A plan is forming: I will choose a book I haven't read and go down the street to the coffee shop and read it.

Coffee or espresso? I can have both, you know. It's called a "Depth Charge" – a shot of espresso unleashed into a cup of otherwise normal coffee. Side-effects include flickering delusions of self-importance and out-of-body experiences. I stopped drinking Depth Charges when I realized that I could still get my frequent buyer's card punched for normal coffee; I had thought that the card was only good for espresso drinks. Evidently I hadn't read the fine print.

25 NOVEMBER

Looks like I might have a cameo on the NBC "reality" show *Average Joe*. I was reading in the coffee shop and in walks the show's star with a quick-talking girlfriend (manager?) and a cameraman. I was the only customer at the time. The camera dude swung his machine at me and the friend asked me if I recognized the star, a blonde named Melana. I gave her a thoughtful stare and admitted ignorance.

I didn't even know there was a show called *Average Joe*. I just now Googled it to know what, exactly, I'm dealing with.[22]

While the group was getting ready to leave, I apologized to Melana: "Don't feel embarrassed that I don't know you. I don't watch TV." She patted my arm and laughed it off.

Here's what she says about her "type" on the show's website:

"I am usually attracted to the guy who walks in and 'lights up the room,' not by his looks, but by his charm and the way he treats others... with a smile. I have been known to become weak for the singer/songwriter/guitar player as well."[23]

---

[22] *Average Joe* was a "reality" television series that ran on NBC from 2003 to 2005. The premise was to to get 16 to 18 ordinary men to win over the heart of a beauty queen.

[23] Melana Scantlin (born December 4, 1977, in Gladstone, Missouri) is an American television co-host, former beauty contestant, and "reality TV" participant. She competed in the Miss Teen USA and Miss USA beauty pageants.

Alas, I don't think my presence precisely "lights up the room." If anything, I add a nuance of caffeinated misanthropy. Charm-wise, I'm probably somewhere between Morrissey and Jeff Goldblum. Definitely not television material.

Anyway, watch *Average Joe* and let me know if I'm in it. I'm the guy in the corner wearing rectangular black-framed glasses and a black leather jacket.

26 NOVEMBER

Dream: Urban decay. Squalid playground equipment, eruptions of weeds through asphalt, the silent carcass of a lobotomized city. An almost tactile sense of abandonment.

27 NOVEMBER

Dubbya, in all of his patriotic glory, blessed U.S. troops with his presence in Iraq on Thanksgiving Day. It was a spectacular photo-op, but it might come back to haunt him. Iraq's been producing dead American soldiers at a respectable rate for a while now. I'm not a Pentagon strategist, but how intelligent can it be to send Air Force One on a top-secret mission so Dubbya can pose with a baked turkey while wearing an Army jacket?

The admiring talking head covering the "story" made Dubbya's secret flight to the Gulf sound like the stuff of action movies – and in Dubbya's eternally child-like mind, talking it up with a bunch of grunts in fatigues while waiting for his private plane to take him back to civilization probably *was* action, in the same way that swaggering around an aircraft carrier in a flight suit seemed oh-so-cool.

Here's an unsettling possibility: What if word of Air Force One's abrupt departure had made it to Iraqi Evil-Doers? And what if they had downed the plane with a rocket-propelled grenade, like they do to U.S. military helicopters on a near-daily basis? Let's be generous and assume that Dubbya survived the crash. Can you imagine him taking on The Enemy under cover of darkness and making it to the nearest U.S. camp, to be greeted with cheers and back-slapping military camaraderie?

Skeptics would pounce. They'd maintain that the "crash" was staged and that the Evil-Doers were actually U.S. soldiers in fake mustaches and phony uniforms following classified orders. Objective: turn Dubbya into a war hero. Of course, there'd be no reason to tell Dubbya. Let him think he really took on Iraqi rebels; then maybe he'd be less likely to let the truth slip at his next press conference.

And then there's the inevitable TV movie: "Behind Enemy Lines" (or some such shit), probably starring Don Johnson as Bush. And of course the obligatory American Hero action figure (fully compatible with Flight Suit Bush and accessories) – just in time for Christmas.

28 NOVEMBER

The Lighting Ceremony for the Plaza Christmas tree really packed them in. There are actually people from out-of-state who flock to the Plaza in trailers and stay overnight to witness the official countdown.

I waited for the crowd to thin while the stage technicians began packing up, and then made for Barnes & Noble. Closed. The coffee shop was jam-packed, so that was out of the question. I ended up just coming home. I've going to brave the masses tomorrow and, contrary to my principles, probably buy something even though it's Buy Nothing Day. In my culture-jamming playbook, it doesn't count if you purchase something from a local, non-corporate store. I'm just making this clear so the Karma Police can't throw me in lock-up.

29 NOVEMBER

It's a zoo outside, a confusion of shoppers and Salvation Army volunteers and horse-drawn carriages. I barely managed to cross the street back to my apartment.

30 NOVEMBER

I received a nice email from a reader in Australia yesterday. He poses a rather pertinent question. In his own words: "I can't believe how many books you read. Are reading and drinking coffee the only things you fill your day with???"

Actually, that's not all I do (appearances aside). I also spend a great deal of time heating up microwave pasta, doing laundry and hatching ambitious schemes involving extra-planetary colonization and uploading brains into computers.

It's a busy life – downright hectic sometimes.

Chapter 12
December 2003

3 DECEMBER

Someone in a nearby apartment has heated up leftover Thanksgiving turkey. Even though I'm vegetarian, it's making me hungry as hell. I haven't had this craving for poultry since I stealthily inhaled cold fried chicken leftovers in the break-room at my old job.

I've hardly eaten anything today, now that I think of it. Two Pop-Tarts, a cup of black bean vegetarian chili and ginger ale. And a $4.00 fruit smoothie called "Lucille's Paradise." With a name like that, I expected at least a modest dose of psychoactives, but no such luck.

4 DECEMBER

Hot off the presses lately it seems is the notion that "Planet X" is in-bound and will wreak havoc upon our planet. I suspect that the rather heavily mythologized version of "Planet X" encountered on the Net doesn't exist, but that's not to say that something isn't out there.[24]

I think the recent online "Planet X" panic has less to do with astronomy than the hideous state of affairs here on Earth. Apocalyptic fictions and predictions are circulating at a rate unprecedented since the Y2K scare. And I think this is ultimately because of the September 11 attacks.

---

[24] Tonnies is referring to the so-called "Nibiru cataclysm," a projected disastrous encounter between the Earth and a large planetary object which some people believe will take place in the early 21st century. Believers in this doomsday event usually refer to this object as *Planet X* or *Nibiru*. See: www.badastronomy.com/bad/misc/planetx/index.html.

We've entered a new epoch, and our fears have been transplanted to the skies. It's fallen on our collective unconscious to seek out patterns in the noise and confusion. But the human mind is more than willing to register false alarms. Thus the modern myth of "Planet X," destroyer of worlds.

Of course, none of this is to say we're safe and have nothing to worry about. Sooner or later a big chunk of rock and ice is going to slam into our planet; the only question is when. So if the possibility of a "Planet X" encourages us to pay attention to the solar neighborhood, then it will have served a very useful purpose.

7 DECEMBER

Francis Fukuyama may have the last, bitter laugh: we may indeed be turning into posthumans, but of the terminally medicated, ineffectual variety prophesied in his book.

The icon of 21st century society may not be the paternal visage of Orwell's "Big Brother," but the looming televised geisha from *Blade Runner*, who drops a pill on her pixelated tongue and smiles with the faintest suggestion of smugness.

"A new life awaits you in the Off-World Colonies!"

Meanwhile, it rains endlessly and we lock horns with the demeaning logic of our own genes.

8 DECEMBER

My name is Senator Victor Kassim Oyofo, the chairman of the Senate committee on Pension, insurance and manpower development in the National Assembly of the Federal Republic Of Nigeria.

Jesus! Why is this crap always (ostensibly) from Nigeria? "Nigeria" is synonymous with "spam." You'd think the brains behind these spam campaigns would relocate. How refreshing, for example, to get some spam from Brazil or Syria or Haiti.

On the subject of extorting money: I've been fielding numerous telephone calls from the Fraternal Order of Police. My position on this is very simple: the police are not some shoe-string volunteer outfit held together by bonhomie and the desire to keep neighborhoods safe from crime. They're a tax-funded entity. Their officers are paid salaries, usually for little more than pulling random cars aside and extorting yet more money in the form of dubious "traffic violations."

Let the police take their little crusade to the sidewalks like a respectable charity.

I want to see them grovel.

9 DECEMBER

BushCo needs to keep a certain critical level of anti-Arab sentiment stoked so it can prolong its illegal war for as long as possible. The "War on Terror" needs nice, neat polarized "good guys" and "bad guys." This leaves no room whatsoever for real terrorists with real explosives if they happen to be home-grown white boys.

No, "terrorists" are from the Middle East and worship Allah. Everyone knows that.

10 DECEMBER

Valiant U.S. troops managed to blow away another six children in Afghanistan.[25] I suppose the logic is that if we kill them early there's less chance of them growing up to be Evil-Doers.

11 DECEMBER

The cold weather has apparently driven the street preachers indoors. What kind of "faith" is that? Shame on them! Nothing would warm my heart like some idiot with frostbite trying to hold onto a giant wooden cross. Get out there and rant, you bastards!

13 DECEMBER

A week ago my watch missed 10-15 minutes. I assumed the

---

[25] Tonnies was referencing the following incident: "More Afghan Children Die In Raids," *BBC News*, 10 December 2003. http://goo.gl/o21qt.

battery was going dead, even though it's a fairly new watch, and have been waiting for it to start lagging again so I'll know for sure. Now, of course, it works perfectly. The problem is that I can no longer trust it. So I'm constantly checking other time-pieces for a "second opinion."

Maybe it's not the watch's fault. Maybe I accidentally lifted the stopper. Maybe I was in a time-warp.

I really need to let this go.

Meanwhile, "Google" the search term "miserable failure" and see what comes up as the number-one match - Dubbya.

I wonder what happens if you enter in "sadistic fuck"?

14 DECEMBER

I bought a LatteLand coffee mug and thermos as Christmas gifts. As I was sitting at a table in the coffee shop doing nothing in particular, the barista on duty reminded me that both items came with a free drink. I had no idea. It was like being awarded a prize. I got a cup of coffee to go and got a ticket for my next one, which I'll use tomorrow. How about that?

15 DECEMBER

We finally got Saddam Hussein. And it only took 8,000+ dead civilians. This is roughly akin to the police chasing down an escaped murderer – moreover, one who is unarmed – and accidentally taking out a small town in the process. I urge anyone who thinks this is a "success" to stand in front of the nearest speeding car.

16 DECEMBER

This evening, I caught my first take of mainstream media coverage of the Saddam thing through the plastic partition of a *Kansas City Star* vending stand ("Special Coverage" emblazoned in blood-red letters). I could really care less. At this late stage in the Iraq mess, capturing Saddam Hussein is so much light entertainment. The Baath regime is no more; we obliterated it as thoroughly as we obliterated Baghdad.

176

Thrusting a grizzled, beleaguered Hussein into the limelight is creepily similar to broadcasting prerecorded footage of Goldstein in *Nineteen Eighty-Four*. We need to be reminded who to hate lest we begin evaluating this whole massively absurd situation for ourselves.

Hussein certainly deserves to stand trial, but I'm not interested in BushCo's inevitable theatrics. *USA Today* loudly reports that Bush wants a public trial. Of course he does. I imagine he'd also endorse a public stoning.

17 DECEMBER

Today's the 17th. The big day when Bush is supposed to announce a new manned venture to the Moon so we can beat the suddenly space-savvy Chinese. I previously predicted that it wouldn't happen. And since it's getting a little late in the day without my inbox being inundated with overjoyed messages saying "I told you so," I'm becoming even more doubtful. At this rate, we'll still be gloating over Hussein's convenient capture when the Helium-3 warheads start raining down from outer space.

20 DECEMBER

The new edifice poised to take the place of the World Trade Center (named, somewhat repugnantly, the "Freedom Tower") is to be topped with tiers of wind-turbines that will provide 20% of the building's energy needs.

I suppose the turbines are meant to express U.S. independence from foreign oil, in which case they're essentially a joke on the American people. But the idea is promising. Wind-energy collectors should be mandatory for all new skyscrapers. Imagine the skyline of a near-future metropolis encapsulated in a mesh of steadily whirring turbines. Why, you might even be able to take a stroll without respiratory gear!

21 DECEMBER

The official U.S. Fear-O-Meter has been raised to "orange" due to the usual unspecified "substantial increase" in whatever exactly it is that precedes terrorist attacks. By "terrorists," I assume the government is referring to Muslim terrorists, as it doesn't appear to give a damn about armed psychopaths right here in the USA, like white supremacists.

So what does this "substantial increase" refer to, anyway? Ex-CIA honchos selling off stock? A sudden, dire need to polarize public opinion against a new batch of faceless Evil-Doers? The guys at NORAD turning off their computer monitors to allow hijacked airliners to fly over major cities unimpeded? Beats me.

Have yourselves a "scared witless for no apparent reason" Christmas.

23 DECEMBER

Here's an urban phenomenon I don't understand: people who come to abrupt stops in the middle of sidewalks so they can talk on their cell phones. You never see it coming, either. The fat woman right in front of you whips out her "designer" Nokia and commuters are forced to make rapid evasive maneuvers or else find themselves in a human pile-up.

All that cell phone use involves is walking and talking. Is this so hard? Is it too much to ask that the self-important drones who must field their calls from heavily trafficked sidewalks and store interiors keep moving while they conduct their business? Are Americans so self-centered and solipsistic that they don't realize when they're in the way? Judging from the U.S. presence in Iraq, I'm guessing the answer is "yes."

Here's something else that's beginning to bother me: Why do the Papa John's pizza delivery guys call to let you know your pizza is on its way? Save us both some time and just call me when it arrives! Unless you can't find my address and need help, I don't really give a damn where it is.

Meanwhile, there's this wildly popular fiddle player here on the Plaza who's steadily grated on my nerves over the years. He sets up shop outside the coffee shop I frequent and starts this god-awful hillbilly routine. How "rustic"! Passersby eat it up, of course, and fling little wads of money into his donation basket.

He fleeces tourists and window-shoppers year-round, but holidays are the worst. To get my coffee, I have to pass through a small crowd of fascinated, tasteless listeners. The other night he was squealing his way through a bone-chilling medley of Christmas songs. Members of his audience were literally slapping their knees in time to the music.

I wanted to vomit, as noisily as possible.

25 DECEMBER

I'm up late – or early, depending on your diurnal sensibilities – wondering if the British-built *Beagle 2* probe has successfully landed on Mars. I just checked the probe's official site and it doesn't look good. Apparently the *Beagle* was to signal NASA's *Mars Odyssey* spacecraft to let it know its status. So far, it hasn't responded. But the game isn't over yet. If I manage to sleep tonight, the first thing I'll do upon waking is check the Net for updates.[26]

Happy holidays to everyone who's taken time out of their day this year to glance over my virtual shoulder.

26 DECEMBER

The good part about all the crashed/disabled/missing probes littering the Martian surface is that they'll provide a lucrative salvage industry for future astronauts (assuming, as always, that we eventually make it to the Red Planet in person). I wonder what the *Mars Polar Lander* would go for on eBay.

I bet that somewhere there's an extremely wealthy person who'd

---

[26] *Beagle 2* was an unsuccessful British landing spacecraft that formed part of the European Space Agency's 2003 *Mars Express* mission. All contact with it was lost upon its separation from the *Mars Express* six days before its scheduled entry into the atmosphere. The *Beagle*-2 website is: www.beagle2.com/index.htm.

like to have the *Mars Pathfinder* displayed in his/her office, perhaps as part of a diorama recreating Sagan Memorial Station. 100% real Martian dirt, of course. Can you imagine what that powdery red stuff would go for here on Earth? My guess is that it would be somewhere up there with cocaine and those military-grade neurotoxins that only Middle Eastern Evil-Doers make.

By the way, bovine spongiform encephalopathy (popularly known as "Mad Cow Disease") has finally found its way into the United States. Contrary to what you might read in the ever-dour mainstream press, this is great news. I hope this really throws corporate behemoths like McDonald's for a loop. The next time you sink your teeth into a quarter-pounder, stop to imagine thousands of deadly, invisible prions inundating your brain and chewing great big holes in it while you inexorably go insane and die a spasmodic death. Not exactly the stuff great ad campaigns are made of, is it?

Of course, the all-knowing folks at McDonald's assure us that there's absolutely nothing to fear. And we all know that giant, politically esteemed corporations never lie or act against the best interests of their clients.

Mad Cow Disease. I'm lovin' it.

27 DECEMBER

One would think a sane society would invest a sizeable percentage of energy and money to the location and prompt destruction of incoming near-Earth asteroids. But no, not us. "Enlightened" Western civilization is just too macho for such things, apparently. Even NASA's official Near-Earth Asteroid Tracking website looks like something thrown together at the last minute by a freshman Computer Science minor.

Even if we happened to locate a "global killer" using the scant resources available, what would we do about it? Have Bush broadcast snide remarks at it? More tax cuts, perhaps? We simply don't have the faintest semblance of an alert/avoidance system.

Compounding the problem, an untold number of people across

the world have been trained to expect and even look forward to the End of the World. Exhibit A: "In Case of Rapture, This Car Will Be Unmanned."

Whether it's a designer virus, climate change, greenhouse emissions, inbound comets, industrial toxins or good old-fashioned nuclear weapons, we'll eventually be done in.

But in the meantime, let's all buy Humvees and watch Monday night football.

28 DECEMBER

Thirteen new "coalition" casualties!? But... but... we got Saddam! "Mission Accomplished" and all that! Could it be that the only people in the world remotely interested in Hussein's capture are right here in the U.S. and that it doesn't amount to anything except a brittle sense of renewed Patriotism and increased approval ratings for Bush?

In other news, there's rekindled hope that Bush will announce a manned lunar/Mars mission at the State of the Union Address. Possible, but unlikely. The tragedy is that even if he does, the Democrats will oppose it as a matter of course and we'll end up nowhere.

Which is, of course, exactly what's supposed to happen in our political system.

29 DECEMBER

This evening a Scientology *Dianetics* auditor, armed with a disappointingly innocuous-looking e-meter, was giving a free "stress-test" to passersby near the Palace Theater.

L. Ron Hubbard's *Dianetics* is one of the only books I've never been able to finish.

I've tried.

Twice.

It's sitting vulture-like on my shelf, daring me to try again.

Meanwhile, I have this inexplicable, absolutely senseless crush on Natalie Portman. On some level, my brain has decided that cultivating a doomed attraction to a captivating young actress is a good idea. I don't have time for this. And yet there's a bittersweet aspect to my infatuation that's not entirely depressing. Maybe that's what my psyche needs right now. Maybe the concept of Natalie Portman is fulfilling some pivotal role in my subconscious.

I wonder what she's doing for New Year's.

30 DECEMBER

I spent a chunk of my day reading a lame science fiction novel called *Wyrmhole*. Now I'm at a crossroads. Do I pick up another book and keep reading or do I start writing fiction in earnest? Can I do both and still write effectively? I charged my laptop the other day and put it on top of my stereo where I can't ignore it. Even so, MacLeod's *Engine City* is exerting an almost narcotic pull on me.

I'm all out of groceries – down to some dehydrated soups. No pop left, so I'm freezing the ice cubes from my last cream soda; they have a faint sugary residue, which is better than nothing. I indulged and ate at Uno's Pizza the other night; now I find myself eyeing Fred P. Ott's out my window and imagining biting into another veggie cheese-steak sandwich. Maybe I should go there. Maybe I'll meet a girl who digs pale, introverted guys who write about Mars.

Maybe Natalie Portman will be there.

31 DECEMBER

It's New Year's Eve. I should write something about my plans for the new year, or describe my resolutions or something. Then again, bloggers everywhere will be doing exactly that. Screw it. Here's something else:

Have you ever been in a store and noticed Amish people walking the aisles, appraising "high-tech" merchandise and sometimes even buying some? Firstly, I have nothing against Amish people. If you want to live your life according to the technological standards of some arbitrary historical period, that's all right with me. In fact, the idea is not without a weird sort of appeal. What I find distasteful is when Amish people cheat. In my opinion, shopping in modern stores is a flagrant violation of the rules. It's a matter of principle, up there with "vegetarians" who order steak and attempt to shrug it off as a dietary anomaly. If you're going to do the Amish thing, do it right.

So rather than making a New Year's resolution for myself, I'll make one on behalf of Amish people everywhere. No more cheating. No more fudging. Be Amish or don't be Amish. Make up your damned mind.

And best wishes for 2004!

Chapter 13
January 2004

1 JANUARY

Fireworks wriggling madly skyward like phosphorescent sperm cells, showers of diminished light playing across the crystalline surfaces of office towers. 2003 dies, moody and faded: a discarded accessory. The future inches nearer — not that it has ever ceased moving nearer, but framed suddenly in a symphony of muffled pyrotechnics and blazing sky-bound chemicals, it seems abruptly and oddly tangible; a presence sensed in the gut and the knot of tissue somewhere between the eyes. A numbing temporal caress; a tectonic shiver. A collective pang of loss and hope and tangled fear. And then the fireworks end and you have slipped through some phantom orifice into a world marked by a brand-new number, bulging with portent. Terra incognita. This slippery thing we call the future, eluding our faculties like a photon engaged in quantum dialogue with itself.

2 JANUARY

Much ado has been made about the "arrival" of "Mad Cow Disease" in the U.S. As dire and newsworthy as this sounds, I doubt that BSE is a newcomer. I think it's been incubating within our population for a long time. Some scientists have even proposed that the infamous "unmarked helicopters" seen in the vicinity of cattle mutilations might be part of a clandestine government effort to trace the spread of BSE. The modern cattle mutilation phenomenon began in the late 1970s, more than enough time for a contagion like BSE to infiltrate the U.S. and take up residence in our spinal tissue.

But why, ask debunkers, would the government use such secretive

185

and costly methods? Why doesn't it simply buy its own cattle-land for research purposes instead of terrifying ranchers and spawning horror stories about Little Gray Men?

Because the horror stories are integral to maintaining secrecy. By conducting tests in the open, the government (or whatever agency is responsible for cattle "mutes") would effectively signal its ignorance and lack of control. Citizens would ask questions. They might even panic.

What better way to avoid public accountability than take the study "deep black"? Sure, ranchers are going to wonder what the hell's going on. But since the underground study hasn't admitted to anything – indeed, it's circumvented Congressional oversight entirely – it can maintain its activity with impunity.

Stories of alien experimentation are bound to arise unassisted. The "alien invasion" meme is incredibly potent. Given its myriad psy-ops applications, it would be foolish not to exploit it. Eventually, in the hands of well-meaning researchers such as Linda Moulton Howe, a merely terrifying top-secret attempt to track a brain-destroying disease becomes the grisly handiwork of ufonauts every bit as cool, unsympathetic and inscrutable as H.G. Wells' Martians.[27]

Or maybe there really is an alien element behind some cattle mutilations. Perhaps the government is using genuine alien experimentation as a cover for more mundane research, or possibly as an attempt to reverse-engineer the aliens' own agenda. Or – and this is truly freaky – aliens and terrestrial biologists are working together. Maybe diseases like BSE really are the culprits, and the

---

[27] Linda Moulton Howe is a conspiracist who has become the leading proponent of the "alien" meme as an explanation for "cattle mutilations" (as well as "abductions," the Roswell incident, and other similar events). A former reporter for mainstream media outlets, she received a 1981 Regional Emmy award for *A Strange Harvest*, a documentary she made about "cattle mutilations" for KMGH-TV, a CBS affiliate in Denver, Colorado. She is a frequent guest on late-night fringe radio talk shows. Her website is: www.earthfiles.com.

aliens have a sincere, ongoing interest in it. In this case, maybe the aliens are OK. Better a bunch of anonymous livestock than us, right?

But there are reports of human mutilations, too. Paranoia? Hoaxes? Disinformation? Whitley Strieber claims that close-encounters with apparent nonhuman beings have taken a decided turn for the malevolent lately. If true, maybe the intelligence behind the "mutes" – human or ET (or both) – is proceeding with the next stage of its project.

5 JANUARY

The Constitution is toast.

Yeah, it lingered for a while in the wake of 9-11-01. It stuck it out like a war-weary soldier, maimed and crippled, but in the end it didn't really have a chance against shits like Ashcroft. Protesters at Bush appearances now have to take their complaints to designated "free-speech zones" or risk the wrath of the Secret Service, whose job seems to have less to do with protecting the president's life than protecting his approval ratings.

This is a travesty. No, it's worse than that – it's the effective end of a democracy that could have been good.

Hail to the thief.

7 JANUARY

We're living in a kleptocratic aristocracy.

Due process?

Freedom of assembly?

Can't have 'em! Got a "War on Terror" to fight here, folks!

8 JANUARY

The FAO Schwartz on the Plaza is going out of business. This is a heartening development, sparing shoppers the seizure-inducing "theme music" that spills from the store's central totem: a twitching plastic monument to prepubescent greed certified to send even the most media-saturated among us clutching at their hair in minutes.

And if that's not enough, there's also an animatronic dinosaur who speaks in "ebonics." Places like FAO deserve to die prolonged deaths.

Across the street, George Brett's has opened up (think: neighborhood sportsbar meets casual elegance), framed in dappled blue neon. Not a place I plan on going. I find quasi-religious worship of sports icons scary as hell.

Of course, on the other end of the Plaza there's The Granfalloon, named after a word coined by none other than Kurt Vonnegut. If The Granfalloon actually had a Vonnegut theme I don't think I could stop myself from going, but sadly it's just another noisy (if nicely designed) place where you're lucky to get a decent seat, and nobody knows who Kurt Vonnegut is.

10 JANUARY

Today the *Kansas City Star* and *USA Today* both have big front-page stories on "Mars Mania." And there's increasingly serious speculation that Bush's Moon-Mars initiative is more than just wishful thinking on behalf of space advocates. Of course, when I say "Bush's Moon-Mars initiative" I'm not really attributing anything to Bush, who I doubt could locate the Red Planet on a map of the Solar System to save his life.

Have you noticed how NASA's Jet Propulsion Lab (JPL) and the mainstream press have turned the *Spirit* rover into something of a personality? Space journalism is suddenly filled with rather desperate attempts to transmogrify a six-wheeled, solar-powered, remote-controlled dune-buggy into an interplanetary showman (or show-woman – I don't think they've given it a gender yet). When *Spirit* stands up on its wheels, it's not performing a basic requirement; it's giving a stand-up performance a la Jerry Seinfeld. It "sleeps," it "wakes up," it sends "postcards" from its new "neighborhood"!

It's alive!

Can we expect Spirit to "do Letterman" anytime soon?

Perhaps the JPL geeks (I use that term respectfully) can make it "wave its hand" to television viewers worldwide during the next big halftime show?

Will Spirit run for president?

As much as I'm savoring the *Spirit* mission, I find attempts to humanize the rover weirdly disturbing, like guys who give their cars (or, worse, their computers) sexy female names. There's definitely a Freudian under-stratum to the public's infatuation with *Spirit* and its cybernetic derring-do. NASA has done more than transplant a bug-like machine to the Red Planet; it's sent a spark of our collective desire to get off this poisoned, treacherous globe we call "home." *Spirit* is nothing less than an avatar of silicon and wire, spared the neuroses and anxieties that plague Earth. Physically distant yet impressively intimate in its media-savvy, it (she?) joins the ranks of "Max Headroom" and "Lara Croft" – postmodern superstars that straddle the dissolving barrier between the real and the unreal.

It's no mistake there's a CD with hundreds of thousands of names on board *Spirit* – and yes, mine's there too, basking in Mars' ultraviolet flux, waiting for some future collector to pop it in his antique CD-ROM drive. It's like some sort of cosmic lottery, or a bid for ersatz immortality.

Ultimately, *Spirit* might have less to do with Mars than it does with the way we identify with our machinery. Perhaps instead of including a plaque commemorating the crew of *Columbia*, JPL should have attached a few choice quotes from J.G. Ballard's *Crash*.

Meanwhile, here's some poetry:

Homeostatic circadian blur
lofty naked dreams bleeding on cold gravel
cracks in the aquaria reveal concrete stars
and trajectories traced in fissured celluloid
Chattering hemispheres, memories of light
seen through a peptide veil
breathing the air of new centuries through
brittle plastic lips and fixated eyes.

11 JANUARY

"I Want to Believe."

You come across this phrase a lot while browsing UFO websites. I don't get it. Why would anyone want to believe in something? "Belief" implies a capacity for self-deception. Perhaps if the human race spent less of its time "believing" in things and more of its time thinking and deducing we wouldn't be forced up against the chilly wall of imminent chaos, vainly pretending all is well.

"Belief" is a sugar-coated suicide pill – attractive in a peculiar way, and not without a certain mystical charm. But I fear it's a luxury we can't afford.

12 JANUARY

I'm up late doing laundry. There's something existentially reassuring about laundry, something earthy and cyclic and zen that speaks to the subconscious. We can launch probes to other planets, explore the subatomic "particle zoo," and map the human genome, but we still have to do laundry. I don't think futurists of the 1950s thought we'd be doing laundry in 2004: much easier to drop your clothes into an ultrasonic cleaner. No detergent, no wrinkles, no static cling, no dryer lint.

But we're still doing laundry pretty much the way we always have. Laundry is exempt from the change that envelops and transforms the rest of waking reality; it's a temporal linchpin, an anchor to sanity.

13 JANUARY

Politicians inevitably counter plans to send humans to the Moon or beyond by relying on a time-honored mantra: "But there are more important things to be done here on Earth!" And the public, sheep-like as always, nods its collective agreement. What wisdom!

Alas, there will always be pressing problems here on Earth. *Always.* Get used to it. Barring the sudden emergence of a global utopia wherein all of our physical, emotional and intellectual needs are met, we will continue to be plagued with violence, poverty, leaking roofs, car accidents, unemployment, homelessness, disease, lost keys, and corrupt leaders.

So why don't we dispense with these disingenuous, imaginatively crippled fucks and get on with it? We don't need NASA. We don't need to await lofty, pointless assurances from the likes of Bush. We need initiative and drive on a grassroots level. Or else one day, possibly quite soon, it will simply be too late. We will have died in the womb, unremembered. And the cosmos' long silence will claim us.

But for now, the sun is certainly shining brightly on the Bush Regime's various administrative atrocities. First "King of Pop" Michael Jackson appears to keep the mainstream media dutifully distracted from anything important. Like the quiet insemination of "Patriot Act II," which basically dismantles the Constitution and then urinates on the pieces.

Now, some ex-baseball player named Pete Rose is all you hear about. Something tells me we'll be hearing about Pete for a long time. Between the spectacle of Jackson's imminent "trial of the century" on child molestation charges, Saddam Hussein's interrogation and Rose's gambling confession, how much room for real news will newspapers and television have time for?

Our military-industrial-entertainment complex is a sad and twisted mockery specifically designed to distract, confuse and move product. Only the product being sold is you.

Turn off your televisions.

This is memetic war to extermination.

16 JANUARY

President Bush has finally voiced his administration's plans for future space exploration. As disappointingly remote as they may seem on first take (and there's every possibility that they will be shot down entirely), it's the first proactive space initiative in memory. It's not "We choose to go to Mars," but it leaves the door open. And it recognizes the dire need for a vehicle to replace the Space Shuttle fleet (or what's left of it) with something that doesn't belong in the

Air and Space Museum.

Of course, we should have had a functioning alternative to the Shuttle a long time ago, but better late than never.

17 JANUARY

What if, due to financial and scientific considerations, NASA was able to launch a manned mission to Mars – but only as a one-way trip? I don't think a strictly one-way trip is necessary; we can have our exploratory cake and eat it, too. But what if, for whatever reasons, a one-way jaunt to Mars was all that was available (or at least foreseeable)? Who would go? Closet fatalists desperate to escape the clutches of Starbucks and Disney or unflagging optimists willing to sacrifice their home world for the prospect of an alien frontier? Does it matter?

More topically: Would I go?

Yes, I would.

In a heartbeat.

Meanwhile, I had another late-night dinner at Panera. They closed at 10:00; I got there at about a quarter till, with the place almost to myself. Panera has a sort of Marxist/Stalinist thread running through its interior décor, with lots of pictures of stolid men engaged in the timeless craft of bread-making, a righteous synergy of muscle and dough.

"I'll have the veggie sandwich and a small drink, comrade."

Blood-red Chinese lanterns sway pendulously over the bridge outside my apartment like plump flying saucers, or perhaps lambent, mildly radioactive tomatoes. The lanterns are guarded by statues of anonymous warriors, silhouetted against a stream of weekend headlights – the usual parade of white limos, oozing blue neon as if the occupants are aliens from some planet of perpetual luminosity.

A double espresso the color of Martian mud and then back across the street (lanterns stirring vaguely in their ranks), past the diligently scrolling Mircom machine and through the freshly painted lobby to the elevator. Someone, presumably on my floor, has cooked fish in my short absence. The hallway, and now my apartment, reeks of it. My cats seem miraculously oblivious.

A conical stellar nursery takes form inside my lava lamp, gooey hatchling stars and molten nebular sludge.

18 JANUARY

I was sifting through my email when the fire alarm went off.

This had happened before, so I didn't panic. Far from it: I kept typing, pretty sure some drunk had tripped the alarm or something equally innocuous; my "building" is actually two identical nine-floor towers. Each floor in each tower possesses at least one smoke detector linked to a general, apartment-wide alarm system, so the odds of a given alarm responding to a conflagration in my immediate vicinity are fairly slim – basically one in eighteen.

"Yes," you might be thinking, "but fire has a curious tendency to spread." But my brain just doesn't assess risks like this. Maybe some of it is my apartment building's sheer age – it's been around since the 1920s, so what are the chances of a towering inferno during my residency? I kept on clicking and looking at pictures of Mars and trying to ignore the ear-splitting wailing and buzzing coming from the hall, which had rudely interrupted the dour electronica of David Bowie's "Outside."

Then I noticed Ebe, one of my cats, perched on top of my monitor and pointedly sniffing the air. That got my attention. I opened the door, saw smoke – not a lot, but enough to suggest a minor kitchen fire on a neighboring floor – opened a window to let in clean air for the cats and trudged down the stairs to the lobby accompanied by a striking short-haired girl from the apartment directly below mine (although I'd never seen her before, which is really quite fucking typical and probably just as well).

Firemen tromped into the lobby within minutes of my arrival. They thoughtfully left the alarm on for the benefit of any coma victims who might not have noticed it and headed for the fire (or the remains of it); I later found out it was a cooking accident on 8.

Meanwhile, I sat on a table next to the girl from floor 8 watching lots of distressed old people who will doubtlessly spend the next few weeks relating this incident to anyone who will listen. And although I was sure my cats would be fine, especially with an open window and the presence of firemen who didn't appear too rattled, I nevertheless felt worthless for not bringing them downstairs with me.

Finally the alarm was shut off and tenants were allowed back in their apartments. I said goodnight to the girl on 8 (probably asleep a few meters beneath me as I type this) and found my cats holding up well, if a bit skittish from the noise. Curiously, I found my door locked. I don't remember locking it, although I suppose I certainly could have in the heat of the moment.

And that's that. The hive was briefly disturbed; now we can all resume our regularly scheduled programming, barricaded in our customized cells of masonry, wiring and groaning pipes. In all probability I'll never know who locked my door. And I predict I'll never see the girl from floor 8 again; homeostasis precludes such neat certainties and happy endings.

It's very late. On the bridge down the street, the bulbous red lanterns have been turned off for the night, and the streets have emptied.

Scattered city lights like suns in a derelict galaxy; the uneasy promise of dawn.

20 JANUARY

The survival of democracy as we know it hinges increasingly on the inherently decentralized nature of the Internet. So I'm annoyed by Netizens who remain forever anonymous behind "clever" usernames and handles in a vainglorious attempt to keep their "real" lives and online lives discreet.

If you have something important to contribute to the data-sphere, speak out! Use your real name! The Net is not one big chat room; it's one of the central forces keeping our world from dissolution at the hands of mega-corporations, chomping-at-the-bit neo-fascists, and "protective" watchdog government agencies out to fulfill the usual list of Big Brother power fantasies.

The childish reliance on Internet nicknames amounts to an admission of guilt. Guilt about what? Taking part in a liberal democracy, however seemingly immaterial or "virtual"? Ideas have always been "virtual'; while the Web has changed many aspects of our lives, it has not supplanted the sheer creative force of new insights and fresh dialogues. It has merely forced the boundaries further into the background.

And if you think that posting "subversive" material online while using an alias somehow disguises your tracks from the aforementioned bad guys, guess again. The odds are you're being watched anyway, if you're sufficiently interesting (or amusing). Which, from a merely statistical viewpoint, you're probably not. Even in Orwell's Oceania, the spooks who eavesdropped via telescreen were forced to perform spot-checks instead of lavishing 24-hour surveillance on a single given Party member.

There is no more "virtual." Conversely, there is no more "real," at least in the pre-cyberpunk sense. Making the leap to an information-driven existence is at least as ontologically bewildering as the advent of quantum mechanics, and every bit as critical for our future.

The government and the media want you faceless and nameless. Why are so many of us, armed with one of the most potent democratic tools imaginable, helping them along?

Meanwhile, I think of the suburbs, where brains go to die, ultimately snuffed out like so many porch lights, carried away like bags of garbage. Boring, identical houses produce boring, identical minds. These places are a mistake, a particularly loathsome eyesore on the American cultural trajectory. Whether they consciously realize it or not, humans require spontaneity, playfulness, novelty.

I like to imagine what America might be like now if the dreary spectacle of suburban sprawl had been abandoned in favor of organic design concepts. I bet our society would be happier, healthier, less subject to distraction, and literally more intelligent. Perhaps fewer

Columbine incidents, or maybe a startling reduction in so-called "attention deficit disorder." At the very least, something interesting to look at. The fact that we attempt to "personalize" suburban homes with yellow ribbons and sports memorabilia and plastic gnomes only accentuates the dilemma.

21 JANUARY

I've got this weird ability to mentally project my surroundings into an unspecified near-future perspective. It's most pronounced while viewing scenery from a moving car, when I'm taking in lots of landscape. I have a cinematic imagination that's constantly panning and zooming behind my forehead, rendering the "present" into something more like a premonition. Nothing is exempt; landmarks, vehicles and buildings can abruptly seem brooding and post-apocalyptic. Apparently my brain has a deep, secret need to occasionally see the world in a desolate, depopulated context, something like the ruinous city explored by Bruce Willis' character in *12 Monkeys*.

On a more overt, conscious level, I dig entropy. I tend to gawk at abandoned movie theaters, neglected, fissured parking lots, seedy roadside motels, derelict buildings with shattered windows. I'm strangely attuned to the colors and hues that signify decay. I marvel at crumbling industrial sites and blighted factories with the zeal of an archaeologist. There's a perverse magic to these places, a palpable sense of the otherworldly.

22 JANUARY

Recently, JPL turned the *Spirit* rover away from a unique, dark-colored rock the science team had nicknamed "Sushi." This rock sports an anomalous geometric cavity, making it an especially interesting find. But JPL elected to abandon Sushi as a target for surface drilling because they claimed it looked too "dusty." This claim is highly suspect; even a cursory examination of the rocks at the *Spirit* site shows that Sushi is not just dust-free, but downright shiny, as if subjected to high heat or glazed with some kind of natural "varnish." What is that stuff? Why not drill?

It's the ultimate irony: we send a survey vehicle to another planet and immediately start seeking the familiar, dismissing any oddities that crop up as "bizarre" or "impossible" and making tracks to the nearest available dune or rock that appears safe for intellectual consumption. JPL's behavior makes even less sense when one remembers that haste is of the essence – *Spirit* could cease transmitting at any time.

The *Spirit Mars Exploration Rover* is an unconditional technical triumph. JPL has shown that it has the engineering mettle to place highly capable surrogate astronauts on the Martian surface. But, disturbingly, the sense of adventure appears to end with the hardware itself.

Conveniently unchallenged by a public conditioned to take the words of "rocket scientists" at face value, JPL is already forming some very bad habits: a refusal to acknowledge the unknown and a crippling immunity to the unexpected.[28]

25 JANUARY

The *Spirit* rover is on the mend and *Opportunity* has landed safely. So why am I in an existential funk?

Robotic astronauts remind us that humans are essentially machine-like. We refuel. We expel waste material. We need down-time. We're constantly performing maintenance on ourselves; I get up, joylessly consume a couple toaster-waffles, chase them with a chug of raspberry lemonade. I shower, scrubbing away disenfranchised skin cells and other microscopic nastiness. I comb my hair, fastidiously clean the interior of my ears with a cotton swab, and subject my teeth to a vigorous session with an ergonomically

---

[28] The *Spirit* rover continued to function until it became stuck in late 2009. Its last communication with Earth was sent on March 22, 2010. It's "twin," *Opportunity*, which landed three weeks after *Spirit*, is still active as of October, 2012.

designed brush. And I do this on a regular basis. Pure mechanical ritual. And that's not taking lunch and dinner into account: more dutiful flexing of jaw muscles, all in the name of combating entropy, inevitable cellular decay, premature senility, the prospect of drooling vegetable-hood.

I'm 28 years-old. I look 20. Biomechanically, I'm not doing too bad. I'm 6'2" and weigh in at 185 lbs, sometimes less. I avoid drugs and seldom drink alcohol; I think I consumed all of five or six beers in 2003. I have a seemingly infinite capacity for caffeine, and enjoy the ability to stop drinking coffee at any time without the withdrawal effects bemoaned by others.

My social existence is appropriately machine-like. I did an interview for a news weekly a few weeks ago and the journalist said something like, "From reading your blog, you paint a picture of a smart guy who reads a lot but doesn't have much of a personal life." I suppose it depends on what he meant by "personal." Socially, I'm borderline solipsistic. The majority of males my age would positively cringe at the private time I require. I venture out into the world of smoke-filled restaurants and bars and coffee-shops and take in masses of inebriated 20-somethings with genuine puzzlement. Who are these people? How did they get this way? Is something wrong with me, or is it the other way around?

But my personal life, as opposed to my social life (the two terms tend to be applied synonymously) is another matter. It's actually pretty rich, at least when I'm in my groove. I suspect there's more going on in my head than in most others. Then again, this could easily be a defense mechanism. Like the late Stephen Jay Gould, I don't think intelligence is quantifiable; I wince when I read about Mensa gatherings, which seem pathetic and desperately elitist.[29]

It's much more likely that my brain simply works differently than

---

[29] Mensa is a non-profit organization open to people who score at the 98th percentile or higher on a standardized, supervised IQ or other approved intelligence test. See: www.mensa.org. Stephen Jay Gould (1941 – 2002) was an American paleontologist, evolutionary biologist, and historian of science.

most others, at least for an appreciable portion of my waking life. I suspect there are two basic kinds of introverts: Those who resent their socially geared counterparts and those who are effectively oblivious to them. I probably straddle both categories.

It's a bit like trying to pin down someone's sexual orientation or ethnic background. For whatever it's worth, I'm hetero, "straight," whatever you want to call it. I'm not "proud" of it, any more than I'm "proud" to be an American; I was never presented with a choice. Occasionally, though, someone assumes I'm gay, which never ceases to disappoint and amuse. Jerry Seinfeld chalked this phenomenon up to the "thin, single and neat" stereotype. If you're obviously unattached, neatly dressed and in reasonably good physical shape, some people actually think they can deduce your sexual polarity.

Thirty years ago no one would have made this bizarre deductive leap. But now my fellow machine-humans are sensitized to the point of paranoia. They're out to slot you into preconceived demographic categories – a task previously left to ad agencies and political campaigns – before taking you on, before accepting you as fully human.

Yes, the human race has always been self-policing when it comes to all things social. But if turning myself into a scrap of easily digestible code is what it takes to kick with the fray, I'm afraid I'm just not interested. I have neither the time nor the energy. I'm machine-like enough already.

26 JANUARY

There's a pervading notion that cryonic suspension isn't "real" since no one has yet to be revived, which is rather like maintaining that Jupiter doesn't exist because no one's ever been there. So the prospect of prolonged life through ultra-low-temperature bio-stasis is marginalized and scoffed at. After all, it infringes on too many social and theological conceits. And it just seems way too macabre, eccentric, far-out. And expensive, which it is.

Some people seem to think that cryonics (almost inevitably

confused with cryogenics) is an improbable and rather ghastly last-ditch miracle cure when in truth it's simply a technically sound attempt to create a sustainable temporal ambulance. Others recoil at the thought of their bodies (or heads, in the case of so-called "neuro-suspension") preserved in industrial canisters and tended by white-smocked technicians.

So when I read a jeering reference to cryonics in the mainstream press, I'm inclined to grit my teeth. Cryonicists make no fanciful claims and will flatly deny any promise of a utopian future existence.

Critics of cryonic suspension tend to harp on the alleged faith cryonicists invest in molecular nanotechnology, which many scientists foresee revolutionizing tissue and cell repair sometime in the next century or two. And perhaps the critics are right, and we won't develop the technology to revive, and repair, cryonics patients before the organizations housing their bodies succumb to bankruptcy. But why not try?

Hardcore transhumanists dismiss people content with "natural" life-spans as "deathists." And they have a point: What constitutes a "natural" life-span? Medical advances continue to push death farther and farther into the future; it's not impossible to imagine a world in which cryonic suspension is rendered obsolete in the next 40 years or so, usurped by genetic therapy and nanotechnologically ensured youth. In that case, the fate of today's cryonics patients will hinge on how effectively modern technology suppresses freezing damage.

It could be that for all of their good intentions, today's cryonicists are irrevocably clumsy when they prepare a de-animated patient for long-term suspension. Or perhaps medical computers of the year 2100 will be sophisticated enough to reconstruct even severely damaged frozen brains, minimizing the frightening specter of memory loss and related dysfunctions.

Mainstreamers balk at cryonics' philosophical implications. Does perpetual youth violate some unspoken tenet? Do cryonics patients forfeit whatever afterlife would otherwise await them (assuming, of course, there is an afterlife)?

And then there are more mundane concerns. Assuming the cryonics gamble pays off and you awake to find yourself alive and (most likely) augmented by future medicine, where do you live? What will you do for money? What good is a brave new world if you don't have any friends or family?

Or what if the future isn't the good place you were expecting? What if, instead of opening your eyes to a world of ecological harmony and cheap space travel, your first sight is of something like the embryo harvesting machines in *The Matrix*?

Ultimately, the so-called "deathists" will live up to their moniker, taking their ideology with them. Which leaves the distinct possibility that today's "cryonauts" will emerge into a world where the line between "alive" and "dead" will be consummately blurred.

27 JANUARY

I was watching gusts of snow falling in front of an outdoor lamp and noticed that the flakes became momentarily elongated as they passed through the middle of my field of vision. As they neared the lamp they would suddenly gain additional "segments" and briefly appear like tiny wingless dragonflies; as they departed they would rapidly "shrink" back into normal windblown crystals.

Apparently the flakes were moving so fast that my eye-brain relay system was forced to compensate by providing this "time-lapse" illusion. Or maybe the effect is more easily explained. In any case, it's unsettling to consider that my brain actually manufactures events – however miniscule or trivial – to avoid potentially sanity-threatening gaps. If an alien intelligence wanted to infiltrate, it could take advantage of this capacity for self-deception, flickering at the threshold of perception, unremarked and serene in its invisibility.

28 JANUARY

Another goddamned computer virus is spreading its unwholesome tentacles across the Net. I can't remember its name, but it's really dumb.

Who names computer viruses, anyway? The hackers themselves, I suppose, although I like the idea of an official Internet weather bureau coming up with names. Like naming hurricanes. Who, specifically, gets to do this? Is it an automated process or does someone actually sit in an office with a baby-name book chewing on a pencil?

Meanwhile, cold has gripped the city like a vice. Everything is hushed, paralyzed, furtive, held together by sheer momentum. Color bleeds away until all is translucent gray. An ectoplasmic varnish coats railings, windows, stairs, rooftops.

30 JANUARY

There are so many ideas and so little time. So I've decided to resume "literary multitasking," my hip term for reading more than book at once. I usually stick to one book of fiction and one nonfiction book. Past attempts to read multiple books have resulted in getting too wrapped up in a single title and losing the narrative thread of others. But this time I'm going to do it right.

31 JANUARY

I thought I'd harness the power of the Web to invite any extraterrestrial beings who may be reading this to come abduct me. No rectal exams or needles in the brain. Just a nice talk. You and me. I'll make coffee. You can even wake me up in the middle of the night and freak me out; if that's the way you work, that's OK. And I won't insist on irrefutable physical evidence, so don't let that scare you off; I just want to satisfy my own curiosity.

Chapter 14
February 2004

1 FEBRUARY

Science has yet to provide the sort of anthropocentric comfort so many human beings are looking for. Most people consider a mechanistic, impersonal cosmos intolerable, harsh, forbidding. They want their ontology cuddly and reassuring. Hence Precious Moments and the 700 Club and "Creation Science." Not to mention more faddish preoccupations like Wicca and predigested Eastern mysticism. If you think Precious Moments should be downgraded to the list of mere fads, guess again. It's a literal cult with surprisingly deep roots.

Carl Sagan argued that there is a numinous grandeur to reality just as we find it. And there is; I experience it on a near-daily basis. I don't need "life after death" to help me sleep at night. I don't need any watchful deities to give me morality. I happen to like and appreciate the fact that I'm a flux of particles forged inside long-exploded stars, a small portion of the universe sculpted in such a way as to reflect on its own beginning and eventual end. I have an innate yearning for the intergalactic abyss, the seminal pyrotechnics of the Big Bang, the distant roar of supernovae.

3 FEBRUARY

It was supposed to storm.
It was all anyone could talk about.
The "big storm."
14 inches.
The meteorological equivalent to the Cuban Missile Crisis.
Schools closed.

Restaurants shut their doors.

Stores sent employees packing.

It never snowed. Not one goddamned inch.

Distended dreams, intimations of fluorescent holocaust.

4 FEBRUARY

Like it or not, elections now hinge on the ability of hackers to infiltrate and falsify data harvested by electronic voting machines. Maybe we should simply drop the pretense that such archaic things as "candidates" and "votes" matter; the party with the best hackers and electronic sabotage techniques wins.

Philip K. Dick's first novel, *Solar Lottery*, is about a future society in which the President is "elected" at random. Winning the Presidency is like being selected for jury duty. It seems to me that this is an increasingly valid model for our own so-called democracy if we're to continue to rely on electronic voting machines. We must become nihilists. We must surrender choice to the caprices of barely understood software.

In this brave new democracy I've proposed, there is no more electioneering, no more posturing on "issues," no more handshaking. You can watch TV confident that you'll never see an ad endorsing a particular candidate or raking "the other guy" over the coals. In fact, you probably won't even know who the candidates are in the first place. And why should you? Ultimately, they're all represented by electronic fluctuations in the guts of some machine. They aren't "people" anymore, but really, were they ever?

The system's been corrupted, infected, fundamentally dismantled. We can't go back. So why not jettison the theatrics and start hacking code?

5 FEBRUARY

I've noticed a near-universal (and perfectly understandable) inability to pronounce or spell my name correctly. For example, at least two sites out there spell my name "Tonnes." No "i." I'm not mad at all. I honestly don't care how my last name is spelled or pronounced, or if I even have a last name, for that matter. If I could just go by "Mac" I'd be happy. Last names are for bureaucrats.

For the insatiably curious, "Tonnies" is pronounced "Tone-ease." Maybe someday, if I'm sufficiently famous, I can go by my first name, or come up with a new name altogether, and retire "Mac Tonnies" in much the same way that online businesses retire Internet domain names.

And, when you think of it, what is a name but a sort of domain name, an "address" that communicates to the world that the addressee occupies space and presumably exists in the same ontological matrix as everybody else? What if I eventually have my mind uploaded into a computer or android body? Does this constitute a change of address? Am I still "Mac" or am I post-"Mac"?

Extropians like to use the "greater than" sign (>) to denote someone with traits that fall under the "transhuman" rubric. So maybe I'm ">Mac." But that seems far too pretentious and clunky for my taste. For good or bad, I think I'm at this particular carbon-based address to stay, at least for a while.

7 FEBRUARY

I have a mild form of synesthesia, a neurological processing "error" that allows me to "see" sounds as patterns, colors and textures. I remember attempting to "draw music" when I was little and wondering why the results were so unsatisfactory. This psychedelic sensual mingling takes many forms, each highly individualized. Some synesthetics can feel tastes; others can hear colors.

Interestingly – and perhaps a bit sadly – my own synesthetic ability has waned as I've grown older. I don't know if this is due to an actual change in my brain's system architecture or if my increasing reliance on words to describe experience has simply drowned out the synesthetic signal. William Burroughs lamented that words are virulent place-holders for authentic experience, an artificial shadow of the sensory world. If so, it could be that my subjectivity have been impregnated with the Word Virus.

Few would argue that we live in a world rendered amenable to words for the sake of quick fulfillment. Information needs to travel quickly; written and spoken language, as opposed to the "mystical" non-grammar of synesthesia, is likely analogous to dial-up Net access vs. broadband. A whole subspectrum of meaning is lost in the act of communication, but we tend to rely on it because it's relatively ubiquitous. Very few contemporary buildings are without telephone jacks. Except for businesses and cyber-cafes, high-bandwidth access is still fairly novel.

Due to neurological budget constraints, words are our interpersonal lowest common denominator.

8 FEBRUARY

Today I drank a great deal of coffee and talked myself hoarse. I feel like I've swallowed a cactus. Salad and French-fries for lunch, micro-waved pasta for dinner.

A pleasant ride home from work listening to instrumental music on NPR. Synesthetic stirrings: seething lattices of blue and silver light, fragments of shimmering chrome.

Not enough time.

I'm battling a tide of machine-reality, mouth barely above water… flesh and asphalt and metal blur into a forbidding gestalt. The cold embrace of circuits; a galaxy reduced to lusterless clockwork and the thoughtless twitching of insects. Giddy compasses and obstinate time-zones, scribbled maps and unnamed streets winding through indeterminate corporate wastelands, strip-malls piled atop one another in silent architectural copulation.

10 FEBRUARY

I'm 28, which is very close to 29. And 29 is, for all intents and purposes, the same as 30. I'd be lying if I said I wasn't having any trouble with this realization. I look back on the last decade of my life with mingled disgust and horror; it went by so quickly, and I have so little to show for it. Lots of self-absorbed scribbling in notebooks, innumerable books read, boxes of drawings, a few stories published, lots of ideas pursued, but it's not enough. There's an aspect of my life that's lacking: a certain warmth, a sense of fully partaking in the human spectacle, a gut-level mammalian belonging.

The damnable thing is that all my hope isn't gone. Not yet. But what am I hoping for? A doctor to awaken me and reveal that I've spent a third of my life immersed in some fiendish virtual reality? Suddenly meeting the woman of my dreams, right on cue for Valentine's Day? Open contact with benign extraterrestrials? All of the above?

14 FEBRUARY

I experienced today as if through borrowed eyes – what robotic telepresence might feel like if we develop sufficiently realistic android stand-in bodies.

I imagine hooking myself up to a tangle of motion sensors and electrodes in the privacy of my apartment and "logging in" to a synthetic body halfway around the world. The foremost technical problem with venturing far from home in my second body is time-lag. The invisible tether that keeps my brain synchronized with my sense organs is stretched to capacity; my surroundings take on a dreamy, half-real quality, the cognitive equivalent to cheap videotape.

To combat this implacable sense of lag, I take drugs designed to modulate my brain's sensory intake. But even telepresence pharmaceuticals are a poor surrogate for actually being there, existing simultaneously in space and time. By the end of a typical session with my rent-a-body I'm addled, clumsy and irritable. The dream-like association between self and the "outside" world persists like a nagging, partially remembered nightmare. My brain has been supplanted, however momentarily, by a new host of rules, forced to adapt to alien parameters.

So, enervated, I log in to my other self once again, seeking communion, starved for reconciliation. I travel the world in a far-flung squadron of rented artificial selves, battling increased doses of time-lag, consuming ever-more-powerful drugs to combat depersonalization.

But at the same time, something in the depths of my bilocated mind craves this novel anonymity. Escaping into the flux of transmissions that comprises my electronically scattered "self" is the only readily available way to bridge the widening fracture between cause and effect. And so I become autonomic, my consciousness diluted into a thin mentational smoke.

One "I" is no longer sufficient.

15 FEBRUARY

I just got this incredible piece of "beatnik" spam. This appears to be source code for the colorfully ambiguous subject headers employed by spammers to evade anti-spam filters. Keep in mind that this is just a portion of the entire email. You have to wonder: Did these tenacious Viagra-peddling drones get the idea from William Burroughs' cut-up technique? I'm seriously thinking about reading this at the next open-mic at Barnes & Noble. Dig it:

Crablike Bloodsucker Booking Reaction Cuckoldom Supercherie=
Ceremonialism Bassetting Adornment Coxcombery Disqualify Reasoner Urc=
eus Disseize Respersion. Dulcorate Bina Tenderness Runnion Plinth Pre=
figuration Scathful Deuced Inseverable Radoteur Crenated Hebetation No=
rther Seppuku Ructation Uxorious Airmanship Trebuchet Quicksands Decad=
ency Bobbery Plexus Operosity. Locular Varuna Operose Lustquencher Im=
poster Unbridled Babblement Beldame Capriciousness

208

Attemper Atheistic =

Nonconformist. Instructions Embellishment Antipodal
Imbibation Riverb=

oat Floss Lorcha Arietation Numberless Supersaturate
Unerring Studded =

Snowdrift Hardened Clearage Libertinage Marbled
Arbitrator Sirkar.

16 FEBRUARY

I'm battling stupefying headaches and waking up with pains in my
back; both maladies can probably be traced to spending too much
time on my computer.

It snowed copiously this evening. I walked down to Panera, had a
sandwich, and savored an espresso at LatteLand in a desperate
attempt to kick-start my psycho-metabolism back into caffeinated
normality.

You know that nasty taste you get in your mouth sometimes when
you fall asleep after eating?

My brain feels like that right now. No kidding.

17 FEBRUARY

I've decided that I really want a decent TV/DVD player. My ban
on TV broadcasting will remain in effect, but I've got movies I'd truly
enjoy watching. Have you ever tried to lose yourself in a Hollywood
film displayed on a laptop? It doesn't work. You have to view the
screen at just the right angle or darker shades turn into
undifferentiated shadow. It's like watching through a veil. And if you
put the machine in your lap you quickly become aware of the thing's
not-inconsiderable heat-output, bringing to mind uneasy thoughts of
testicular cancer. All so I can watch *Dead Ringers* for the fiftieth time.

18 FEBRUARY

Late dinner at Winstead's. Ceiling lights like art-deco flying
saucers; bubbles in the Wurlitzer like buoyant souls encapsulated in

some gaudy liquid purgatory.

19 FEBRUARY

I was sitting in front of 47th Street watching motorcycles go by, nursing a coffee and trying to ignore my still-sore back when I suddenly found myself staring into the pastel-and-neon maw of The Sharper Image one block over. The weather is beautiful today, hence the open doors.

Inspiration struck. I sauntered inside doing my "I'm a customer" act and collapsed into one of the robotic massage recliners. Heavenly. I tested out "PERCUSSION." Not bad. I sampled a few minutes of "KNEAD," briefly transported by mechanical fists and tireless, disembodied fingers.

Not wanting to overstay my welcome (as good as it is, my "serious customer" act dissolves pretty quickly once I'm comfortably seated, staring at the ceiling like a happy corpse), I feigned interest in portable DVD players until an employee winked the store's lights, signaling that my relaxation session was at an end. Otherwise, I might still be there.

21 FEBRUARY

In an ideal world, laptop computers would be completely impervious to inclement conditions. Extremes of temperature wouldn't faze them; you could leave one lying in Death Valley, screen open, and come back a month later to find it operating perfectly. An ideal laptop could shrug off falls from great heights and body-blows from enraged gorillas: in effect, the sort of unrelenting percussion associated with professional hockey. And it would look correspondingly tough, constructed of ergonomically contoured black Kevlar and titanium, among other military-spec materials. Imagine something like the famously rugged "black boxes" carried aboard commercial airliners, but downsized into something you could strap comfortably to your shoulder.

Alas, we don't live in an ideal world. Laptops, even the high-end ones, are still worryingly fragile. You can't casually knock them around as you would a mountain bicycle, or even a weather-proofed cordless phone. Drop a laptop onto the sidewalk and something critical is going to shatter. Inadvertently dunk one in a body of water and you might as well leave it there.

So tonight I bought a small notebook and set of wafer-thin pens that double as bookmarks. This is my backup system – imminently portable, reasonably coffee-resistant and a hell of a lot less conspicuous. Not that I'm especially afraid of a mugger relieving me of my Gateway, but still.

In the not-unforeseeable future, of course, it's possible no one will have laptops. Or, for that matter, PDAs or cell phones. With the exception of neophobes and the occasional eccentric who finds the clacking of plastic keys and the heft of warm silicon in his palm a reassuring anchor to brick-and-mortar reality, we'll be packing the hardware in our skulls, wielding high-bandwidth digital telepathy as nonchalantly as a teenager scrolling through the contact list on her color-coordinated Nokia.

22 FEBRUARY

One thing I just can't take: MINDLESS CHATTER. It's everywhere, like a reeking aural fog. I'm pretty adept at tuning it out but sometimes my defenses are weakened by its sheer inanity.

Have you ever stopped to really listen to the stuff people "discuss" while sipping lattes and window-shopping? It's not real dialogue; it's canned, vacuous, recursive. Eavesdropping on this prattle leaves me feeling like I'm surrounded by chittering bipedal insects that just happen to look human.

Way too many of us are addicted to this pointless facsimile of conversation. Maybe we've seen too many talking heads on local news shows and mistaken "happy talk" for the real thing. Maybe losing one's personality in endless sessions of automatized "discussion," however superficially earnest, is merely an innocuous retreat from the stark horrors of a world still wobbling from its violent emergence into the 21st century.

Am I being elitist and whiny? Possibly. But I invite you to take up the challenge for yourself. Sit in a coffee shop for an hour consciously listening to what people talk about, and how they talk about it.

Within five minutes you'll be searching for the lobotomy stitches.

24 FEBRUARY

I have a class reunion coming up. In keeping with the general tone of misanthropy of several recent posts: Why should I care? What would possess a sane person to "relive" one's high-school experience?

I had a decent time in high-school, so I don't have anything to be particularly bitter about. I actually had a pretty fun senior year. But the reunion concept just seems absurd. High-school reunions are synthetic experiences defined by the same formalized sentimentality that makes weddings and funerals so tiring. If I had any genuine interest in keeping up with former classmates, I'd be emailing them right now instead of blogging.

Invitations to class reunions are classic guilt-trips, ritualized ways of saying: "We realize perfectly well that none of us really give a damn about what everyone else is up to, but we're having this event so all of us, virtual strangers now, will have the opportunity to ease our consciences and revel in a few hours of ersatz camaraderie. Go Bears!"

Meanwhile, I'm totally out of it. Clueless. Square. Unhip.

Examples: I don't give a damn about perusing new/emerging bands. I see maybe two or three new movies a year. I don't think Britney Spears is sexy. I have literally no idea when sport seasons begin or end. I don't know who was in the Super Bowl. The last time I saw a music video was sometime in '98. I have yet to sample fondue or make a pilgrimage to a hyper-mall. I don't especially like beer.

By the standards of the military-industrial-entertainment complex, I'm an abject failure, destined for unpersonhood. I fully expect men in black suits to come knocking at my door wearing expressions of mixed disdain and sympathy: "Mr. Tonnies, if you'll just come with us. We know who can help you."

I am the dead.

25 FEBRUARY

Wouldn't it be cool if blogs came with soundtracks, just like movies? Here's a hand-picked line-up for Posthuman Blues:

1. "Burning Down the House" (Talking Heads)
2. "Country Feedback" (R.E.M.)
3. "Mysterons" (Portishead)
4. "Wide to Receive" (Morrissey)
5. "Human Behavior" (Bjork)
6. "The Pretty Things Are Going To Hell" (David Bowie)
7. "I Know It's Over" (The Smiths)
8. "Planet Claire" (The B-52s)
9. "Enjoy the Silence" (Depeche Mode)
10. "Don't Give Up" (Peter Gabriel)
11. "Maybe Someday" (The Cure)
12. "Idioteque" (Radiohead)
13. "Hazy Shade of Winter" (Simon and Garfunkel)
14. "Like the Weather" (10,000 Maniacs)

26 FEBRUARY

We're overdue for a good old-fashioned meteor impact. I'm not saying it will be a huge one, like the one that ejected the dinosaurs from the evolutionary stage, but it will be significant. When you have a chunk of metal plunging into a planet's gravity well, it doesn't have to be all that big to pack a hell of a punch.

Earth has been narrowly missing these things for decades. The last time we got hit was in 1908, really not that long ago at all when you think about it. Fortunately it exploded over Siberia instead of, say, Paris or New York City, in which case the history of the world would be quite different.

So let's get morbid. Say we get hit by a 40-meter rock, and we're unlucky enough for it to land in an industrialized country instead of the middle of the ocean or Antarctica. There's a lot more industrialized territory than there was in 1908, so the odds of a catastrophic strike have risen. Yet despite our expansion, we're woefully unprepared to divert, or even detect, incoming meteors. One of our only prospects for advance warning, the Hubble Space Telescope, is probably going to be scrapped, apparently so Dubbya can invest more skull-sweat into the pressing issue of steroid-use in professional sports.

So if we get hit, it's likely no one will know what's happening. And remember that many of us live in a culture trained to be perpetually afraid. Yellow alerts. Orange alerts. We've been conditioned, with ruthless efficiency, to attribute Western society's ills to terrorists and "Evil Doers."

By now you probably see where I'm going with this. A nickel-iron meteorite obliterates a major city. Before the cause of the blast can be determined, some foreign power has been targeted by what's left of the afflicted nation's nuclear arsenal. The beleaguered nation fires in a white-hot rage. The recipient state collapses in a "shock and awe" thermonuclear inferno. Sympathizers immediately retaliate in whatever way they can. Dirty nukes, poison gas, hijacked planes, you-name-it.

Suddenly, while the dust settles around the epicenter of what will later be revealed to be a chance collision with an unallied celestial body, the world is wracked by spasms of self-inflicted mass destruction. Like a forest fire, the spread of retaliation may be too swift to stomp out. And even if we do manage to get a positive ID on the original culprit within the first few hours of conflict, who's going to believe it?

Even more ominously, who's going to care? By then, we will have reached critical mass. Mob mentality takes over, fueled by fear, devastation, and millennia of self-fulfilling Armageddon stories.

Surely I'm not the only one who's thought of this. I'd like to think that somewhere in the halls of power, contingency plans have been drafted to deal with such an event, in which case we might make it out of a collision-retaliation event not wholly incapacitated.

Or the truth might be even darker: Someone indeed realizes the danger, but has chosen not to educate us. The idea of being exterminated from above has a powerful mythical resonance; perhaps we collectively long to be sterilized. Given the option of mere oblivion or dreadful knowing, we may well elect to die in ignorance.

27 FEBRUARY

I'm becoming less concerned with the possibility that our reality is a simulation and more concerned with the probability that it's a simulation within a simulation within a simulation within a simulation, etc. We could be virtually anywhere in a near-endless regression of "nested" universes, about as note-worthy as microbes at the bottom of a mineshaft – and that could be glorifying ourselves considerably.

The nested universe cosmology makes the future of *The Matrix* seem almost utopian. At least in *The Matrix* a "Red Pill" brings you face to face with authentic reality, however unpalatable. Assuming our universe is located at random in some regressive "stack" of simulated universes, it's doubtful we're anywhere close to the "top." Chances are we're located somewhere in the middle. But how many higher (more "real") universes encompass our own? How many Red Pills do we need to swallow in order to extricate ourselves? How much truth can we tolerate before our status becomes hopelessly abstract, forever beyond our grasp?

And we're faced with another disorienting prospect: Ultimate reality – if we should ever come close to reaching it – may not be amenable to human existence, just as the vast realm beyond the ocean is off-limits to water-breathing fish. A simulated universe may be a prison, but it may also be the only substrate capable of sustaining us.

29 FEBRUARY

I woke up late last night in a state of panic, unnerved at the implications of a "nested simulation" cosmology. Although I was exhausted, my mind was functioning lucidly enough. But the protective veil offered by daylight had been peeled away, and I seemed immersed in remote blackness, trapped within numberless Chinese boxes.

If we're living in a simulation – or I am (for all I know solipsism may have the last laugh) – then what good are efforts to reach the "next level"? No matter how hard one tries, one is still condemned to the computational substrate that houses his or her particular tier on the cosmic shelf; my own sense of confinement was almost visceral, governed by the recursive grammar of bad dreams.

My attempts at insight, my nagging desire to transcend merely human perception, whether couched in quantum physics, neuroscience or arcane philosophy, seemed (and still seem) flimsy and ineffectual. The abyss wasn't merely staring back at me; it was leering into my face, so close I could feel its breath.

Chapter 15
March 2004

1 MARCH

Cryptic chalk graffiti: Oversized spermatozoa wriggling away from the center of a pendulous pastel egg cell, igniting like meteors as they gain distance.

4 MARCH

I rarely leave home without at least one book to read. So I'm naturally curious when I see someone else reading in public. Unfortunately, I've noticed that Books Read In Public fall into a few considerably less-than-interesting categories. Almost without fail, people are reading either:

1. the Bible, or something to do with it;
2. something involving weight-loss;
3. the latest John Grisham; or, perhaps worst of all…
4. books about TV.

This is a disastrous state of affairs. There are so many worthwhile, relatively esoteric books out there I can only wish I had the time to read, and these bastards are perfectly content to read fluff.

I've always been rather amazed at the spectacle presented by Barnes & Noble and Borders. These are stores stocked ceiling-high with books by almost every note-worthy author. With one inexplicable exception: One of the best writers in America today, Steve Erickson, is utterly absent from the shelves at my local B&N.

But from what I can tell, no one's buying anything new and interesting. Instead, readers obligingly head for the bestsellers, the Atkins Diet section, and the "Christian Inspiration" aisle. Or worse, the "graphic novels," or the so-called "news" stands.

I remember an interview with Norman Mailer on NPR. He predicted the novel would soon become obsolete, just how poetry is generally perceived as somewhat obscure and archaic by contemporary readers. In the near-future, actual novel-reading might be an almost unbearable eccentricity.

There are a number of ominous trends within the publishing industry that appear to support Mailer's prediction. Did you know that there's a spin-off of the ghastly Christian Fundamentalist *Left Behind* saga targeted at juveniles? No kidding. It's called, accurately enough, *Left Behind: The Kids.*

The point of this series – and the point I'm trying to make about so much of today's "literature" – is that it's not even remotely intended to provide an aesthetic experience, but to sow ideological seeds. I find it distinctly amusing that so much of this garbage is co-authored, as if recycled Armageddon fantasies require the combined mental might of two authors – and I suppose since we're talking about Fundamentalists, they very well might.

Most of the time the ideology being packaged is laughable and harmless, as in the case of Atkins devotees. But then there's the truly detestable stuff: masochistic biblical fantasies masquerading as Tom Clancy-esque thrillers; demeaning supernatural claptrap disguised as "inspiration" or "self-help." Once upon a time, you found cheaply printed gospel tracts in restroom stalls; now you find their elegantly bound and savvily marketed descendents combating for shelf-space in actual stores.

And people can't get enough. Like the "reality TV" craze, spin-offs proliferate with the tenacity of kudzu vine. Any day now, I expect to find "Chicken Soup for the Soul for Dummies" staring back at me from a prominent display. The Wal-Mart-ization of the written word will have triumphed, leaving an embittered subculture to hoard the few remaining works of Kafka and Philip K. Dick and Kurt Vonnegut.

But, as usual, I'm getting ahead of myself.

Parting thought: Isn't it odd that, for a series about the End of the

World, the *Left Behind* books just keep coming? There are like 50 of the fucking things now.

5 MARCH

A criminally boring day.

It was my own fault, of course. My major accomplishments consisted of consuming strawberry apple sauce, berating my cat for tipping over my lava lamp (for which I immediately felt guilty), and playing *Asteroids Alive*.

I just swilled Beer Number Three at the joint across the street. *The Family Guy* (a show I've never seen) was playing on the overhead TV, muted. I watched the entire thing, my head a riot of imagined cartoon voices.

I've unearthed Ani DiFranco's *Dilate* from my CD collection. I've got Portishead's first record playing now. It doesn't get much better. And it's confirmed – Morrissey's first new record in seven years is due out soon. That warrants at least some excitement.

Who said my life was all weird books and caffeine abuse?

6 MARCH

Well, I relented. Caved. Succumbed. I forked over eight dollars to see what the Mel Gibson Jesus movie was all about. Why? Maybe because I felt a little sheepish about bad-mouthing it without having seen it. Perhaps because I thought that its bad rap might be unfair. After all, it's a movie about religion; of course it's going to be controversial.

Having said that, the movie was god-awful. I intended to write a proper review, but what's the point? The reviews calling *The Passion of the Christ* gruesome and exploitative are right on the money. If anything, they're being kind. So instead of a review, per se, I'll share a few random impressions and get back to more important subjects.

Firstly, no characterization. No pretense of humanity. In Gibson's defense, *The Passion* simply doesn't have time for it. The entirety of this movie, except a murky first scene in which a brooding Jesus is apprehended by snarling Jews, consists of stomach-wrenching torture sequences. *The Passion* is a distended spectacle of aerosolized blood, flayed flesh, poked-out eyes, weeping onlookers and occasional blink-and-they're-over flashbacks.

Shame on Ebert and Roeper for branding this movie an "epic"; there's a palpable lack of depth to this eyesore, an utter absence of narrative meat (unless you count those sheets of ruined skin and muscle dangling from Jesus' mutilated torso).[30] Compared to this, Japanese manga has the complexity and substance of Thomas Pynchon.

The Passion proceeds with malignant inevitability. At least fifteen minutes of the film consist of yawn-inducing scenes of Jesus, blood-drenched and oozing, collapsing to the ground in slow motion, accompanied by a so-dramatic-it's-comical musical score. The intention, I guess, is to pound home the title character's spiritual resolve, but it was all I could do to refrain from glancing at my watch. At one point, as Jesus once more toppled to the dirt under the crushing blows of Roman soldiers, I actually stifled laughter.

This movie doesn't merely approach self-parody – it revels in it like maggots in shit. Not a good thing.

On the other hand, this cinematic atrocity isn't meant to withstand criticism. It's meant to provide the faithful with a high-budget retelling of their favorite bedtime story. And if the only way Jesus can sell tickets is to bathe in artificial blood, then so be it. Give 'em what they want.

I could go on. I could mention the distinct and ironic lack of

---

[30] *Chicago Sun-Times* critic Roger Ebert gave the film 4 stars out of 4. He wrote, "This isn't a movie about performances, although it has powerful ones, or about technique, although it is awesome, or about cinematography (although Caleb Deschanel paints with an artist's eye), or music (although John Debney supports the content without distracting from it). It is a film about an idea. An idea that it is necessary to fully comprehend the Passion if Christianity is to make any sense. Gibson has communicated his idea with a single-minded urgency." See: www.goo.gl/VNkW6.

passion that went into Gibson's insufferable vision. I could harp on the completely unnecessary and gratuitous FX scenes depicting what I took to be an androgynous Satan, or the way the sound of whips cracking just gets, well, fucking old after 45 minutes. I could even present my case for *The Passion* being the product of a somewhat disturbed mind. But I won't, because I have the feeling that's partly what Gibson and company want. Instead of feeding the meaningless controversy already blazing around this forgettable piece of Celluloid, I choose to let it die the quiet, unremarked death it deserves.

Yet I can't resist mentioning the final scene. Yes, I'm about to issue a "spoiler," but it's not like there's anything vaguely innovative to report, so bear with me. After a brief dramatic silence, we see Jesus' gravestone rolled away, a conspicuously unoccupied burial cloth. Then the J-Man suddenly appears in profile, scar-free, while the soundtrack escalates into a militant staccato unmistakably reminiscent of the opening credits for *The Terminator*. And, in an uncanny "Terminator" impersonation that challenges viewers not to fall into the aisles screaming with laughter, the naked, robot-like Jesus proceeds to hasten off the screen, but not before we get a good look at one of the bloody holes left over from his crucifixion.

Cue closing credits.

Eight dollars, squandered.

Get me the hell out of here.

7 MARCH

So far tonight I've experienced two intense episodes of deja vu, the first while looking at a picture of a fossil-like formation photographed on Mars and the next after changing CDs in my stereo.

I very, very rarely experience deja vu. So when I do it's rather unsettling. Especially so since the sensation tends to come in successive "waves." It's a little scary, especially since neuroscience is still basically clueless about its origins. I personally think that "real" deja vu is a minor seizure, a momentary glitch in the synaptic matrix. There's no evidence that it's harmful or symptomatic of any undiagnosed malady. In fact, it's easy to understand the mystical, "shamanic" connotations the phenomenon has acquired. Though brief, it's an actual altered state – a dizzy certainty that everything exists in some inaccessible holographic "Now," an unannounced perforation in causal reality.

8 MARCH

The other night I was sitting outside the coffee shop listening to the weekend motorcyclists compare bikes when I realized that I was dressed quite similarly to the bikers sitting next to me: black leather jackets, blue jeans, black shoes. Even my hair was a little rebellious. It occurred to me that anyone passing by might, for a moment at least, assume I was one of the gang.

Then the biker nearest me, a guy with arcane patches sewn onto his midnight-leather jacket and an Australian accent, leaned over and asked if I'd kindly keep an eye on the silver helmet on the sidewalk while he and his friend went inside for lattes. Not having anything better to do, I took his place.

Suddenly the transformation was complete: I looked like a plausible owner of the chrome BMW cycle on the curb a few feet away.

Cool.

Very Brando.

So I sat there for a minute until the Australian's friend reclaimed the chairs.

Sorry; that's the end of the story. No moral.

10 MARCH

I got the galleys for my *After The Martian Apocalypse* for last-minute corrections. Formatted, it's about 300 pages. One thing I'm certain of: If nothing else, the book looks cool. I like the fonts, typestyle, etc. I lugged it to Starbucks this evening and managed to get about half-way through. The first half suffers from some repetition that needs to be cut, or at least downplayed, but overall I'm pretty happy with it.

There are a couple nagging style issues, but it's little stuff. Parts of it are too wordy. I need to tighten up the prose a bit, at least in the first section. This should help minimize repeated references.

But at the same time, I can't simplify too much; the first several chapters consist of walking readers through alien territory, showing them the sights (often without benefit of illustrations). So maybe I'm being too hard on myself. Time will tell.

At least I can rest easy knowing that Martha Stewart is behind bars (or as good as)! That menace to society! Finally, justice!

What a joke. Martha, love her or hate her, is harmless. She's checking into the cinderblock hotel because she acted on an insider stock tip, for Christ's sake. Meanwhile, that bastard from Enron, who deliberately and maliciously screwed people out of their life savings, is going free because he had the good fortune to be chums with Dubbya's clan.[31]

There are industrialists reaping the Bush administration's environmental myopia by unleashing toxic substances into our air and water. No questions asked. They get away with it. As John Shirley has bluntly and repeatedly pointed out for the benefit of those who can't accept we're living in a dystopia, "they just don't care if you die." Keeping the herd distracted by sending interior decorators to jail while actual criminals trash the planet and compromise the well-being of entire populations because of sheer neglect and greed: It's a good thing.

---

[31] Martha Stewart, a businesswoman and television personality, was imprisoned from 8 October, 2004 until 4 March, 2005 after she was convicted in an insider stock trading case (in which she avoided a loss of just over $45,000) of conspiracy, obstruction of an agency proceeding, and making false statements to federal investigators. Kenneth Lay, the CEO and Chairman of the Board of Enron, was convicted on multiple counts related to securities fraud that led to the company's bankruptcy in December, 2001. Each of the convictions would have carried a 5 to 10 year prison term, but Lay died before he could be sentenced. Conspiracy theories quickly arose as to the true cause of his death, given his close ties to the Bush family.

12 MARCH

A letter in Arabic claiming responsibility for the Madrid train bombings on behalf of al Qaeda has reinforced fears of another imminent attack on the United States, Homeland Security chief Tom Ridge says.[32]

If this happens before November, everything changes. There will be no pretense of an election. The Bush administration will try to convince United States citizens that it needs to "finish what it's started," and we will have begun the fall into a politically crippled, xenophobic police-state. Even now, anti-Bush demonstrators must take their signs to conveniently distant free-speech zones designated by the Secret Service.

Patriot Act Two will be quickly and unceremoniously made law. The inevitable policing of U.S. dissidents may very well be "outsourced" to private contractors unrestrained by Constitutional triviality. And bad news for Ashcroft-haters: You'll be seeing a lot more of his cadaverous jowls and hungry reptile eyes on TV.[33]

13 MARCH

Don't you just fucking hate that "motivational" crap you find in sterile cube-farms and corporate lunchrooms? You know, those cloying, infantile posters of don't-you-wish-you-were-there nature scenes accompanied by abrasive "go get 'em" mottos?

---

[32] The Madrid train bombings were nearly simultaneous, coordinated bombings against the commuter train system of Madrid, Spain on the morning of 11 March, 2004 – three days before Spain's general elections. The explosions killed 191 people and wounded 1,800.

[33] On 9 November, 2004, following George W. Bush's re-election, John Ashcroft announced his resignation as Attorney General, which took effect on 3 February, 2005 when the Senate confirmed White House Counsel Alberto Gonzales as the next attorney general. Gonzales' tenure as Attorney General was marked by several conflicts with Congress. Following bipartisan calls for his removal, and threats of impeachment, Gonzales resigned in September, 2007.

14 MARCH

Most people who read this blog or my book review pages probably assume I read a staple diet of science fiction. And while SF is my favorite genre, some of my very favorite books aren't SF at all. Some, like J.G. Ballard's *Crash*, hover in the twilight zone between science fiction and "mainstream." Although "Crash" employs no emphatically science fictional elements, Ballard himself refers to it as an SF novel – read it and you'll understand immediately why David Cronenberg was compelled to turn it into a film.

Among my very favorite novels of all time is Ken Kesey's *One Flew Over the Cuckoo's Nest*. The movie's not bad at all, but doesn't compare to the book. And I really like Margaret Atwood's *The Handmaid's Tale*, which, technically, is science fiction, even though I dare you to find it marketed as such. I read the back cover of one of her newer books – *The Blind Assassin* – and the publisher even uses the term "science fiction" to describe it. But like *The Handmaid's Tale*, *The Blind Assassin* (which I'll get around to reading eventually) has circumvented genre; it is Literature with a capital "L."

Likewise, Jonathan Lethem's back catalogue, containing the hilarious future noir *Gun, With Occasional Music*, has been reincarnated as "mainstream" literature, complete with an inscrutably bland new cover illustration (the first was an inspired knock-off of 1940s detective pulp). When this book first came out, no one attempted to disguise the fact that it was satirical SF; after all, one of the primary characters is a genetically augmented kangaroo. Lethem is one of those authors of the fantastic whose work mysteriously disappears from science fiction shelves, strategically repackaged for those who dismiss SF as so much juvenile escapism.

Kurt Vonnegut's fiction is often explicitly science fiction, yet Vonnegut recoils at the use of the term, scared off, I suppose, by the books written by Kilgore Trout, his fictional alter-ego. So you won't find Vonnegut in the science fiction department either, even though *The Sirens of Titan* is about flying saucers, *Player Piano* is about the effects of automization in a near-future society, and *Cat's Cradle* is about a lab-created crystal with the capacity to plunge Earth into a permanent Ice Age. These are science fiction themes, whether Vonnegut wishes to admit it or not. And since his books are so readily available, I won't complain. At least I know where to go in the bookstore to find his books, which is less than I can say about "slipstream" writers like Lethem and Steve Erickson.

Where does Franz Kafka fit into this scattered pantheon? His books are located under "Literature," but they're so unique and elusive that they all-but demand a classification of their own. *The Trial* and *The Castle* certainly aren't science fiction, although I think there's a case for Kafka's short-story "In the Penal Colony" being borderline SF, but they're certainly not mainstream in any acceptable sense.

Maybe in an alternate universe Kafka took up science fiction. Or maybe, somewhere, there's an unopened crate of never-before-seen SF manuscripts drafted in his characteristic spiky handwriting.

15 MARCH

Up early. New short-story idea: "The Other Room," based on a futuristic version of "looking glass" technology. In the story, venturing outdoors is rendered virtually impossible due to genetically contrived airborne diseases and pollution. Interpersonal contact is limited to communing with "neighbors" via high-res wall screens. The screens are so advanced that they're easily mistakable for actual separate rooms, fostering a sense of enhanced personal space.

The main character has lived his adult life "sharing" his germicidally insulated apartment with a female love interest. But all they can do is look at each other and talk; it's as if they're on opposite sides of an invisible glass barrier (which, in a very real sense, they are).

Anyway, toward the end of his life something goes wrong with the programming of his homeostatic apartment building and he realizes that the woman in the "other room" is a computer program designed to keep him from going crazy – she never existed; he's wasted his life pining away over a simulacrum. And the World Outside is worse than he's imagined.

And they all lived happily ever after.

16 MARCH

When you're piloting a car from one location to another, you cease to be "you" in the normal sense. You become an extension of the vehicle, a meat-based nerve center for two tons of metal, glass and plastic. The concentration demanded by driving forfeits thinking the sort of thoughts that make you an individual, if only briefly.

So the driving experience is rather like teleportation; you get in the car, casually surrender your normal self-hood in exchange for speed and convenience, and (barring a crash) emerge at your destination, where you can "rematerialize." The "person" driving the car wasn't you: it was a subsystem, a drone summoned genie-like from the brain for a specific purpose.

I think the entirety of a normal day can be viewed as a succession of somewhat exclusive subsystems. The "you" on lunch break is a distinctly different entity than the "you" surfing the Web at 2:00 in the morning or the "you" dining out with friends. Maybe the notion of a central, indomitable Self is so much quaint wishful thinking. It seems more likely that we're composites, each transitory "disposable" self vying for supremacy in much the same way that the genes in an individual's own body compete for expression.

17 MARCH

Man, I hate St. Patrick's Day.

18 MARCH

I can't stop browsing my book now that it's actually bound and portable. Fortunately, I'm finding moments of poor phrasing and dumb word-choice which, in theory, can be corrected before the finalized edition is shipped. I basically have to force myself to put it aside for fear of finding yet more to correct; it's easy to get carried away. After all, this book is going to represent me to (hopefully) many thousands of readers. The last thing I need is to come across as needlessly verbose, pretentious or repetitive.

Then again, I think I'm my toughest critic. I'm positively anal-retentive when it comes to reading my own stuff, this blog included. Sometimes I get the overwhelming urge to alter posts for increased readability, but I typically desist because it seems somehow unethical, a bit like Winston Smith creating "unpersons" at the Ministry of Truth.[34]

20 MARCH

My biorhythms have been thrown into utter disarray. I feel like a superhero in some comic book panting, "no... energy – can't... move..." after being doused in some superpower-retarding substance. So I'm guzzling caffeine and reading and hoping this fog lifts so I can do some laundry later tonight.

21 MARCH

We are here to fail.

How's that for fatalism?

Remember the revelatory scene in *The Matrix Reloaded* where the Architect tells Neo that the Matrix (i.e., reality as we know it) has been repeatedly allowed to fail so that the AI in charge of the world as it really is can anticipate and thwart any glitches? It's tempting to consider the possibility that the increasingly fast-paced and forbidding geopolitical milieu is somehow engineered – that consensus reality is destined to split noisily at the seams because, as the great Charles Fort speculated, "we are property."

Perhaps our unseen overseers – call them "aliens" – are deliberately allowing terrestrial civilization to fail so they can take preventive steps to ensure their own immortality. It might not even

---

[34] In Orwell's *Nineteen Eighty-Four*, an "unperson" is someone who has not only been killed by the state, but effectively erased from existence. The unperson was written out of books, photographs, and articles so that no trace of their existence could be found. The central character in the novel, Winston Smith, was a clerk charged with removing unpersons from the historical record.

be the first time this has been enacted; scattered evidence of previous technological civilizations on Earth may indicate a grisly succession of self-destructive global societies. Perhaps we're merely the latest permutation, destined to fail in the service of an intelligence we'll never meet.

An arbitrarily advanced space-faring (or trans-dimensional) culture could have every reason to experiment with a hapless backwater civilization like our own. For an industrious alien scientist, creating a new version of humanity might be as simple as a conjuring an experimental regime in the video game *NationStates*. Adjust the parameters, sit back and enjoy the humans' apocalyptic antics until the final credits roll. Rewind, make a few changes, and repeat.

A psychology professor, using the pseudonym John Norman, once wrote a fairly exasperating series of novels in which god-like aliens periodically transplant Earth civilizations to a world of their own devising. Technologically omniscient, they subject entire populations to what author Brian Stableford correctly identifies as a long-term existential experiment.

To the delight of many male readers, Norman's recipe for utopia requires that most women function as eager sex slaves. Ken MacLeod's *Engines of Light* trilogy provides a very similar (if substantially brainier) version. But the aliens of Norman and MacLeod act out of various altruistic (or at least politically merciful) motives; while they might be interested in keeping humanity in its place, at least for the time-being, they have no plans to see their "pet" species render itself extinct.

Right now, religion seems to be the most obvious precursor to our own planetary destruction; we wade through a thicket of theologically entrenched doomsday memes. What if geneticists discover that our capacity for belief is an artificially encoded trait? What if humanity has been altered to conform to some long-term experiment? What if religion has been "implanted" as a means of hastening our own demise? Imagine an oncologist grafting cancerous tissue into the body of a lab animal and dispassionately watching it grow.

The UFO phenomenon appears to have roots in prehistory. If, as argued by Jacques Vallee and John Keel, UFOs and "aliens" represent a form of psychological warfare, then the long list of reality-transforming events chronicled by theologians and neurologists may signal nonhuman manipulation. Our defining mythologies, so often based on "divine" messages, may be no more than experiments enacted to test our psychosocial endurance in the face of steadily escalating absurdity.

In a few thousand years of "progress," our inherent flaws will rise boiling to the surface for casual inspection. There's no need to terminate the experiment, since the experiment will effectively terminate itself. And within "mere" millennia, a new, amnesiac society will have spilled itself across the planet, perhaps endowed with a slightly different cerebral architecture. And, as always, the Others wait to see what mistakes will be made, cataloguing every atrocity with the cool reserve of clipboard-wielding lab technicians. It's the ultimate diabolical expression of Nietzsche's Eternal Return.

In the words of The Cure: "Over and over we die, one after the other."

22 MARCH

Nigerian spammers are getting smarter. Please note the following personalized spam, revealing that I'm related to a guy named "Pitt":

Dear Mac Tonnies,
I am Lawyer GARUBA MOHAMMED, a solicitor at law. I am the personal Attorney to Mr. Pitt Tonnies, a national of your country, who usedto work with Chevron Oil Producing Company in Nigeria. Here in After shall be referred to as my client. On the 21st of April 2002, my client, his wife and their only daughter were involved in a car accident along Lagos; Ibadan Expressway. All occupants of the vehicle unfortunately lost their lives. Since then I have made several inquiries to your embassy here to Locate any of my client's extended

relatives, this has also Proved unsuccessful. After these several unsuccessful attempts, I decided to track his Last name over the Internet, to locate any member of his family Hence I contacted you. I have contacted you to assist in Repatriating the fund valued at US$18 million Left behind by my Client before it gets Confiscated or declared unserviceable by the Finance Firm where these huge amounts were deposited. The said Finance company has issued me a notice to provide the next of kin or have the account confiscated within the next fourteen official Working days.

[et cetera]

24 MARCH

I've got a sudden obscure urge for a double espresso macchiato at Starbucks. Indie coffee won't do; it has to be Starbucks. Some fragile component in my psyche craves the reassuring corporate iconography that's part of the Starbucks experience. It's frightening, but I'm succumbing.

26 MARCH

Ufologist Stanton Friedman quips that "SETI" stands for "Silly Effort to Investigate."[35]

I disagree; I think a vigorous search for ET radio/laser emissions is well worth our time. But daring to take the UFO phenomenon seriously and scanning the sky for intelligent signals are not mutually exclusive, as both sides of the dichotomy will typically have you believe. It's yet another symptom of Western society's addiction to binary thought, in which all eggs must necessarily be thrown into

---

[35] Stanton Friedman is a long-time UFO researcher, most famous for his belief that the "Roswell incident" of 1947 was the crash of two alien spacecraft, and in what he has called a "Cosmic Watergate" – the cover-up of an extraterrestrial presence on Earth.

either one basket or the other.

An emerging thread in SETI discourse (as well as informed science fiction) is the notion of a post-biological cosmos. The majority of advanced aliens aren't likely to be flesh-and-blood; I suspect they'll be more like thought-forms than anything familiar to terrestrial biologists. This catapults Arthur C. Clarke's maxim that "any sufficiently advanced technology is indistinguishable from magic" to truly dizzying heights. In a cosmos populated by machine-based life, we are most definitely not alone; the Earth itself could be under siege by stealthy intruders. Even traveling at sub-relativistic speeds, miniaturized probes designed to reproduce using raw materials encountered on their travels could overwhelm the galactic disk in "mere" billions of years.

Trends in electronics manufacturing strongly suggest that elements of the cosmic diaspora could be exceedingly small, even microscopic. It's not inconceivable that we inhabit an airborne sea of alien machinery, a voracious "smart dust" taking up residence in our brains to understand how we think, or distributed throughout the oceans in order to track our planet's ecological plight. Of course, this assumes that the alien intelligence is interested in such things; perhaps by achieving machine-hood, ETI forfeits its stake in all matters biological. Carbon-based life might not be worthy of any special attention.

Some UFOs might be a manifestation of a machine-based alien presence. But this begs the question: If stealth is of the essence, why do so many UFOs and their ostensible "occupants" often seek out our attention? The literature brims with credible cases of pilots closing in on uncorrelated targets, only for them to scatter playfully in what seems to be a deliberate display of technological superiority. Maybe the alien intelligence is showing us something we can comprehend (i.e., humanoid aliens in metal spacecraft) in a gradual scheme designed to bring us up to speed.

A post-biological ET intelligence might be god-like but still yearn for companionship. So it's not unthinkable that our own evolution has been bootstrapped, psychosocially as well as genetically, in order to accelerate our own transition into machines. A version of this scenario can be glimpsed in the writings of Whitley Strieber, whose book *Confirmation* posits that UFO technology is ours for the taking, but only if we're able to wrestle with its technical and political implications.

Like a lofty Olympian god, the UFO intelligence seems content to simply let us gape in wonder. But at the same time it must surely know that we're furiously trying to duplicate the bizarre physics seen in our skies.

27 MARCH

Imagine human consciousness as a palpable, visually arresting substance, a vibrant flowing stuff emanating from our minds and blending into fractal auras and impossible hues. From the air, cities would appear as congested, pulsating domes of color; up close, streets would writhe with brief, fantastic forms, office towers and apartment buildings bleeding livid Technicolor awareness into the night like vaporous portals into the mind itself.

An evening's stroll through an electric fog of roiling, mercuric awareness, tides of phosphorescence mingling, perpetually replenished.

28 MARCH

I feel an absurd affinity for Starbucks, an ersatz nostalgia. I'm drawn to simulations, lured by attempts to reproduce authentic experience that deftly exclude the very humanity they're designed to commemorate. Starbucks franchises are like tiny bubble universes where the rigors of reality are temporarily suspended and dissolved. All is plush furniture, shimmering, overpriced merchandise, yuppies intent in front of color-coordinated laptops, and the omnipresent susurration of cell phone conversation.

Of course, the entire production is synthetic, up to and including the brittle smiles of the baristas, who almost invariably screw up my order. But I don't mind; Starbucks lulls me into an uncharacteristically accepting stupor. I want so direly to sit in those absorbing, womb-like chairs savoring the smell of espresso, categorizing the faces behind their inscrutable flat-screens. I sometimes find myself ordering coffee simply as an excuse to linger, entranced by the almost library-like hush that predominates between outbursts of anonymous laughter.

Starbucks straddles the zone between crass commercialization and authenticity, or at least pretends to. Like an airport or a hotel room, a Starbucks is reassuring because it's implicitly transitional, an easily discarded prop stripped of sentiment.

I walk into a Starbucks and find my own alienation abruptly justified, my ego severed and allowed to float, disembodied, amidst the canned music and aromatic steam.

29 MARCH

The great thing about living on the 9th floor is watching the car wrecks. I'm not kidding. I mean, I rarely see them happen, but I commonly hear the telltale SQUEAL-THUNK of frantic tires and colliding metal and stop what I'm doing to observe the aftermath.

There was a crash just a couple minutes ago in the intersection below my kitchen. I'm listening to the sirens now. Last night there was another one in almost exactly the same spot. White cars each time. It's like there's some electromagnetic anomaly buried in the street that causes drivers to space out and lose control.

And while I stand in my kitchen laughing with smug disdain, I'm not without sympathy. The truth is that driving scares me. I'd rather not do it, given the choice.

I wish we had telepods like the ones in "The Fly": instant, petroleum-free molecular reconstitution for the masses.

But on the other hand, look what happened to Jeff Goldblum. Do you honestly think public telepods could be kept insect-free?

I personally doubt it.

30 MARCH

If we can hasten the demise of our biosphere using primitive industrial technology, just imagine what poorly understood stuff like nanotech is likely to do if stupidly unleashed into the environment.

The upshot is that we can eventually design nanobots programmed to seek out pollutants and render them harmless. But by the time we develop a technological immune system for our oceans and atmosphere, the ecological bedrock may have crumbled beneath us. It will be too late; our only option will be to terra-form our own planet, just as some optimists hope to "revive" Mars (which, ironically, doesn't appear to be quite as dead as everyone's assumed).

In any case, a massive human dieback is inevitable. Millions, perhaps billions, will probably die in the next few hundred years. Those "dead zones" out in the oceans may seem comfortably distant now, but wait until the United States finds itself situated in the middle of one. Wait until Europe is one big ecological Chernobyl, drenched in greenhouse heat. And do you really think everyone's going to peacefully wait for high-tech deliverance? No, there will be wars.

We are bounding blindly into the twilight.

31 MARCH

To anyone who's seen David Cronenberg's *Dead Ringers*, this may come as a somewhat disturbing revelation, but I can relate to the twin gynecologists played with freaky artistry by Jeremy Irons. Cronenberg's psychological vivisection is a singular metaphor, alarmingly identifiable.

Dead Ringers is probably Hollywood's most successful portrait of psychology stretched to aberrant extremes. The "identical" twins at the film's core form a composite organism, each the cerebral mirror of the other. One is socially cunning and icy-suave; the other is painfully shy, awkward, and self-absorbed.

Despite their glaring differences, each is utterly dependent on the other. Functioning in stealthy unison, they comprise an integrated if chillingly synthetic self.

Only when this duality is shaken by a love interest does their shared world begin to disintegrate. If each brother represents a respective brain hemisphere, any attempt at individual autonomy is like severing the knot of tissue that makes an anatomically bifurcated mind function as an undifferentiated whole. For the twins, escape from symbiosis equals suicide.

Reality fractures when the two hemispheres fall out of synch. In *Dead Ringers*, Cronenberg illustrates this schism by assigning left- and right-brain attributes to each twin. Esteemed doctors, they both live in the same swank apartment, ritualistically regrouping at the end of each day to synchronize. Their lives are carefully modulated so each can reap the other's experience – an automatic process in an organic brain, but one that the twins must manage with incredible finesse lest their composite-self begin to fracture.

Dead Ringers may be disturbing, but the central concept is enacted within our minds on a near-constant basis. Cronenberg and Irons humanize a process most of us would prefer to consign to neurology textbooks, revealing how fragile that link between the hemispheres really is – how something as trivial as a romantic obsession can cut deeper and more exactingly than the sharpest scalpel.

Chapter 16
April 2004

2 APRIL

I know it may seem trite for the subject of a blog entry, but today was remarkably pleasant. Great weather, so I spent the afternoon strolling the Plaza, circumnavigating the giant bipedal rabbits and pausing to take a group photo for tourists who entrusted me with their camera. The world seemed anomalously shiny and happy.

Of course, I know damned well it's not. The biosphere is faltering. The Bush administration is lying its way to another election "victory." A new study reveals that humans are inundated with industrial neurotoxins deemed "acceptable" despite unknown long-term effects. Our "best and brightest" are committed to designing grotesque new ways to kill or disable large numbers of people while relatively small-budget projects such as the Hubble Space Telescope are abandoned due to a presumed lack of funds. I don't have a girlfriend. The bodies of American civilians are being dragged behind cars in Iraq. And to top it all off, the new *Left Behind* book just came out.

Armageddon is in the details.

3 APRIL

While most debilitating viruses are crafted, Frankenstein-like, by conniving hackers, the Internet is aswarm with the hardy remnants of a silicon ecology that so far only occasionally manages to precipitate dire alerts in the pages of non-specialty newspapers.

But the problem is escalating. I read somewhere that email as we know it may fall out of favor due to memory-eating deluges of spam. I like to think that's so much wringing of slightly neophobic hands. In any case, what can replace email? And spam, for all of its ugly excess, is for the most part consciously perpetuated by humans, members of a species whose caprices we can at least begin to identify and comprehend.

If the Internet is ultimately incapacitated, I predict digital "wildlife" will be responsible. As computers and Internet connections become more varied and versatile, new viruses will emerge, the binary equivalent of SARS and BSE. Aspiring viruses will engage in incredibly selective Darwinian competition, breeding fierce new strains that may well prove uncrackable and worryingly alien.

Computation will continue to thrive alongside efforts to link the nervous system directly to the Net. Which means that we may be faced with a crop of particularly savvy viruses capable of jumping the "substrate barrier," existing as smatterings of machine code in one instant and manifesting as flesh-and-blood symptoms the next.

The transition from chip to meat isn't likely to have a high success rate – at first. But as viruses learn from experience, a dire and unwanted compatibility may emerge. The battle will have migrated from the abstract realm of "cyberspace" to the trauma wards of hospitals.

The first "transgenic" viruses will probably be hobbyist variations of DARPA-inspired electronic warfare programs, good for little more than brute-force nerve damage. As we augment our organs with ever-more flexible, user-friendly electronics, we bore a tunnel from the organic world to the intricate havens of machine-life, redefining cherished philosophical notions and making ourselves newly vulnerable.

As technology improves, so do the stakes. Transgenic viruses will be no more content to cause random, superficial damage than human hackers content to merely cripple a mainframe when they have the capacity to enter it and seek the informational gems within. Enter the age of "neurophreaking" and identity wars, viruses that incubate in the snarl of meat and silicon behind your forehead in order to profile your habits and consumer preferences.

Most "smart" transgenic viruses will have roots in today's Internet spyware. Others will seek to actively take over their victim's nervous system, if only for brief periods. In theory, strangers could be selected and stealthily programmed to act as terrorists, or commanded to sympathize with a given cultural or political agenda. The motives behind the viral siege will be thoroughly familiar to anyone who's screened pop-up ads or been forced to install expensive firewalls.

But how to firewall a human being, granted that a human being can be identified by the arsenal of synapses and circuits lurking in his or her central nervous system? And what happens once the digital ecology threatens to slip beyond our control, just as spam now threatens the viability of online communication?

Substrate-hopping viruses will arguably make a bid for dominant species-hood in the next couple hundred years. What plans might they have for humanity?

4 APRIL

I just coined a new term – *Spangst*: the state induced by wading through unacceptable quantities of unsolicited email. The techno-intelligentsia will be saying it in no time!

6 APRIL

I'd like to take this opportunity to announce my "write-in" candidacy for President of the United States. I haven't decided on a running mate yet. I might just do without one. Seriously: Who cares? "Politics" is simply a convenient label for the process by which stark realities are assigned numbers and filed away for the benefit of speech-writers.

By now you're probably telling yourself, "I bet Mac would make an ideal President, but where does he stand on the issues?" I think that's a fair question. But before I start in on a bunch of nebulous political concerns (of which I honestly know quite little), I think it's fair to examine these vague, frequently abstruse, self-perpetuating phenomena we call "issues."

What, exactly, constitutes an "issue"? And why do we keep hearing about the same "issues" every four years? Granted, I have no former experience in the political arena, but it seems to me that the defining nature of an "issue" is its subsequent resolution. The fact that the so-called "issues" that dominate presidential elections are never satisfactorily resolved strikes me as extremely curious. If I didn't know any better, I'd even consider the possibility that there's an implicit vested interest in perpetuating various problematic "issues" so that voters can be more easily manipulated.

I also hear a great deal about "values." You're probably wondering right now where I stand on the issue of "values." And yes, as far as I can discern, the very prospect of "values" constitutes an "issue" of its own; conversely, "issues" can take the form of a pressing "value." I think. It's all quite complicated. And again, it often seems as if this state of near-terminal abstraction is willfully perpetuated, like a gear in a machine that's lovingly oiled lest the entire mechanism come screaming to a disastrous halt.

Forgive me for sounding cavalier, but my stand on the "issues" is that there are no issues, at least as popularly conceived. I think issues are flimsy thought-viruses, mere gears in the electoral machine. Deeming something an "issue" is a way of distancing oneself from it.

As President, I'll do away with "issues."

Completely.

8 APRIL

I was first really turned onto the universe-as-hologram concept by Michael Talbot's highly engaging *The Holographic Universe*, a book I consider must-reading for anyone who gives a damn about what reality actually is – or isn't.

At the end of Gregory Benford's *In the Ocean of Night*, the astronaut hero experiences an epiphany (via an alien computer discovered buried on the Moon) that dissolves his sense of separateness from the Cosmos; he suddenly experiences everything as a unified Now, observed and observer forged into a single entity.

I wonder if we can achieve this without ET intervention. Really achieve it, in a way that makes us recoil in visceral horror at the way we routinely abuse ourselves and our environment. A person wholly aware of his quantum-entanglement with the universe (a universe that just happens to encapsulate his mind and body) would certainly be an improvement on the current breed.

Visionary physicist David Bohm proposed a new syntax designed to eliminate the illusion of duality. I don't foresee it becoming popular, but he was thinking in the right direction. Bohm's experimental language reminds me of William Burroughs' tireless attempts to "rub out the word." Words, after all, are artifacts, pale substitutes for reality.

Or are they? As a writer, or at least as someone who writes, I have a certain affinity for them. Reading a choice passage from a William Gibson novel has the ability to heighten sensory experience by juxtaposition; good writing rewires your brain, gently forces you to see the world anew, if only for a moment.

Burroughs considered Egyptian hieroglyphics a superior alternative to the written word. But even a graphical language fails to capture the quantum unity that Bohm sought. I suspect that beyond "deep structure" there is an existential lingua franca; instead of representing something else, it simply *is*, resolute and abiding, antedating attempts to share experience via words and images. It's the Cosmos' own source code, the white light of creation, mistakenly anthropomorphized and deified.

11 APRIL

A few minutes ago I noticed that my cats were staring oddly at nothing in particular, or perhaps at each other in preparation for one of their frequent good-natured duels. As I waited for one of them to make the first move (my money was on Spook, the oldest), I noticed that they had become enraptured by a longish, many-legged "something" that had somehow managed to penetrate my ninth-floor apartment.

Suddenly this insectoid phantasm started skittering my way; I mustered the courage to stomp it before it could disappear beneath any furniture. I examined the thing's flaccid corpse, antennae still flexing listlessly, before I disposed of it. It was roughly an inch long, with about six legs on either side of its disturbingly meaty body.

The perverse thing is that my cats spent several minutes in a state of denial. They missed the horrid thing. They staked out the area where it had made its last stand and scraped pitifully at the carpet in a futile attempt at feline necromancy.

Other than the bug incident, this was an uneventful Easter. I slept late, started Neil Gaiman's *Neverwhere*, and managed the singular task of microwaving a jumbo bean-and-cheese burrito without the ends messily exploding.

13 APRIL

Today was… pleasant. New furniture in my apartment lobby after months of tedious remodeling. The chatter of Starbucks patrons. A not altogether unpleasant day at work.

And yet – that persistent feeling that I'm wading through a clever hologram… that all is a solipsistic delusion that could come crashing to pieces at any moment, like a film committed to brittle Celluloid.

I will myself numb so that I can't feel the blade cleaving my brain into pieces.

14 APRIL

Getting rid of the meat. Jettisoning obsolete human baggage. When to say "when"? Is there a critical threshold where the route to transhuman ascendancy takes an abrupt downward fork?

It's conceivable humans will eventually have the technology to edit their own memories, rearranging their mental furniture as casually as dragging icons across a computer desktop. Can we trust ourselves with such ability? What will we decide to delete?

Click and drag… Click and drag…

Are you sure you want to delete the contents of the Recycle Bin?

Assuming you click "yes," the "you" that ponders the outcome is a new and different "you." Maybe not a substantially different "you," but then again, how will "you" ever know?

Some hobbyist technophiles buy ancient computers so they can pore over the contents of their hard drives, upon which all sorts of esoteric (and sometimes useful) data can be found languishing. I can imagine neuro-hackers 50 years from now lopping the heads off fresh corpses and purging their brains of recoverable memories. Recycling them. Sifting through the sensory debris of subjective centuries. Blood from a stone.

Maybe this has already happened. Maybe I'm already dead and someone is simply rummaging through the contents of my brain. Looking for something, perhaps. Or maybe simply for the vicarious hacker thrill: What did this guy think about? Talk about voyeurism; it doesn't get any more intimate than that.

More disturbing is the prospect that probing a nonliving mind can actually trick the dead person's synapses into a spurious sense of autonomy, the tragic misconception that this is real when in fact reality bears no resemblance to the images and sensations triggered by the scanning process. And what is consciousness, really, but a sensation?

Dead frogs can be made to jump by jolts of electricity applied to the right muscles in the proper sequence. In a strictly biomechanical sense, the frog is tugged back in time, restored to a clumsy semblance of functionality. A dormant human brain may not be as sacrosanct as we assume. "Dead" brains may even be a valuable commodity for a near-future information economy.

So what do we call this technologically assisted parody of thought? Can the brain being hacked be made to experience new stimuli or is it read-only-memory? Perhaps more pertinently, is there a qualitative difference between the thoughts of a living brain and the synaptic acrobatics of a dead brain commanded to believe it's actually alive?

If not, then the definition of "alive" begs redefinition. As proponents of cryonic suspension are justly fond of pointing out, it certainly wouldn't be the first time in medical history that we've been forced to revise our criteria for death.

15 APRIL

The entire point of television is to reduce us to compliant drones incapable of harnessing the mind-power to form an independent thought – and it's working awfully well.

Wal-Mart!

Home Depot!

Budweiser!

Sprint long-distance!

Get out there and consume!

We've got product to move!

Buy, buy, buy!

17 APRIL

Today is a bright, sunny day, so of course the Street Preacher was outside Pottery Barn yelling his head off. His children have been trained to hand out gospel tracts, so you have to thread your way carefully while in his presence.

It really struck me today what a lame street preacher this guy is. I paused and actually listened to him for a few moments while waiting for a walk light; he seemed unsure as to what he was railing about. I heard him yell: "You can be Born Again twice! [pause] Three times!" Like it's an amusement park ride, which I suppose isn't a completely bad analogy.

If I ever start audio blogging, you can bet I'll webcast this idiot.

I'm wrestling with the prospect of taking out an Internet personal ad. If there's one thing I've learned about romance, it's that drinking coffee and reading is a terrible way to find it. I've actually tried online personals before with disappointing results. But perhaps the biggest reason I don't like them is because they're far too time-consuming than they have any right to be. I hate wading through all those "scientific" match-maker filters, trying to locate my "type."

My "type"? I have a type?

Come again?

It's fair to say that all I really want when I'm browsing personal ads is to be drinking coffee and reading.

22 APRIL

I'm groping for words virulent enough to express my disgust with the United States, with its phony president, media-soaked voters, morbid religiosity, and utter disregard for truth. Many long-forgotten societies mused that they were living in the "end times," but I have the horrible sense that this time it might be for real. The future looks unnervingly bleak; if we're lucky, in fifteen years we'll be living in a world that's a particularly stomach-wrenching rendition of John Brunner's *The Sheep Look Up*.[36]

It's no accident that religious "fundamentalism" is looking so bright. It promises the ultimate easy escape. Dreams of the "Rapture" – the premise behind the *Left Behind* phenomenon – are the intellectual equivalent to an all-expenses-paid trip to Disney World, where nothing is as it seems but everything is imminently agreeable. Why care about the oceans dying if you know that you'll be whisked to safety when disaster strikes? Why give a fuck about anything?

One way or another, the milieu that's been developing since 9-11-01 will end. But we're past the point of controlling how it will end with any degree of accuracy. We've tossed our rationality onto the bonfire like so much kindling. We wait like passengers on some vertiginous malfunctioning ride. The unseen technicians in the control room know the ride is doomed; they can see the widening

---

[36] First published in 1972, *The Sheep Looks Up* painted a dystopian portrait of the United States in the near future, wracked by civil unrest and riots, controlled by a corporate-sponsored government, and faced with a rapidly deteriorating environment. The title references the poem *Lycidas* by John Milton: "The hungry sheep look up, and are not fed, but swollen with wind and the rank mist they draw, rot inwardly, and foul contagion spread."

hole in the tracks. But they've weathered disasters before and see no purpose in heeding their senses when previous debacles have been so successfully marginalized and erased from public conscience.

Now the ride is nearing its end. And if you pay careful attention to the faces of the passengers in those last cataclysmic moments of rending metal and oily smoke, you'll notice that almost all of them will still be smiling.

23 APRIL

I find myself confused by and disgusted with teenagers. I don't understand them. It's not enough to say they simply inhabit a liminal realm between childhood and adulthood – it's weirder than that. It's like they're only peripherally alive, human only in a basic anatomical sense. What's really unnerving is the knowledge that I was once one of them. I feel obscurely ashamed of the fact; I'm trying to keep it secret. Heaven forbid if word of this closeted skeleton gets out.

26 APRIL

I chanced upon a solution to the "not enough troops" problem. You see these goddamned "Hummers" everywhere, right? I figure the only reason anyone would purchase one of these aesthetic monstrosities is out of a sublimated desire to be in the armed forces. So here it is: Humvee dealers and Army recruitment offices should join forces.

Want to be a bad-ass soldier? Want to drive a Humvee? Then get your fat urbanite ass over to Iraq and start weathering sandstorms and rocket-propelled grenades like a real patriot so desperate kids who can't afford to buy their own custom military assault vehicles don't have to. Get back alive – exact date subject to change – and we'll give you a Hummer.

And maybe a free pack of G.I. Joe action figures to boot.

27 APRIL

What sort of blog is this, anyway? Blogs are, after all, subject to genre. There are personal blogs. War blogs. Political blogs. Industry-specific blogs and blogs devoted to emerging technologies. I know of a belly-dancing blog that's quite good.

So where does *Posthuman Blues* fit in the topical spectrum? What the hell is this? My psyche eviscerated? An extended confession for never-committed crimes? An elitist soapbox? A simple plea for attention?

28 APRIL

I enjoy disturbing things. Things that give epistemologists headaches and send "skeptics" running for the nearest cognitive fallout shelter. Franz Kafka, for example, saw no point in books that failed to disturb; to Kafka, a book should be "an ax to break the frozen sea within us." The same applies to memes in general. I take special pains to purge my brain of the ordinary. It's like wringing some noxious liquid from a sponge.

29 APRIL

Sometimes I wax nostalgic for really good books. I recall bits of character and setting and they ramble about in my head like thought-viruses. Lately I've been thinking about China Mieville's *Perdido Street Station*. Neil Gaiman's *Neverwhere*, which I'm about to finish, strikes me as a distant cousin to Mieville's novel; both share some of the same dingy "steampunk" trappings and fascination with ruinous architecture.

John Brunner's *Quicksand* is another I can't shake. It's a little-remarked book about a psychiatrist who falls in love with a mysterious patient – intensely interesting and utterly haunting. As actual storytelling, it's probably better than his breakthrough novels (*The Shockwave Rider*, *Stand on Zanzibar*, *The Sheep Look Up*).

I make a point never to reread books. But if I did, I have a half-realized list of titles I'd revisit: William Gibson's *Neuromancer*, Jack Womack's *Elvissey* and a few others. Possibly *The Difference Engine*, which I read in high-school and would probably appreciate a lot more now having immersed myself in cyberpunk. And Kim Stanley Robinson's *Red Mars*, if for no other reason than I could move on to the sequel, *Green Mars*, without feeling quite so amnesiac.

30 APRIL

A news article today: "To stop sex in space from happening they are trying to develop a drug that will temporarily reduce sex drive but not leave the crew permanently impotent."

The key to dealing with sex in space is to shelve the Puritan antics and realize that humans are going to remain sexual beings regardless what planet they're on. Instead of spending untold thousands of dollars turning astronauts into high-tech eunuchs, we should just give them condoms. They could even put the NASA logo on each pack.

But why stop there?

NASA could take out ad space for contraceptives right on the sides of Mars-bound rockets!

Meanwhile, for the past 48 hours or so, my body has been valiantly fending off a nasty cold virus. I've been acutely aware of its stages; first, the itch in the throat; then the sneezing; then the nasal leakage (arguably the worst part, especially when you're trying to edit manuscript galleys). Finally, the disturbing impression that my sinuses and brain have been packed with industrial epoxy.

Chapter 17
May 2004

5 MAY

Today's news item: "Cats can now have more than nine lives thanks to a Californian company that is the first US firm to go commercial and offer the public a pet cloning service."

At least cloned cats won't be subjected to the misplaced expectations and neurotic fervor of parents who plan to have their dead children Xeroxed. Can you imagine being a cloned teenager forever trying (or, more likely, explicitly not trying) to live up to the achievements of your deceased doppelganger, knowing that you're a fertilized-on-command biological rerun, a nostalgic whim in the guise of flesh?

6 MAY

I like coming up with paranoid conspiracy theories. One of them, never before posted, involves the growing concern over ominous-looking jet contrails, sometimes dubbed "chemtrails" because of presumed nefarious chemical properties.

Contrails are taken seriously because they alter climate. We inhabit an age of ubiquitous air-travel; just as our cars contribute to global warming, jet exhaust wreaks its own havoc in our atmosphere. And the more planes there are up there spewing exhaust, the more the atmosphere is disturbed.

Imagine, for a moment, that a secret group of U.S. government scientists produced compelling evidence that jet contrails threatened to produce a cataclysmic effect on Earth's ecosystem, and that the only way to test their notion was to suspend a substantial portion of the Earth's air traffic in order to compare clear skies to polluted ones.

Suppose that this is a dire study in need of immediate results. How to stop planes from flying? What would the government research group do? Petition major airlines all over the globe to refrain from flying for a week or so in the name of science? Hardly. Besides, the study is secret; telling airlines that they should forego their livelihood for the sake of an atmospheric study would immediately clue everyone in to the fact that the U.S. government is terrifically concerned about something having to do with the environmental impact of commercial air flight.

So the group would have to act behind the curtain, somehow bringing world commercial aviation to a virtual halt without letting anyone know why.

Enter the 9-11-01 attacks on the World Trade Center and Pentagon.

Forget everything you ever heard about Osama bin Laden, the Taliban and Muslim extremists. What if the entire 9-11 debacle was an epic sleight of hand contrived to help desperate scientists understand something far scarier than the most anti-American Evil-Doer? What if something horrible is happening to our atmosphere, something so potentially apocalyptic that the deaths of several thousand New Yorkers were considered a justifiable expense?

Finally, a few words of caution. Do I really think the above scenario is for real? No, I don't. But I think it makes a weird sort of logic; it wouldn't surprise me if some people did believe it. And there are all sorts of phenomena just waiting to be added to the central theme: UFOs, anomalous solar flares (of which there have been quite a few recently), HAARP, ozone depletion.

There. I've committed the meme to the Web.

Now it's your turn.

8 MAY

I'm pleased to no end that the senseless torture and murder of Iraqi POWs is infecting front pages everywhere. The governing assumptions in our dealings with the Mid-East are defined by an unspoken, condescending certainty that the Arab world is something rather less than human. The West has always trained itself to think of Arabs as somewhat barbaric characters – uncouth "B"-movie villains whose claim to civilization is little more than a PR facade. Maintaining this stereotype was definitely the agenda behind the *Saving Private Lyn*ch drama. The public was expected to blanch at the notion of a God-fearing white girl in the clutches of psychopathically misogynistic dark-skinned rapists.

Now the rules have been upturned. Suddenly we're forced to stare at a reflection of ourselves that is so unshakably ugly that our most entrenched misconceptions require revision.

We are the monsters.

We are the sadists, the brutes, the savages.

9 MAY

I spent today ghosting in and out of stores, unable to focus, not in the mood to read and just barely tasting my coffee. I felt like a cheap hologram.

The sidewalks were thick with teenagers in prom formal-wear.

Fat girls in ludicrous backless dresses, pale flesh rippling.

10 MAY

I've had a mostly broken TV/VCR combo languishing in my closet for a few years. Tonight, on a whim, I hauled it out and managed to get an old *Seinfeld* tape playing (the one where Kramer visits Elaine's psychiatrist and George almost ruins Jerry's deal with NBC).

Then, waxing nostalgic, I watched *Beneath the Planet of the Apes*.

Beneath is a stupid movie on several levels. But at the same time it has a strangely implacable ambient menace.

I'm forever fascinated by the scene in which the main astronaut character, accompanied by Nova, discovers the New York City tunnel system while fleeing from a pack of gun-toting gorillas.

13 MAY

Here's another common language error that drives me absolutely nuts: the utterly misguided notion that apostrophes denote emphasis. I see this on signs all the time. The other day I walked out of Wild Oats Market (which serves "Entree's [sic] to Go") and there was a car in the parking lot covered with professionally made signs advertising how to:

WORK FROM "HOME"

Just like that.

"Home" in goddamned apostrophes.

The funny thing here is that the apostrophes convey exactly the opposite of what the sign-maker intended. Putting "home" in apostrophes makes it sound like "home" isn't really "home." Like there's some fiendish trick lying in wait for unsuspecting job-seekers. Maybe if you take the job, whatever it is, you'll be "relocated." I can imagine being led to some sweatshop with decaying mattresses strewn in some roach-infested back-room and a chain-smoking supervisor sizing you up from behind a cluttered desk:

"Welcome 'home,' pal. Now get to work."

14 MAY

The Nick Berg killing dominates the news.[37] No, I haven't seen the much-discussed decapitation footage. But I've been tracking the inevitable conspiracy memes. There's a medical doctor who doesn't think the severed neck spurts blood correctly, implying that Berg was already dead at the time of the beheading. Some think the murder was perpetrated by BushCo loyalists intent on distracting the public from the mounting evidence of wide-scale prison abuse.

I sincerely doubt both scenarios. But the latter almost makes

---

[37] Nick Berg (1978 – 2004) was an American businessman who was abducted by Islamist militants in Iraq in April 2004 and later beheaded in response to the Abu Ghraib torture and prisoner abuse scandal involving the United States Army and Iraqi prisoners. The decapitation video was released on the Internet.

sense, if you're willing to pay a passing visit to Tinfoil Hat Land. Occam's Razor suggests that we're seeing plain, imbecilic "revenge." But the timing of the beheading's release is certainly convenient ammunition for a mainstream press forced to deal with the spectacle of American troops behaving like savages. After all, these are the same troops we're constantly reminded to "support" (apparently by ensuring Bush's election).

The Berg killing helps make the Arabs look more like the popularly conceived caricature: thugs who revel in American blood. And in a perverse, subconscious way it might even help to "justify" the pointless abuses and killings doled out by occupying American forces; war supporters will seize on the Berg footage as evidence that "war is hell" and that the prison abuse should go unpunished.

The "logic" will go like this: Conditions in Iraq are so aberrant and awful that we should expect U.S. troops to "lose it." Hell, those grinning men and women in uniform hooking up battery cables to Iraqi genitals are the real victims – just look what they've been reduced to by those Arab bastards!

I fully expect to read variations on the above theme for months to come.

16 MAY

I've never had a "song of the day" on this blog, but I think I might start, beginning tonight.

How about "A Hazy Shade of Winter" by Simon and Garfunkel?

17 MAY

My fiction writing took a decided turn for the morose after I first really watched *Blade Runner*. Now I'm almost incapable of writing a story that isn't set in a bleak, urban near-future where it rains a lot and characters have conspicuously easy access to consciousness-altering technologies ranging from particle accelerators to funky designer drugs.

Here's an excerpt from a blessedly unpublished novel about

neurology and quantum physics I wrote in 1998/1999. This particular project, while educational, ultimately failed because of Kitchen-Sink Syndrome. I was trying to graft way too many weird ideas into one story, producing more than a few scenes like the following:

It was worse than Zak had expected.

The dim lights of Roma's apartment revealed mountains of rubbish: sheaves of CD-ROMs, dismantled hard-drives. Screens scrolled enigmatically in the corners of the living room, which had been converted into a bewildering shrine. The animatrons, dressed in rags of dying skin, knelt meditatively in a pile of microchips and torn cables, eyes pinched shut, pubices encrusted with discordant bits of metal and silicon.

Roma led him through the door. The omnipresent alien, now crowned in fiber-optics and wadded electrical tape, shut it with a four-fingered hand.

"Roma..."

Zak swallowed and stared mutely. Every inch had been transformed. Fastidiously arranged ZIP drives had turned the walls into gleaming murals; shredded diskettes carpeted the floor like matted leaves. His every step crunched, as if he walked on a thick layer of beetle husks.

Roma led him closer to the dormant simulacra, hands cool and restless as she ritualistically kneaded his arm, testing his solidity. The skin below her eyes nicitated. Zak noted with alarm that her lips had completely lost their color; they had adopted the predominating off-white of the computer shells throughout the apartment.

Roma became very still and put a finger to her lips. Her pupils contracted into dusky pearls as she crossed an apron of plastic and knelt among the animatrons.

Zak gasped as he saw her body for the first time. Roma had streaked her skin with liquid crystal, skewered her nipples with blunt plastic screws. Dried blood striped her abdomen, neck and thighs. Buds of metal and plastic poked through her skin like stunted quills.

"I came to see what you're doing here," Zak said. He almost mentioned Michael's referral but caught himself at the last second.

Roma began leaning to one side. One of the animatrons broke her fall, cradling her in chapped hands. The nutrient tanks Michael had used to keep the cloned skin alive had run empty, leaving the skin to slough away from the elaborately wrought armature beneath.

Even from where he stood, Zak thought he smelled decay. He wanted to retch, to fall on his knees and cry.

Roma had opened the door without the slightest glimmer of recognition. Her face, pinched by slow starvation, had become a rictus of numb piety. No emotion... Zak couldn't fathom the change that had eclipsed her eyes, stripping them down to flat circles. She had the guileless look of an ancient tomb painting.

He crossed the living room, shoes crushing shoots of brittle wire and panes of glass from gutted flat-screens. Mosaics of burned circuitry gleamed in his peripheral vision. Through some trick of perspective, the wires seemed to reach out at him, offering him some rare understanding. When he turned his head they fell away like weary insect feelers and resumed their usual two-dimensionality.

He looked up at a ceiling festooned with video cable, a kind of sloppy fish-net used to suspend the few books and videocassettes left over from the Roma he used to know. She had reduced them to squalid ornaments.

To what purpose? Zak thought. He felt he was traipsing through some piece of misguided conceptual art. He looked back at Roma, who slowly detached herself from the mothering animatrons and walked toward him, bare feet unscathed by the debris covering the floor. Flecks of dried blood fell from her thighs as she walked. Zak could see the illicit dance of sinew in her neck and calves.

He forced himself to stand still. Roma walked within touching distance and spread her palm, revealing a single Pentium chip. Only on second glance did he realize it had been pressed deeply into her flesh, and even then he wanted desperately to believe it was simply trompe l'oiel, something to be wiped away with a warm, soapy cloth.

"Look," Roma said.

"I'm looking"

She leaned closer until Zak feared she would collapse into him. "Look closer."

He did. And for the first time he saw the shimmering matrix embedded in her skin, a rambling fractal composed of strands thinner than spider silk. The strands, faint but unmistakable, branched from the Pentium chip and traced riotous patterns up her wrist, arm and shoulder.

Roma pivoted like a runway model striking a pose, letting the light reveal the matrix in its entirety. It spanned her entire body: galaxies of triangles and squares that caught the light and threw it back at him in eye-scalding clarity.

Zak knelt in wonder. The schematic continued undaunted across the insides of her legs and knees. The lines didn't seem to follow any recognizable pattern. They reiterated themselves in their own private logic, unconfined by symmetry.

20 MAY

As I've mentioned before, the odds of our inhabiting the "original" universe (assuming there is such a thing) are infinitesimally low. We're probably "nested" within multiplex universes – simulations running within simulations within simulations. I'm also intrigued by the idea that universes are best viewed as living organisms; instead of passing along genes, a universe "seeks" to pass on its physical infrastructure – its "ontological fabric," for lack of a better term – via singularities that give birth to new universes.

Of course, to get the singularities, you need mass, which is where black holes come in. Massive stars collapsing into "black holes" may seem like stellar casualties to Earth-bound astronomers, but perhaps they're actually the multiverse's way of achieving cosmic posterity. Of course, not all black holes and gravitational anomalies necessarily translate to baby universes; the best a universe can do is produce lots of singularities in the hope (and yes, I'm anthropomorphizing) that at least some of them will spawn brand-new universes.

Stars are quite striking to look at – after all, we evolved because of the steady flow of energy from our own Sun. But it could be that stars are essentially cosmic ejaculations. Celibate universes that lack stars inevitably lack the mass necessary to procreate. Presumably, they're rare, if not altogether extinct.

Ultimately, the Cosmos appears asexual.

21 MAY

Puddles of dried, colorless wax greet pedestrians on the bridge: the relics of blood-red candles burned in silent homage or memoriam. The accompanying rose petals have long since succumbed to the thick medicinal waters of the creek below. The air is stagnant, unmoving, oddly selfish. Ragged symphonies of asphalt and sun-baked concrete clash with too-perfect lawns and rows of fastidiously watered flowers. The glow of digital cameras, screens like small blue flames tricked into unlikely geometries. The cool depths of parking garages, where the air is held captive and breathable.

23 MAY

Last night I went to bed really late. Part of my brain was already engaged in the dreaming process – becoming pliant, malleable-on-command – so that when I turned out the light I could conjure images into my mind's eye and set them to motion. I could actually "see" what I was imagining, and knowing it for what it was made it no less interesting.

I spent a few minutes "looking" at what appeared to be a simian hand (although I'm pretty sure it only had four fingers), commanding it to flex and curl and rotate. It reacted at the speed of thought, showing texture and detail that I hadn't (consciously) imagined. And that was what made the exercise so fun; every second offered new discoveries. My brain was creating this thing partly of its own volition, triggered by the breakdown of workaday consciousness.

I got bored with the ape-hand and tried modeling what I thought the hand of a "Gray" alien might look like: thin, bloodless, with tapering chitinous points on the ends of the four fingers. This effort wasn't as successful as the previous one because it was forced; I wanted it to look a certain way, and my mind was having none of that. So I had to reconcile myself to the fact that my control over the experience was confined to offering cues. I had to relax or else the experiment would dissolve utterly under the familiar scrutiny of wakefulness.

I never achieved a satisfactory "alien" hand. I had too many preconceptions. I tried too hard when I should have let my subconscious continue with its own inscrutable flow.

This semi-lucid state reminded me of Whitley Strieber's account of discovering a compliant, bug-eyed woman fixed in his mind. By consciously directing it, he could examine the entity's anatomy. He had a professional artist draw the being as he "watched" it in his mind and the result is the archetypal alien featured on the cover of *Communion*, which became a number-one bestseller. Strieber's "vision" occurred during a state of otherwise normal wakefulness, whereas mine was decidedly dream-like and tenuous.

I wonder: If there are nonhuman intelligences hovering at the periphery of human consciousness, could waking thought form a perceptual shell around us, rendering them invisible?

Maybe the cessation of ego that accompanies dreaming and related processes helps to "melt" the shell, turning it into something like a selectively permeable membrane.

24 MAY

I took my laptop to Starbucks, stood in line for coffee, and got some Actual Writing done – specifically, the opening portion of an eco-dystopian alien invasion story that's been incubating in my head ever since I saw a photo of large, anemic-looking insects (or were they spiders?) in Iraq. There are a few touches I'm proud of; for example, the escalating homeless population is pacified by cheap virtual reality gear and accident-prone wi-fi. And city life is so noisy and chaotic that people are willing to pay handsomely to relax for a few moments in soundproofed theme-rooms.

25 MAY

I just took the Honest Bloggers Quiz.

It goes like this:

1. Which political party do you typically agree with?

Democrats.

2. Which political party do you typically vote for?

Honestly, I have yet to vote in a presidential election. But that changes this year.

3. List the last five presidents that you voted for.

See above.

4. Which party do you think is smarter about the economy?

It would depend on the administration, but again I have to go with the Democrats – not because I'm in love with them but because they're the lesser of two evils. Or three evils, if you count Ralph Nader.

5. Which party do you think is smarter about domestic affairs?

See above.

6. Do you think we should keep our troops in Iraq or pull them out?

Phase out our military presence in a hurry. The Iraqis see us as occupiers, and rightly so.

7. Who, or what country, do you think is most responsible for 9/11?

Islamic extremists for actually doing it, and the Bush administration for making it so goddamned easy.

8. Do you think we will find weapons of mass destruction in Iraq?

Not a chance in hell.

9. Yes or no, should the U.S. legalize marijuana?

Yes.

10. Do you think the Republicans stole the last presidental election?

Yes.

11. Do you think Bill Clinton should have been impeached because of what he did with Monica Lewinski?

No.

12. Do you think Hillary Clinton would make a good president?

Frankly, she sort of gives me the creeps. But she just might make a decent political leader.

13. Name a current Democrat who would make a great president.

"Great"? That's asking a bit much. All I want is someone who isn't blatantly dysfunctional.

14. Name a current Republican who would make a great president.

See above.

15. Do you think that women should have the right to have an abortion?

Yes.

16. What religion are you?

None.

17. Have you read the Bible all the way through?

No.

18. What's your favorite book?

Neuromancer.

19. Who is your favorite band?

R.E.M.

20. Who do you think you'll vote for president in the next election?

Kerry.

No, wait. I meant me. I'm running as a write-in.

26 MAY

I have no tattoos. But I've thought about it. Franz Kafka inked several mesmerizing stick-figures in various angst-ridden postures and I've considered having them emblazoned on my arm. Well, one of them anyway.

28 MAY

I glanced at a mainstream "news" publication the other day and was shocked to discover that America is facing a "gay marriage crisis."

Crisis?

Gays wanting legal recognition as couples constitutes a "crisis"? Who sold this moronic idea?

You want a crisis? Ocean life has started dying in what could very well be the first stage in a global ecological nightmare. That's a crisis.

The Bush administration is controlled by biblical fundamentalists who believe in a literal interpretation of Armageddon – and it has nukes. I think that qualifies as a crisis.

But – silly me – it's those gays I should be losing sleep over. Forget mercury poisoning, ozone depletion, escalating carbon dioxide levels, melting ice-caps, "missing" plutonium, and our cheerful disregard for near-Earth asteroids.

Boy, I had it all wrong.

Good thing I saw that newspaper.

29 MAY

Look at the garbage shoveled out by the entertainment industry: vacuous, banal, vulgar, boundlessly stupid – but viewers don't even realize that they're being insulted. How can anyone expect an appropriately outraged response to far-away POW abuse when voters have been dumbed down into cell phone-wielding idiot savants who just want to see who wins *American Idol?*

30 MAY

I just saw *The Day After Tomorrow*, which was precisely the kind of movie I was in the mood for. I wanted to see it because I generally like high-budget disaster movies and also because I'd read the book upon which it was loosely based, *The Coming Global Superstorm*, by Art Bell and Whitley Strieber.

Tomorrow is an FX-driven movie. I knew that going in and I got what I wanted. Not that the acting was appalling; Dennis Quaid was good, and I was relieved that Jake Gyllenhaal (*Donnie Darko*) was chosen to play his son rather than a more conventional heart-throb. Thankfully, the teen romance angle was kept at a healthy minimum and the scenes of global climate chaos were mostly entrancing. Who doesn't want to see New York City flash-frozen by a super-hurricane?

My main complaint is that I wanted the disasters to be worse than they actually were. I wasn't content to see the Northern Hemisphere buried under a mantel of ice; I wanted the whole goddamned planet to get what was coming to it. If I'd written the screenplay, I would have invoked quantum mechanics and had the storm cells achieve sentience.

But no one asked.

31 MAY

Project me forward in time several decades and I just might be something like British author Colin Wilson. I've never read Wilson's most famous book, *The Outsider*, but I read *Alien Dawn* (an omnivorous look at paranormal phenomena) and loved it.

Unlike Wilson, I'm not a panty fetishist (although, coincidentally, I frequent a blog devoted, in part, to all things sock-related), but socially we fit the same profile. Outwardly, I was never exactly the pariah depicted by Wilson. I actually enjoyed grade school. And I survived high-school pretty much unharmed; nevertheless, I found myself identifying with "Edward Scissorhands."[38]

College was a Kafka-esque fever-dream. I didn't fit in; with few exceptions, I didn't like anyone (up to and including myself). I never dated, never precisely hit it off as I had expected; I certainly didn't meet the girl of my dreams. Quite the opposite: I was bullied, made fun of by complete strangers. I was in a small town and the reasoning

---

[38] The eponymous main character in Tim Burton's 1990 film, which dealt with themes of self-discovery and isolation in a romantic fantasy setting.

seemed to be that if you weren't seen in the constant presence of others then something was "different" about you and that difference was almost certainly being gay, which I emphatically wasn't.

I've been in an almost Pynchon-like cocoon ever since – but I haven't realized it until fairly recently. No, that's a lie: I've sensed it in my bones for years. I feel like a science fiction alien whose intellect has caused one side of his brain to inflate into a gnarled, imposing mass, leaving the emotional half withered and flaccid.

Quite truthfully, I feel more mechanical than mammalian most of the time. It's a sense of imprisonment coupled with a genuinely eager desire to expand that swollen hemisphere of my brain to the breaking point, a game of cerebral "chicken." Please – let me be anything but merely human.

And yet the deprived hemisphere isn't quite dead.

I feel a vague synaptical stirring.

Chapter 18
June 2004

11 JUNE

Today was a special day. *After the Martian Apocalypse* has been printed, and I got an express-mail envelope stuffed with some of the first copies to be seen by human eyes. The cover looks really good.

Michael Stipe has commented on the feeling of relief that accompanies the release of a new album. Getting "ATMA" out of the "vaporware" stage and into the hands of readers – actually seeing it in meat-space as opposed to text on a computer screen – is similarly satisfying. "ATMA" is no longer "my" book in the same sense as it's been for the last year or so.

Have I mentioned you can order it from Amazon?

13 JUNE

B&N has a fresh stock of titles by Aleister Crowley, which I've had my eye on. On the way to the bookstore today I passed a guy with a "Crowley Furniture" shopping bag. I consider this a nominal synchronicity – certainly nothing spectacular.

I'm intrigued by the synchronicities that accompany "high strangeness" UFO/entity reports. Trying to fathom reality's "deep structure" with normal human consciousness is like trying to study nano-bacteria with a pair of reading glasses.

15 JUNE

Some band has produced a misguided and frighteningly bad remake of The Cure's "Lovesong." What were they thinking? "Lovesong" is a perfect pop song; you can't hope to improve on it.

And I don't buy the notion that the remake is a "tribute" to The Cure for a moment. I think the band that recorded it is secretly hoping its audience won't be that familiar with the original. They're hoping some of The Cure's brilliance will somehow inflect their own songs by some act of musical osmosis.

Dream on.

Meanwhile, the inventor of an 'invisibility' cloak has said that his next project will be to develop the technology to allow people to see through walls. The potential for technologies like this makes me giddy. If we can make things like this now, what could a civilization a few million years ahead of us be capable of? "They" could be here and we'd never know. Unless they wanted us to; I suspect the theatric behavior exhibited by UFOs is a deliberate ploy to get our attention without overloading us.

I'm reasonably certain we're being visited by an intelligence so thoroughly mated with its technology that we lack the syntax to accurately describe it.

18 JUNE

Memorable scene today at Starbucks: Some young corporate type was demonstrating the voice-recognition feature on a new slate-style laptop.

The damned thing wouldn't work.

"Start Menu," he kept saying, tersely. His clients watched impassively. "Start Menu. Start Menu..."

Finally the computer managed to display the Start Menu, at which point the salesman repeated the same routine, this time with "All Programs."

"Voice recognition isn't perfect," I heard him say in a reasonable voice. "But it's getting better."

I sipped my coffee and smiled.

19 JUNE

The Cosmos as pure sentience. Is matter simply a convenient metaphor provided by our senses? What do you "see" when you strip away the veil?

Anonymous smile outside the museum. The distant glow of traffic; the endless susurration of fountains; consciousness like an odorless smoke hanging in the cool evening air.

The aftertaste of strange endorphins.

I'm really in a maudlin mood right now. Can you tell?

20 JUNE

I've gradually become aware of a few words I probably use too much.

One of them is "imminently," which I've been using in place of "eminently." This heinous error even made it into my book. D'oh!

Another is "innocuous." Don't ask me why, but I like this word. It's eminently useful.

Here's another: "portentous." I over-use the hell out of this word. Not because I think it makes me look "smart"; I genuinely like it. If words were condiments, "portentous" and "innocuous" would be like Grey Poupon mustard – unless I monitor my dosage I tend to go overboard.

What is it they say in addiction-recovery groups? "Awareness is the first step to recovery?"

Earlier today, I chanced upon an unpublished story on my hard-drive, which I just emailed to an "erotic" e-zine. It's more satire than an authentic attempt to write something "sexy." Nevertheless, it asks not-insignificant questions: Assuming we eventually make convincing sex androids, what might the experience be like? And who, exactly, will be having these experiences?

Excerpt:

Jason ran his fingers possessively through Trisha's lank, braided hair as she kissed at his groin and unrolled the hem of his beer-stained T-shirt with cool, thin fingers. When he removed his hands from her once-famous coif, some of Trisha's hair came away glued to the sweat on his palms. He frowned elaborately and clutched Trisha's shoulders, kneading her skin and relieved to find it warmly human-like, as advertised.

In my story, Jason is a loser living in the "apotheosis of mid-21st century suburbia." And "Trisha" – a high-tech sex-doll based upon a has-been pop idol – is decidedly less than state-of-the-art: her lips are disintegrating; her hair is falling out. And she's in urgent need of a sound-card.

> When he'd bought Trisha, she'd been pretty much indistinguishable from the original: slim, curvy, with braided black hair and eyes so soulfully large they resembled Japanese anime. Her flawless olive skin denied attempts to decipher ethnicity. Trisha had been expensive – more than the Hyundai he'd bought when he was seventeen. Four years later, the sedan graced the apartment's lawn like a decrepit shrine, tires shredded, hubcaps stacked nearby like dirty dishes. Trisha was faring better than the car, but not by much.

21 JUNE

In the news today:

> NASA has given a Topeka-based group of amateur astronomers $56,060 to use optical parts of the so-called Pitt telescope to search for asteroids that could hit the Earth.

It's a start, I guess. But what happens if they find one? Suppose they find a murderous chunk of rock heading our way and astronomers are unanimous that it will extinguish all life as we know it. Further suppose that we have ten years until impact.

What changes? What will we do?

For many, a civilization-destroying threat from space would probably be welcomed as justification for religious rhetoric. And although I'm not 100% sure, I think George W. Bush is probably among them. I'm sure "End Times scholar" Tim LaHaye and company could work annihilation from space into their masturbatory apocalyptic forecasts just as Jerry Falwell rationalized the September 11 attacks as evidence of God's displeasure with secular humanists and other liberals.

23 JUNE

I recently had a cavity filled (sans anesthetic) while wearing wireless headphones and watching scuba-diving footage on a flat-screen a couple feet above my head. While watching a passive DVD is a far cry from virtual reality, I was nonetheless able to transfer my senses to the world on the screen with some success. The familiar meat-based "me" that surfs the Web and reads books was lying in a dentist's chair while some other aspect of myself – a more synaptic, abstract "me" – was pursuing schools of brightly colored fish through inviting waters.

One of my favorite solutions to the so-called "Fermi Paradox" involves VR.[39] Might a sufficiently capable alien civilization transplant itself into a simulated world, severing its ties with the outside universe in the process? I see increasing numbers of people who seem quite literally addicted to their cell phones and personal digital assistants.

Is this the beginning of a silicon-based collective solipsism? Instead of expanding into space, might we instead choose the frontiers of our boundless information ecology?

24 JUNE

My reactions to the "afterlife" debate have changed significantly over the years. While I've always been agnostic, I've been generally inclined to view death as final and all-encompassing. For example, I was angry at Timothy Leary when he opted not to have his brain cryonically preserved; I interpreted his sentiment that death was "the ultimate trip" as so much pseudo-religious bullshit.

---

[39] The Fermi Paradox is the apparent contradiction between the high probability of the existence of extraterrestrial civilizations, and the lack of contact with such civilizations. It was first raised in 1950 by physicist Enrico Fermi.

My viewpoint is more flexible now. Perhaps it's possible for some form of consciousness to survive biological death. At this point it wouldn't surprise me. I suspect that aliens, if they're here, have probably refined consciousness into an actual technology, and that we may be getting closer to the point where communication with the dead (assuming it's possible) is removed from the realm of wishful thinking.

This isn't to say I necessarily buy the concept of individual "souls" (a word, like "spiritual," that I find maddeningly vague). Perhaps awareness is more along the lines of a universal commodity, like mass or energy; it's only natural to try to anthropomorphize it.

On a related note: Is it possible that some of the "places" I routinely visit in my dreams are, in some way, actual locations? Sometimes I experience an overwhelming nostalgia for places I've never been. Not all of these places seem entirely Earth-like; nevertheless they can seem suffocatingly familiar. On one hand, these bizarre locales could be electrochemically derived; on the other, they could represent something beyond our ability to properly define. Nodes on some cosmic Internet?

Supposedly the normal everyday world is "real." I'm not so sure. I have a hunch that "reality" is the ultimate con.

27 JUNE

I was browsing at Barnes & Noble tonight and, lo and behold, there's *After the Martian Apocalypse* on a wall display containing a sheaf of coming events notices.

Here's what they have to say about me: "Detailing the very latest Mars discoveries, local author Mac Tonnies steps away from his usual science fiction into science fact. Meet him tonight."

What the sheet doesn't say is that you can "meet" me at Barnes & Noble almost every night.

They've got *Apocalypse* filed under "Metaphysical." Evidently I am a writer of metaphysics; I was not aware of this.

Mis-labeled writers of the world unite!

28 JUNE

I drink lots of espresso. I prefer to drink it out of ceramic cups; those Dixie-sized paper ones are somehow demeaning. I think $1.80 warrants the classy white porcelain treatment.

The problem is that ceramic drinkware (is that a word?) scarcely keeps the espresso any warmer than the corporate paper substitute.

So I have an idea. Why not run toaster-like electrical filaments through the ceramic to keep the drink hot? Power source, you ask? No problem. I think a lithium-ion battery, similar to those used in the matchbook-sized cell phones you see everywhere, should suffice nicely. The manufacturer could even attach an activation button to the handle so the discerning espresso-drinker could use coveted battery power when s/he needs it most, which is typically right before you're finished, and there's only a shallow pool of rapidly cooling, inky-dark espresso at the bottom of the cup.

Meanwhile, I've decided that I really don't care to see *Fahrenheit 9/11*. I thought I did. Upon reflection, though, I couldn't possibly care less about it. I'm tired of Michael Moore. I'm tired of Bush. Why in hell would I want to spend two whole hours of my life watching the latter's antics and policies lampooned and denigrated? I mean, how hard can that possibly be?

For that matter, no more political/anti-war commentary on this blog. Honestly, I'm sick to death of the subject.

Fuck it.

I've got bigger fish to fry.

Chapter 19
July 2004

12 JULY

I just coined a brand-new term that, as of a minute ago, didn't appear at all when I ran a Google search. The term is "neo-extropianism."

13 JULY

Animated media and clothing will invariably merge – this is just the start. I foresee contact lenses with customized video loops, clothing that ripples and flashes with movie clips and commercials (think of the "flicker cladding" in Rudy Rucker's *Ware* novels), and accessories that automatically adopt the wearer's mood and broadcast them to passersby.

You think that car with the thumping bass stereo is annoying? Wait until flat-screens become flat (and durable) enough to be molded to the bodies of cars. In time, every available surface will writhe with video imagery of every conceivable variety. The work of hackers and digital graffiti artists will proliferate.

It's possible that the written word will begin to decline in importance; people will rely increasingly on ubiquitous televised "e-glyphs" to conduct business. Nonverbal communication will become more dynamic and expansive; entire dialogues will take the form of rapidly changing footage projected onto clothing and even skin in much the same way that online conversation is (arguably) facilitated by the use of animated "smilies."

We may even begin to think differently. William Burroughs feared the power of words because they were, at best, artificial stand-ins for real experience. A predominantly visual vocabulary will have massive ramifications for linguistics and aesthetics as we know them.

If a beautiful woman with a TV emblazoned on her chest ever approaches me, you can be sure I'll tell her this.

14 JULY

Tonight I wandered to my apartment lobby and perused the "library" – a few shelves of dusty paperbacks and arcane reference materials. Whitley Strieber and James Kunetka's 1984 novel *Warday* was there; I remember plowing through it while riding buses in Florida on the way to the Space Coast. It's a simply told chronicle of life after a "limited" nuclear exchange with the USSR; strangely, it seems as frighteningly topical in the 21st century world of suitcase nukes and fundamentalist political leaders as it was during the actual Cold War.

So I sat on one of the lobby's new chairs, my back facing the entrance, and reread Strieber's uncanny depiction of a nuclear attack on New York City and Washington, D.C. And, quite frankly, found myself deeply afraid.

15 JULY

I read Hermann Hesse's *Siddhartha* today, inspired by Colin Wilson's treatment of Hesse in *The Outsider*.

The conflict I encounter with books on Eastern thought is the presumed need to permanently dispense with the Self. Can't one somehow have both? How to reconcile the ego (William Burroughs' "excess baggage") with the need to become as one with the Cosmos, obliterating the illusion of time and plunging into David Bohm's "implicate order"?

Being philosophically omnivorous doesn't help matters. I like Ayn Rand and Timothy Leary; Nietzsche and Gurdjieff. As Hesse's Siddhartha would have said, each route is an equally valid, if limited, way of understanding.

I sympathize completely with Burroughs' efforts to "rub out the word."

Words, for their pragmatic beauty, are a stumbling block, a transitory phenomenon to be overcome.

17 JULY

Anna Kournikova played tennis below my building today. I had half an urge to wait outside the court complex just to see her walk to her car, and simultaneously realized the utter futility of it.

Plus, it just would have been too "stalker." I'm not a tennis fan, let alone a Kournikova devotee; I'm quite convinced my passing desire to catch a glimpse of her had a lot more to do with the sheer allure of fame than personal infatuation.

So I settled for coffee and book-browsing.

18 JULY

The grotesque irony about the imminent Fundamentalist "Rapture" ("imminent" now for a couple thousand years) is that aficionados believe that it's an entirely physical event.

For the uninitiated: The "Rapture" is when Jesus appears and the bodies of righteous Christians are physically levitated into the sky, sans clothing – a distinctly stomach-turning notion in itself. For believers, ascending into the sky is synonymous with ascending into heaven. So I can't help but wonder what would be in store for these poor bastards if the Rapture actually occurred as scripted.

Firstly, you can only "ascend" so far. Then the air starts getting really thin. Before you know it you're in outer space, and by then you're quite dead. Does one's corpse continue to "ascend" once beyond Earth's atmosphere? I mean, how far does it need to travel to reach the "kingdom of heaven"?

Not that it matters, because by this point Fundamentalists will be nastily suffocated and disfigured from exposure to hard vacuum. And in any case, there's no "up" or "down" in space. So, based on my careful study of gospel tracts and the rantings of sidewalk preachers, I've deduced that the naked, bloated bodies of True Believers will begin a short-lived orbit around the planet.

Why "short-lived"? Because I figure that once Jesus realizes that his faithful are messily dying instead of rejoicing in heaven, he will abort the spectacle ASAP. So, just like the space-junk they are, the millions of righteous cadavers in low Earth orbit will plunge back into Earth's atmospheric envelope within a matter of hours, illuminating the sky as they burst into flame.

Those of us "left behind" get to watch.

Meanwhile, I keep returning to John Mack's notion of "reified metaphor."[40] The "aliens" may not be what they seem. Of course, to most, they don't seem like anything, except perhaps a useful portal into aberrant psychology or pop-culture run riot.

The "conventional wisdom": Gray aliens are harvesting us for our genes. It's possible. But Mack's reasoning (which is admittedly elliptical) suggests there's something else going on, something that transcends mere genetics. We latch onto the "genetic harvesting" scenario because it makes sense to us; we live in an age of exponentiating biotech, so it seems sensible to assume that extraterrestrial visitors will be obsessed with similar concerns.

But a careful look at world folklore reveals that "aliens" have always been with us in one form or another. There are two immediate explanations:

1. Extraterrestrials have been here for a long time and humans have tended to address them in terms of their own techno-mythological vocabulary. Thus the "little people" of Celtic myth were perfectly real but not "supernatural." Arthur C. Clarke: "Any sufficiently advanced technology would appear indistinguishable from magic."

2. Humans have simply been projecting their fears and hopes onto the collective unconscious; yesterday's faeries and kobolds are today's

---

[40] John Mack (1929 - 2004) was an American psychiatrist, writer, and professor at Harvard Medical School. He won the Pulitzer Prize in 1977 for his biography of T. E. Lawrence. In later years, he became a leading (and controversial) researcher into the spiritual or transformational effects of alleged alien abduction experiences.

aliens. We simply use what we know to define the notion of the Other; it's inevitable that a technological society like our own would latch onto a scientifically informed vision of alien geneticists, even if the model rings hollow upon close inspection.

This was how Carl Sagan left matters in *The Demon-Haunted World*, grossly misrepresenting Jacques Vallee's "multiverse" thesis, which posits that we are somehow involved with an unseen intelligence that camouflages itself to fit the reigning zeitgeist. According to Vallee, both "aliens" and "faeries" are equally misleading labels for something that can't be properly addressed using a single-universe model.

Are our perceptions so fragile that our brains are forced to manufacture new and better disguises for our visitors? Is the "visiting" intelligence (given that it exists) responsible for its apparent cultural camouflage, or do we effectively hide its true nature from ourselves, as reflexively as we might swat at a bothersome fly?

Mack's concept of "reified metaphor" might help to excavate something real from the desert of illusion. Perhaps human consciousness exists on several levels at once. "Reality" – the world we think we inhabit – might represent a relatively low level of awareness, a crude virtual reality designed to keep us from over-taxing our seemingly meat-based brains.

The computer I'm writing this on may only be a shade more "real" than the "My Computer" icon on my screen's desktop. In the same way, genes might be mere symbols – elements in a "Matrix"-style consensual hallucination.

So what are the "aliens" trying to tell us? We're told they extract ova and semen; that they're keen on "punch biopsies" and nasal implants. Is there an intelligible symbolism at work behind the forever-rippling veil of sensationalism? If so, can we even hope to decode it?

20 JULY

Ecopalypse is breathing down our necks. I've been giving the human species less than 300 years until it simply becomes too late to relocate; we will have become yet another failed evolutionary experiment.

I'm beginning to wonder if I was being hopelessly optimistic. When stuff starts happening to the oceanic food-chain, I get scared. The oceans are the bedrock of life as we understand it. One extinguished species might be all it takes to turn the biosphere against us.

And yet we just keep pushing it. We're like locusts, forever gnashing our mandibles while the world disintegrates around us.

21 JULY

I developed this weird nervous tick about a year ago. It faded over a period of months, but now it's back.

You know how sometimes when you're under strain or tired one or both of your eyelids will flutter uncontrollably? It's like that, but amplified and near-constant. It feels like there are delicate wires running through the skin around my right eye, and that some sadistic homunculus is randomly tugging at them as if to wrest control of some cyclopean marionette.

You can actually see it if you look closely: an oddly reptile-like nicitating. Christopher Walken would be envious.

24 JULY

I just saw *I, Robot*, which was essentially what I expected from a near-future suspense-thriller starring Will Smith. Not that it's a bad movie; it's just that I spent most of it roaming over the CGI scenery and taking only peripheral interest in the actual goings-on.

The successes in *I, Robot* are minor triumphs in post-*Blade Runner* visual futurism: the artful decrepitude of antique 'bots going about servile tasks; the subtly arresting motion of clockwork behind the robots' translucent skulls; the consummately ergonomic contours of futuristic cars (Smith drives a fetchingly believable self-driving Audi).

At least one reviewer has stupidly commented that the future society depicted in the film is "dystopian." Far from it. Slender color-coordinated robots do humankind's dirty work with perpetual hardwired smiles; the Chicago skyline, unlike the smoke-clotted industrial hell of *Blade Runner*'s cyberpunk Los Angeles, is bright, sunny, and fundamentally optimistic. We can only hope 2035 is really like this.

The humans, perhaps unavoidably, fail to elicit any real interest. They function solely, and possibly even appropriately, as foils for the robots, and allusions to their personal histories invariably come across as clichés. Will Smith's detective, Del Spooner, is likeable but disorienting: Is he a brooding policeman (a la Harrison Ford's Rick Deckard in *Blade Runner*) or an affable wise-ass who just happens to wield a cool looking electronic badge? At one point in the film, a minor character informs us that Spooner has a history of psychiatric problems – could have fooled me. That future Prozac must be damned good stuff.

I, Robot itself suffers from a dose of cinematic schizophrenia. Is the robot theme intended as commentary on ethnic barriers, the commodification of nominally useful handheld gadgets, or a carnivalesque monument to technological hubris?

Robots are a challenging subject; just because they can be convincingly rendered in a digital studio doesn't mean they can be expended as props. *I, Robot* doesn't exactly waste the potential inherent in simulacra, but it's mainly content to casually strip-mine it instead of really digging.

Go see it. Enjoy the sights (those new 'bots really do look like iMacs). But expect a narrative with the same brittle, unsubtle tone of the Asimov short-story collection from which it took its ideological cues.

28 JULY

I had an interesting hallucination last night. I had just woken up and was lying in bed. I felt fully awake, but of course when you're sufficiently tired your mind can make you feel or think just about anything. For what seemed to be about three seconds, two massive, soundless, forking bolts of blue lightning appeared outside my window – absolutely archetypal lightning bolts that lasted much longer than the real thing, defying the relatively clear night sky.

At first there was no doubt in my mind that I was observing some weird meteorological phenomenon. I wasn't scared, precisely, but I was shaken – those brilliant blue stalks looked close, and they were unlike any normal lightning I've seen. They looked more like special effects than real lightning, and the lack of thunder made them doubly surreal.

Within moments I was questioning if I'd actually seen them; a few seconds later I'd comfortably filed the "sighting" away as a brief waking dream. But for all of three seconds they had seemed menacing, and all-too-real.

I remember once, years ago, waking up to a particularly red dawn sky and, for a paralyzed moment, absolutely believing there had been a nuclear explosion.

30 JULY

Remember zines, those innumerable, cheap, joyously eclectic Xerox indie magazines that predated the Web? I do. I miss them. My first full-length story ("Pulling Strings," about a neurosurgeon who suffers a psychotic breakdown while in the OR) appeared in *Meshuggah*, where I shared page space with the likes of Simeon Stylites (editor of FEH! Press) and "Blaster" Al Ackerman, whose legendary "mail art" has since appeared in galleries.

I discovered zines in high school. No email, no websites, just a far-flung network of similarly minded anti-establishment types who reveled in oddball humor, literary esoterica and comix. This was before Googling, so you never knew where your memes were taking root. I remember receiving a cassette tape from England; it turned out to be a spoken-word small-press review (Andrew Savage's *Super Trouper*) containing, among many other things, a musical rendition of my poem "Elvis In My Pants," which had originally appeared in

FEH!: A Journal of Odious Poetry.

The last I knew, *Meshuggah* had changed editorship and had moved from New York City to Athens, GA. This was in the early 90s, and I had hopes that some member of R.E.M. would chance across it at a local bookshop.

I haven't exactly checked lately, but I imagine zines are still a thriving industry. But the Web has stripped them of their once subversive status; I suspect they're less "samizdat" than badly penned self-indulgence.

Maybe I'm wrong. Maybe all the hip blogs I monitor are missing out on some fundamental vibe; maybe electronic publishing can never precisely outgun the sheer memetic impact of a cheaply stapled zine, with its shoddy typography and anarchic leanings.

Strangely, the names I remember from the zine era (of which I caught only the tail end) don't seem to produce too many Google results. Did *Super Trouper* take its act online? Is Blaster Al still furiously grinding out pen-and-ink mail art, or has he traded in his arsenal of envelopes for a wi-fi enabled laptop?

31 JULY

I have this vague theory that human consciousness is being somehow altered by the proliferation of wireless technology. UFOs might be part of it; perceived aliens might be another aspect. Remember that the modern UFO era began shortly after the widespread use of radar. If we inhabit a "superspectrum" of co-existing terrestrial intelligences, as suggested by John Keel, then our EM leakage may have disturbed the pecking order. When "aliens" warn us of the dangers of nuclear weapons they may be quite sincerely concerned, although for purely selfish reasons.

Meanwhile, we're busily and heedlessly wrapping our planet in a veritable fog of EM pollution. Cell phone towers, for example. How much do we really know about the long-term effects of cell phone transmissions? In any case, it's probably too late; we're marinated in a flickering stew of pointless dialogue. Victorian factory workers obliviously breathing lungs full of soot.

We could be hastening a new ecology – call it the "electrosphere," although surely someone's beaten me to the term – that interacts with the conventional biosphere in potentially strange, even psychedelic ways.

And all of this is excluding outright malicious intent. We hear more and more about microelectronics and "nonlethal weapons"; I think we're at the threshold of an age in which effective lobotomization of "the enemy" is deemed preferable to actual killing.

Chapter 20
August 2004

1 AUGUST

My apartment needs a new look. I still like the ubiquitous weird postcards, but I want to move on, and reinvent. Actual framed art would be nice. There's a killer decorating store down the street; they have a mind-boggling stock of really cool prints. Of course, they're incredibly over-priced.

I have a few "nice" things to work with: a reasonably stylish black up-lamp, a rather industrial-looking futon; an androgynous life-size glass head; the obligatory lava lamp (with tripod "rocket-ship" fins); rock specimens from an alleged UFO crash site in New Mexico (not Roswell – another one). And then there are the knick-knacks: glow-in-the-dark aliens; plastic dinosaurs; King Tut; Mr. Peanut; the Mars *Pathfinder* mission ensemble. On a bookshelf, diminutive injection-molded astronauts diligently inspect an omnipresent layer of dust.

Meanwhile, my wall and ceiling have succumbed to an engagingly organic-looking decay as leaking rain moistens the plaster, causing it to swell into strange shapes. The paint traps most of it in blisters, which are subject to uncontrolled growth. One of them has grown quite large in recent weeks; it looks cyst-like, something from a David Cronenberg movie. I half-suspect it will rupture noisily at any moment.

The inside of my main closet is actively disintegrating – a whole chunk of wall is easing out of place like the lid of a horror-movie coffin, announcing its emergence with the intermittent patter of plaster on videocassettes and obsolescent computer hardware (which I've since moved).

I've told the management, so I assume they're going to come in and basically re-do the entire north-facing wall. They could have spared themselves the trouble if they'd actually fixed the roof-leak the first time this happened, but I don't blame them for not wanting to tackle this at the source. I imagine the ensuing confrontation will be the remodeling equivalent of Sigourney Weaver single-handedly storming the hive at the end of *Aliens*.

3 AUGUST

The entire Midwest is a vast stew of self-righteous bores.

Even the relatively urbane Country Club Plaza in Kansas City is regularly besieged by religious nuts. For example, a month or so ago I saw a woman lugging a life-size cross down the sidewalk. Nothing new there; Jesus impersonators have long become part of the weekend landscape here.

But this particular cross had actual wheels jutting from the bottom. You know, like airport luggage. As unwitting metaphor, the Cross On Wheels very accurately sums up "What's Happening in Kansas": the unimpeded infantilization of the American mind.

There's a Segway store opening where the boarded-up carcass of F.A.O. Schwartz now stands; will I soon see gyroscopically assisted cross-wielding idiots trucking across town?

4 AUGUST

I heard a news report today titled, "Disappearance of Eels Worldwide Puzzles Scientists."[41] A few thoughts come to mind. Some eels are electric, right? In light on the Missing Homing Pigeon Mystery, perhaps the eels are not so much missing as simply lost, unable to orient themselves because of the planet's unstable magnetic poles.

Of course, when species get "lost" in the wild, they die because they're cut off from their normal diet. This could be a brief prelude to an ecological domino effect; species that rely on the

---

[41] "Disappearance of Eels Worldwide Puzzles Scientists," *NPR*, 1 August 2004. www.npr.org/templates/story/story.php?storyId=3808641.

magnetosphere for navigation wander off, never to be seen again. Pretty soon, those oceanic "dead zones" the American press has been so good at ignoring grow exponentially larger. Then everything starts dying, seemingly out of nowhere – an ecological 9/11.

So by all means keep on pouring that mercury into the water supply. I love a good game of chicken.

6 AUGUST

It's no longer possible to escape the clutches of The Election. Pictures of Kerry, pictures of Bush, each looking as Patriotic as humanly possible. The tension mounts. Remarkably, it seems a growing number of people think Kerry might actually win, or at least has a sporting chance.

Quite honestly, I'm apathetic. I think The Election is a monstrous "phildickian" distraction. I actually suspect we intuit, deep within the collective American unconscious, that Bush will remain in the White House. Note that I didn't say he would "win" – simply that he's not going anywhere. The zeitgeist doesn't have room for Kerry; he will be industriously discarded and forgotten like a contestant in a particularly grueling "reality" TV program.

That's why I'm not spending any of my time reading political weblogs or attempting to analyze campaign strategies or quoting lengthily from the mass of inflammatory partisan literature that dominates bookshelves.

The Election is pseudo real, illusory, a bit of post-democratic theater.

But you already knew this.

8 AUGUST

In the news today, this headline: "Prozac 'found in drinking water.'" An excerpt: "A spokesman for the Drinking Water Inspectorate (DWI) said the Prozac found was most likely highly diluted."[42]

---

[42] "Prozac 'found in drinking water,'" *BBC News*, 8 August 2004.

Well, then there's absolutely nothing to worry about. After all, it's "highly diluted." Meanwhile, back on Planet Earth: *What the fuck is a potent commercial psychoactive drug doing in the water supply?* I can imagine several scenarios, and none of them are exactly cheerful.

Could this be a government experiment of the MK ULTRA variety?[43] I'm serious. Perhaps it's not as overtly heinous as doping unsuspecting citizens with LSD or performing unsolicited lobotomies, but there would have to be a concerted "national security" interest in something like this. Or maybe it's simply corporate greed. What better way to get an entire country conditioned to "need" expensive antidepressants than force-feeding them in small, "highly diluted" dosages?

Say "no" to drugs, kids – except the ones your government puts in your drinking water.

9 AUGUST

I just wrote a really, really short as-yet-untitled short-story. It's about the Roswell crash. Here it is:

Some short bald guys build a time machine so they can go back to 1947 and view the Roswell crash in person. The time machine crashes.

ba-da-BOOM!

10 AUGUST

I suspect that one of the many reasons we haven't received an irrefutable ET signal is because some – perhaps even all – advanced alien civilizations upload themselves into custom-tailored virtual

www.goo.gl/WZV6S.

[43] MK-Ultra was a covert, illegal human research program into behavioral modification run by the Central Intelligence Agency from the early 1950s until it was finally halted in 1973. See: www.abuse-of-power.org/foia-mkultra-document-archive/.

universes, effectively leaving this one behind.

Of course, this isn't to say that we're not inhabiting a virtual universe. In fact, I think there's an extremely good chance we are.

That might also explain why the universe doesn't behave as SETI theorists would prefer.

11 AUGUST

Two odd, foreign-looking men visited me today.*

"Well, by now you've got it figured out," said the first one, helping himself to a seat.

"Got what figured out?"

The two men exchanged a knowing glance. "Surely you realize," said the second man, still standing, "that there's, well, something different about you."

"You feel out-of-place, like you don't really belong here," offered the seated man helpfully.

"Well, I think everyone experiences something of the sort…"

"Lay off the existential rhetoric, Tonnies," the seated man said. "You don't relate. You read weird books. You don't like Bush or Kerry. It's time to face the facts."

"I really have no idea what you're talking about," I said, flustered.

"Oh, but you do." The standing man smiled as I fidgeted. "Tell me, Mr. Tonnies: Does the term 'UFO' mean anything to you?"

"Well, uh, sure. I mean…"

The seated man shot a quick confirming glance at his counterpart. "Thought so," he said.

"Thought what, exactly?" I said, increasingly perturbed. "Just say whatever you're here to say and get the hell out of here."

"Mr. Tonnies, you are an alien from outer space." The seated man let the last two words hover in the air as he studied my face, waiting for a reaction.

"It all fits," said the other man. "The preoccupation with cosmology. The weird books. Your anomalously high capacity for caffeine. That rambling book about Mars you wrote."

"That weird blog of yours," suggested the seated man. "Every minute detail of your life leads inexorably to the same conclusion. You can deny it if you wish. But in the end you will find your efforts are futile."

TO BE CONTINUED...?

*This is, of course, entirely made up.

13 AUGUST

I spent most of today in waiting rooms and having various medical tests performed, all of which was quite dull. One good thing came of it: thanks to a fluorescent dye, my urine is a garish orange-red, like Gatorade. I found this rather funny. And – lucky me – I'll continue to excrete neon urine for a couple of days as my kidneys filter this stuff out of my system.

Meanwhile, something I'm extremely goddamned sick of: self-righteous movie-goers who extol the brilliance of "documentary" films like *Supersize Me* and *Fahrenheit 9/11*, lazy efforts at pseudo-journalism that play it safe by telling us things we already know in such a way as to seem somehow subversive or revelatory.

Supersize Me reveals – gasp! – that a steady diet of McDonald's hamburgers leads to health problems and weight gain; *Fahrenheit* exposes George W. Bush as a crooked, lying bastard.

Big surprises. Wow. I never knew.

Of course McDonald's food is unhealthy, and it's equally obvious that, given the chance, McDonald's would attempt to obscure the fact. Similarly, every thinking person knows – on some level, at least – that Bush is a fraud; *Fahrenheit 9/11* should be perceived in the context of light infotainment instead as some sort of authentic "Statement."

All of this would be harmless enough if debilitating hidden agendas weren't studiously unnoted in favor of Celluloid treatises on french fries. I'd like to see a film-maker attempt to make sense of the Congressional "black budget," or reveal the monstrous manner in which the US "news" media avoids stories dealing with pollution, ecology and global warming. But of course we won't be viewing any of that. Or, for that matter, reading about it. Best to stick to easier targets.

I find it deeply troubling that fluff like Michael Moore's "exposé" becomes the stuff of actual public controversy. Far too many Americans profess concern about the fate of their environment, or at least the fate of their tax-dollars. But they'd rather not expend any actual thought, and this is where limp, pretentious films like *Fahrenheit 9/11* come in so handy. They provide an ersatz sense of worldliness by systematically confirming pre-existing fears. It's the best of both worlds: a smug sense of "I told you so" righteousness with none of the headache, questioning or moral conundrum that defines real problems.

But it's the fears we're not so conscious of that are doing us in. And we are ignoring them.

14 AUGUST

Various People I Loathe (Part One):

1. UFO nuts who "want to believe";
2. Religious people of any kind;
3. Anyone over the age of 10 who wears Starter merchandise;
4. Anyone under the age of 10 who wears Starter merchandise;
5. Anyone who thinks politics make a difference;
6. Journalists who lie;
7. Glad-handing corporate types;
8. Anyone who "counts carbs";
9. Wal-Mart "greeters";
10. People who never read science fiction unless it's by Margaret Atwood;
11. Anyone with "anti-establishment" bumper stickers on their car ;
12. People who don't know the difference between "its" and "it's";
13. Television news anchormen;
14. "Meteorologists";

15. Anyone who indulges in public displays of affection;

16. Meat-eaters;

17. Paris Hilton;

18. Anyone who's ever read a *Left Behind* novel;

19. Anyone who's ever considered buying a *Left Behind* novel;

20. Old people;

21. Anyone who's ever "joined a frat";

22. Anyone who identifies with the term "metrosexual";

23. People who say "sci-fi" instead of "science fiction";

24. Couples who marry and expect you to drop everything to attend their wedding;

25. Couples who reproduce;

26. Parents who bring their children into coffee shops;

27. Anyone with a Humvee;

28. People who don't know who Portishead is;

29. 600-pound women who have to be surgically removed from couches; and

30. Anyone who gives a damn about the Olympics.

15 AUGUST

Have you ever noticed it's the same cars with "Goddess Worshipper," "Pagan and Proud," etc. bumper-stickers that also feature stickers proclaiming "Don't Label Me"?

Hmmm.

Meanwhile, the weather was excellent today. I had a hemp bracelet assembled before my very eyes by a shoeless hippie girl who'd set up a work-station on the sidewalk near Barnes & Noble. $5.00. Not bad. Passersby handed her friends styrofoam containers of left-over food as I sat on the pavement. Very bohemian. I was surprised when the girl mentioned that she kept in touch with friends via email. Evidently they'd amassed enough gas money shortly after my purchase, because when I came out of the bookstore some time later they were gone.

I fished through her selection of beads while she worked on the bracelet. All sorts of interesting stuff: geodes harvested from the Ozarks; a conspicuous pewter skull; a fertility goddess figurine; beads that looked like they'd been hewn from cork. I asked her if she'd ever thought of using cannibalized electronics – capacitors, IC chips, etc. – along with her usual materials, and she gave me a strange look.

17 AUGUST

I've become almost stodgily skeptical about crop glyphs. I think the cerealogical signal-to-noise ratio is even more withering than that of raw UFO sightings, which is all the more depressing because crop circles are undeniably physical and amenable to empirical investigation.

You can actually take your time and walk around a crop formation taking measurements, which is more than you can say for the study of UFOs. Or at least the ones we know about.

I'm certainly open to the possibility that some circles are actual anomalies. But I suspect "real" circles are almost vanishingly scarce. Colin Andrews, self-professed circle "expert" (and believer), amazed field-watchers when he estimated that 80% of all formations were hoaxes. But 80% is most likely a wild understatement; I'd put the figure much closer to 99%.

Despite the endless proclamations of devout crop circle enthusiasts, these things can be faked surprisingly easily, and I fear the more elaborate specimens are hoaxes capitalizing on the misguided belief that manufacturing a circle is superhumanly difficult.

18 AUGUST

It's my theory that humankind, by and large, is dumber than it's ever been. Literally, organically dumber, as evidenced by flickering attention spans and widespread preoccupation with distraction. It's a combination of cultural and chemical factors, and it couldn't have come at a worse damned time.

The chapter in *Planet of the Apes* in which human subjects recite past-life narratives comes to mind. In the original novel, humanity's downfall wasn't due to The Bomb, but to apathetically losing the "brain race" to chimps and orangutans.

Meanwhile, here's my list of 30 things that I really like:

1. The smell of ozone after a storm;
2. Cardboard "java jackets";
3. Chalk graffiti;
4. Deserted places;
5. Fountains;
6. Mexican beer;
7. A full moon;
8. The blast of air-conditioning from open storefronts while strolling in 90-degree weather;
9. Shoot-'em-up arcade games;
10. The smell of old paperbacks;
11. Cats;
12. Airports;
13. The floral-looking designs that drift to the top of well-made espresso;
14. Flickering neon signs;
15. Those walls made of stacked glass cubes;
16. Existentialism;
17. Writing;
18. Sound-proof walls;
19. Ergonomic design;
20. Drawing;
21. Thunderstorms;
22. Cyberpunk novels written before "cyberpunk" was a word;
23. Dr. Martens;
24. Lava lamps;
25. Violins;
26. Lightning bugs;
27. Photos of UFOs;
28. *Seinfeld*;
29. Department-store mannequins; and

30. Fusion cuisine.

20 AUGUST

I'm 29 years old today. I've got the same birthday as H.P. Lovecraft (!).

And Connie Chung.[44]

22 AUGUST

Uh-oh. Yesterday a sloppy-looking woman in a T-shirt passed me on the sidewalk. The shirt read: "B.I.G.: Believe In God." And yes, the woman was indeed "big."

Could this be the next "WWJD"?[45] Should I hide in my fallout shelter and wait this one out?

23 AUGUST

Actually seen: a plume of kitchen smoke in the shape of a quintessential mushroom cloud rising from a Japanese steakhouse.

24 AUGUST

This evening found me chatting with Scientologists (I got my hands on a no-kidding e-meter) and watching *Alien vs. Predator*, which isn't half-bad. It's most definitely a big-screen movie; if you miss the theater release, I don't see much point in rushing to watch it on the small-screen.

Like all *Alien* movies, it suffers from the "biomass problem," which I was relieved to find Roger Ebert noted in his justifiably scathing review of *Alien: Resurrection*. The Giger-aliens (or xenomorphs – call them whatever you like) use humans as incubators, not food. In none of the *Alien* movies have I seen an alien actually chow down on anything. Yet, defying basic physics, they grow many orders of magnitude within minutes of erupting

---

[44] An American journalist, and wife of tabloid talk show host Maury Povich.

[45] "What Would Jesus Do?"

from a host's chest.

What gives?

25 AUGUST

I don't know enough about jet aircraft or structural engineering to make an educated determination about what precisely happened on September 11, 2001. Yes, there seem to be anomalies. I don't think for a moment that we've been told the entire story.

But was it really an "inside job" in the conspiracy-mongering sense? And if it were, then why risk blowing it by using improper planes that could be identified as such by anyone watching? The mind reels. And maybe that's the point: Create a locus of such overwhelming confusion and duplicity that only the most fervent "nuts" will begin to make sense of it all.

I think the '00s will be looked back on as the "Philip K. Dick decade."

27 AUGUST

Brand-new word: conspirinate (verb) – to make the object of a perceived conspiracy (see "assassinate").

Example: "Stanton Friedman helped conspirinate the Roswell Incident by claiming the MJ-12 briefing document was authentic."

And yes, I Googled it to make sure no one had beaten me to it. My only reservation is that it sounds quite a bit like "urinate."

Meanwhile, apropos of nothing, I remember a trip I took to Galveston a few years ago. The local vacationing industry had placed a giant inflatable simulacrum of the Titanic caught in the act of sinking out in the ocean, and throngs of kids were merrily climbing up a ladder to slide down the fatally canted deck.

This was just after 9-11-01, and I remarked to my girlfriend (yes, I had a girlfriend) that it was only a matter of time until Disney wielded its magic to transform two jets slamming into the World Trade Center into an amusement park ride.

Actually, I still haven't quite given up on Disney-Auschwitz.

28 AUGUST

It's increasingly ironic that mainstream critics refuse to acknowledge there's more to literary science fiction that Orwell and Huxley, especially as Gibson has become a lauded cultural fixture on a par with Burroughs. *Pattern Recognition* wasn't even SF, and elicited comparison to Thomas Pynchon, of all authors.

But the stuffy critical establishment won't bite; contemporary mainstream reviewers will go to their graves clutching moth-eaten copies of "acceptable" genre fiction, never knowing what "cyberpunk" is.

Nothing against *Nineteen Eighty-Four*, by the way – it's one of my all-time favorites.

Chapter 21
September 2004

6 SEPTEMBER

I've been fretting over the Synaptics TouchPad built into my laptop. It's temperamental. The cursor floats merrily across the screen, seemingly of its own volition; I lift my finger and the arrow shoots away like a frightened hummingbird. This afternoon I was acutely tempted to put my fist through the LCD screen.

Anyway, I think I've discovered a way to keep the cursor under control: I cool my fingertip by gently blowing on it. Apparently the touchpad registers the heat, as well as the heft, of the controlling fingertip, and if you're on edge – as I was this afternoon, trying to point and click with the accuracy provided by a mouse – your skin tends to grow hotter, confusing the touchpad interface.

I've actually seen the cursor drifting and meandering across the screen when I'm not even touching the computer; I still have no clear explanation for this poltergeist-like phenomenon.

7 SEPTEMBER

Probability strongly suggests that SETI's best bet is to eavesdrop on a stray transmission, something the program is presently unwilling to consider. And we probably don't even have the technology to search for stray signals anyway. SETI as it is now envisioned will only succeed if and when an extraterrestrial civilization takes an exclusive interest in our solar system.

Meanwhile, who knows how many actual transmissions we might miss out on because our criteria are so depressingly slim and anthropomorphic. A venture like this can only work if we follow up on everything; we can't afford to wait for a greeting intended for us.

9 SEPTEMBER

I saw a news article today about a robot that eats flies as a way of generating its own power.

Robots that eat vermin – I love it. And think of the potential military applications. Drop a platoon of flesh-eating 'bots into enemy territory and watch the feeding frenzy. Plus, the military brass doesn't have to worry about troublesome body counts, as all human corpses will have been processed into fuel that can be used to launch new offenses against The Enemy.

Quick – what's DARPA's phone number?

10 SEPTEMBER

I was just on a New York radio show called *Beyond Strange and Mysterious*. I tried Googling it to no avail. This was the first show I've done in a while with call-ins, so I got to ramble a bit about two subjects that otherwise weren't on the usual list of talking points.

The first caller asked if I thought aliens were walking among us in an attempt to learn the nuances of human existence. I mentioned the work of Dr. David Jacobs, a smart guy who thinks that an extraterrestrial hybridization program begun in the 1940s is now producing viable transgenic offspring who are quietly infiltrating human society (I don't agree with Jacobs, but that's another post). I offered my opinion that if advanced ETs wanted to secretly observe us they could probably do so using a form of nanotech that would elude 21st century science; disguising themselves in order to work and live among us unnoted seems unlikely.

Then again, who am I to outguess bona fide aliens? I like Whitley Strieber's telling of two apparent "visitors" in a bookstore shortly after the release of *Communion*, covered in scarves, hats and sunglasses.

The second caller asked me if there were such things as Men In Black. I replied that there were, although exactly who these frequently bizarre characters are is the subject of debate. Keel's *The Mothman Prophecies* and Jenny Randles' *The Truth Behind Men In Black* are probably the best books I've read on the phenomenon.

11 SEPTEMBER

Various unsorted thoughts:

1. Zines are not dead! Not quite, anyway. I got a print rag called *Bizarre Bazaar* in the mail. It's basically a cheaply produced catalogue for Fortean/New Age/conspiracy merchandise, but there's at least one article in it. The complete works of David Icke, anyone?

2. LatteLand (my coffee shop of choice) now has satellite radio. With any luck, this means not listening to the same damned thing every time I stop by for a caffeine fix. Tonight the playlist was entirely 80s, highlighted by The Smiths' "Ask."

3. I've come to realize I have a weird habit of clarifying perfectly obvious spoken references with "illustrative" hand-gestures. A couple hours ago, for instance, I was discussing CDs and discovered that I was pretending to hold a CD in my hand (gripped at the edges between thumb and forefinger). Lame nervous tick, or genuine eccentricity?

4. Tonight I noticed a horde of blond party-girls clambering down the stairs of what appeared to be an airport shuttle or "senior" bus. On the side of the vehicle was the name for some limousine service. I couldn't help but wonder if these girls knew they had been gypped. A "senior trolley," no matter how ostentatious, is not a limousine. It might be an eminently practical means of transporting a gaggle of vacuous 20 year-olds, but please don't call it a "limousine" when any schmuck can plainly see that it isn't.

5. After viewing the original release of *Donnie Darko* for the first time since 2001, I have to agree that the opening song by Echo and the Bunnymen was an inspired choice. INXS's "Never Tear Us Apart" (substituted for the director's cut) works nicely, but "The Killing Moon" works better. Plus it's performed by a band with "bunny" in their name, and the film involves a forbidding six-foot rabbit. Come on – you're not going to do any better than that.

6. I finally rode a Segway. It's pretty fun; they're surprisingly

speedy. Learning to navigate is basically intuitive, but not quite as automatic as I'd expected – it's actually closer to learning to drive a car than learning to ride a bike. If I had a spare $5,000 lying around, I might just get one; as it was, I winced when I forked over $5 for the test-drive.

12 SEPTEMBER

It's football season! Or pre-season, or whatever the hell they call it. And you know what they means? That's right – even more pathetic jock-sniffing nobodies strolling around in officially licensed NFL gear than usual! Some of these idiots have already started decorating their vehicles. And to top it all off, everyone's doting on a completely fictitious presidential election.

Orwell couldn't have come up with this shit in his wildest dreams.

13 SEPTEMBER

I don't care for protests. In a digital age, I think they're an insufficiently savvy means of self-expression. They're along the lines of big street parties, the quintessential Vonnegutian "granfalloon." The mass protests at the Republican National Convention, for example, were a complete waste of time. But I have to wonder if there would have been any effect if anti-Bush protesters had taken their act to Diebold. Probably not; I think we all know the score here.

The irony is that even if this were a real election, Bush would probably win.

Grotesque, indeed.

Meanwhile, I was driving through the suburbs on my way home from my parents' house and glimpsed what looked like a luminous four-foot humanoid figure standing by the roadside. The illusion persisted for about a second: I was actually seeing a reflective stripe on the side of a newspaper vending machine. It must have had a design on it that suggested a tiny person standing in profile, and when my headlights played over it it seemed to materialize out of the dark. Acutely disappointing.

17 SEPTEMBER

A teacher was arrested last month while trying to board a plane carrying an 8.5 inch leather strip bookmark with small lead weights at each end.

Something tells me the boneheads who arrested her don't spend a lot of time at Barnes & Noble. Although if someone were to just describe the bookmark to me without telling me what it actually was, I'd probably guess bondage paraphernalia.

18 SEPTEMBER

This evening I walked down to LatteLand and was greeted by a swarm of milling pedestrians and a black stretch limo. I didn't think much of it at first. I bought a latte and sat down to read. Then I tuned into the ambient conversation and discovered the limo belonged to none other than *Wheel of Fortune* sidekick Vanna White, who was shooting a promo for the show outside "Steve's Shoes" next door.

I was disappointed; I irrationally hoped it might be Natalie Portman. Even so, I found myself joining the crowd outside, where technicians with high-definition cameras and eye-scalding lights were preparing for the shoot. Vanna was sauntering around blankly, like a Disney World animatron with a head-wound. She looked like, well, Vanna White – older and shorter than I had expected, but still very pretty. I shuddered with concealed laughter as security personnel attempted to corral the small mob of rubberneckers. The black guy who asked me to step back a few feet had a name-badge reading "White."

"Any relation . . . ?" I asked.

Vanna's script, if one could call it that, involved strolling past LatteLand clutching perfectly empty shopping bags from various stores on the Country Club Plaza. I experienced a fierce urge to run down 47th Street to Barnes & Noble and slip her a copy of *After the*

Martian Apocalypse.

The first shoot done, a crew member from *Wheel* informed my section of the crowd we would be videotaped. It was then that I realized I was about to appear in a *Wheel of Fortune* commercial. Everything became quite surreal; Vanna passed right in front of me next to the locally famous "boar sculpture," a forbiddingly life-like bronze über-pig whose lustrous nose is due to untold thousands of hands rubbing it for good luck.

She uttered something about "from Kansas City" and timidly rubbed the boar's nose, bidding *Wheel* contestants good luck.

Clever.

Then, on the director's cue, everyone yelled "WHEEL . . . OF . . . FORTUNE!" Including me. I was right there, immediately behind Vanna yelling and applauding like a mind-control casualty.

The moral? Set your VCRs, because I honestly don't see how I can fail to be in this commercial. I'm wearing a long-sleeve pale-green checkered shirt.

19 SEPTEMBER

For a blog that frequently dwells in "the unknown," Posthuman Blues has been conspicuously silent on the Afterlife Question. I'll try to remedy that.

Simply, I don't know. I don't pretend to know. I haven't a fucking clue. My hunch is that "afterlife" is a bloated oxymoron and that once the meat-machines we call our brains cease working, so do we. It's tough to conceive what it might be like to not exist, but should it be? After all, how many of us remember anything prior to our own birth?

Part of me likes the idea that I somehow persist after biological death; it might even be possible, albeit in ways currently antithetical to materialistic science. Empirical science (as currently practiced) may be missing something crucial; if consciousness exists after the demise of its neurological substrate, then it's likely our current definition of consciousness is simply wrong-headed. Maybe brains are more akin to receivers than computers and we're all tuned to the same channel, or at least the same spectrum.

Another part of me finds the prospect of an "afterlife" thoroughly unnecessary. Simply ceasing to exist, in whatever form, seems so much more economical than lingering in some non-biological state. Or maybe, upon death, you're presented with the option to "terminate program."

Eternal life or blissful oblivion – what would you do?

I should point out that none of this logically entails the existence of "God"; if there's a "next world," then I assume it's every bit as much a part of our Cosmos as black holes and quasars. In this context, the "soul" should be viewed as a phenomenon intrinsic to sentient organisms, perhaps amenable to technological intervention.

22 SEPTEMBER

One of my biggest flaws is my desire to be approachable and accommodating to strangers. The trouble, simply, is that I'm not discerning enough, and the Crashing Bores of the world universally see this as a select opportunity to take advantage. I'm burdened by this naively Mr. Roger-ish view that because I perceive myself as fundamentally decent, everyone else must be, too. I want to be liked. And I pay dearly for it.

This was pounded home a couple months back when I was signing books at Borders. It was a weeknight and the turnout was far from outrageous, but I found myself signing more copies than I'd expected and basically enjoying myself. Enter two Crashing Bores: a young married couple with this inexplicable – and in hindsight, totally spurious – interest in Martian archaeology. They nodded over my book, commending my intelligence. That should have been the tip-off; strangers don't go around attempting to boost someone's ego unless there's something in it for them. In this case, all I could offer was a signed copy of a book they'd never heard of which, to my surprise, they actually purchased.

But not before dropping veiled references to a lucrative "work from home" scheme they thought would be up my alley.

"What's involved?" I asked, politely skeptical.

"It's basically e-commerce," the male Bore replied.

"What's your email address?"

The Bore conceded that he didn't have one. Strange for someone supposedly making big money in e-commerce, I thought, but since he and his wife were talking Mars and making to buy my book, I let it pass and let the husband hand me a very unimpressive business card with the original address in Lawrence, Kansas scribbled out and the new one scrawled in its place. Finally they departed and I resumed my evening.

A few days later I get a message on my answering machine. It's the male Bore wanting to discuss his business and requesting a call back. I groaned and promptly deleted it.

Then one morning the phone splinters my sleep. I answered groggily, defenses in limbic shambles. It's the Crashing Bore again, wanting to meet me at the Borders where he bought my book.

"Can you explain what, exactly, this is?"

The Bore informed me that it was "mostly visual" in nature and that it "wouldn't make sense" over the phone. Half-asleep, I didn't summon the will-power to question this absurdity. Instead, I agreed to meet him and his wife to hear out whatever they had in mind – furious at myself but placated by the thought of strolling the aisles at Borders after they'd finished their spiel.

I met them as planned. The spiel was indeed "mostly visual," consisting of the male Bore drawing crudely annotated diagrams in a spiral notebook. I smiled over my coffee and said "no." He persisted. So did his disturbingly Stepford-like wife, whom I abruptly felt like kicking forcibly in the shins.

Again, I politely declined, to no avail.

The husband, with a tepid show of good cheer, handed me a CD and color leaflet. I looked at it briefly: lots of condescending stock imagery of guys 'n' gals conducting "business" in the privacy of nicely furnished living rooms. Lying, I said that I would be happy to peruse it and contact him if interested. No good; the leaflet and CD, it seemed, were quite valuable materials that needed to be returned as soon as possible – preferably that very Saturday when a local work-from-home/e-commerce convention was to take place.

Bing!

Then the guy tried to leave in a hurry, letting me know that he wants his materials returned and that he'll see me Saturday. I finally had to virtually shove the fucking brochure into his hands.

"Take it now, please; this isn't for me and I'm not going to able to return it."

The two of them stalked off, visibly discomfited, and I watched them conversing from the cafe as they walked rapidly to their car.

Then I looked at books.

23 SEPTEMBER

John Shirley writes:

When I was having thyroid problems, I began having visions of suicide and a feeling of "do it, do it." When I got thyroid medication, those suicidal images and urges went away. Certain people (often teens) taking certain antidepressants, paradoxically get suicidal urges. Men who are very territorial and possessive of their families often – when their chosen mate decides to leave them – fall victim to a "I must kill my family and myself" syndrome. It seems triggered by a specific set of circumstances. This pattern of self destruction, prompted with such cerebral automaticity, suggests that suicide is designed into us by nature. There may be a "suicide program" wired into the brain, which is triggered at times, sometimes accidentally. This to me also argues that nature is up to something – that it has intention. It is willing to make us kill ourselves if we don't get with the reproductive program. It is more winnowing.

I bang my head against this issue all the time; am I a merely a convenient receptacle for selfish DNA molecules, or am I a sentient individual fortuitously perpetuated by the machinations of DNA? Both, quite possibly. If so, which is the more important aspect of my being? What's the raison d'etre of intelligent carbon-based life?

Maybe it's a yin-yang sort of thing. Life and death; the solace of the inanimate waging perpetual war against the sense of individuality and purpose (however ill-defined) taking place inside our skulls — and, just possibly, elsewhere.

Like Shirley, I've wanted to cash it in. At times there's an almost palpable drop in what can only be called "life energy," a sort of subjective energy-level maintained by the subconscious. Think of it as one of those little glowing meters that accompany characters in video games. You take so many bullets, or lasers, or punches to the face, and the meter drops to zero and you "die."

To Freud, the psyche was ruled by the immutable laws of Sex. I suspect the mind cares less about actual sex than it does the perpetuation of DNA. Superficially, of course, they're one and the same, but the ensured output of viable genetic material is far more abstract and depersonalized. It's as if we share our bodies with mechanistic genies with their own purely selfish agendas, and when our own agendas begin to conflict with the deoxyribonucleic overmind, our "life meters" start to plunge, maybe just a little bit, enough to produce a bit of existential unease, or maybe a considerable fraction all at once, like blowing a tire.

It's then that the genetic overmind plants its roots in the fertile soil that once housed your volition and identity. You become a husk, loping android-like from once task to another until effectively lobotomized. As G.I. Gurdjieff stressed, we are literal machines. And although he didn't specifically invoke biochemistry, he may as well have harped on Richard Dawkins' inspired notion of the "selfish gene," had the idea existed in his time.

The irony is that a being constructed (and in certain critical respects defined) by genes bent on self-preservation can be lured to (or actually programmed for) self-destruction. I wonder if other planetary ecologies have produced intelligent creatures to whom suicide is a physiological impossibility; such creatures may exist among us in coming decades, and we will know them as robots.

Maybe that's the answer. Perhaps we are larvae, subject to incurable neuroses that will cease to exist only when we ourselves cease to exist, supplanted by something new, and – in strictly Darwinian terms – fundamentally better. Maybe Shirley's "winnowing," seemingly psychotic from our narrow vantage on the evolutionary bridge, is an essential instrument in the betterment of our species, or at least a lens through which to glimpse where we're headed.

24 SEPTEMBER

"Creationism" is BS. What bothers me is that the various skeptics groups that help deflate Fundamentalist Creation mythology tend to attack UFOs with equal vigor, and they lie, whether by intentional omission of data, willful ignorance or simple disingenuousness.

There's no need to duck the "points" made by so-called Creation Scientists; they're intentionally fabricated by feeble-minded people for feeble-minded people. The UFO problem is much more complex. Debunkers typically attack the existence of unexplained objects in our skies by attempting to confuse the core phenomenon with the mythology it has spawned. This goes generally unquestioned by academe; you never read articles in science magazines decrying the limp, anthropomorphic biases that show up again and again in anti-UFO literature.

Ideally, politically inclined groups such as CSICOP would like to stereotype "UFO believers" as mindless dolts who also believe an omnipotent being created the world in seven days and molded humans in his own image.[46] My own findings reveal a genuine, but unfocused, dissatisfaction with Darwinism among some "UFO

---

[46] The Committee for the Scientific Investigation of Claims of the Paranormal, now known as the Committee for Skeptical Inquiry. See: www.csicop.com.

types." But the issues under question are generally scientific, not metaphysical, even if the controversy shares a common origin. It appears most of us share a common need to be part of something larger, whether that something is a bearded caricature of ourselves or a galactic super-cluster.

For example, many in the UFO "community" advance the idea that Homo sapiens was genetically facilitated or modified by an extraterrestrial intelligence. To some, this sounds preposterous, little better than Creationist rhetoric. But at worst, it's mere bad science, even if the proposed explanation strives to turn the human legacy into something bigger than it really is – and, of course, to some, the idea that we're basically livestock at the mercy of super-intelligent ETs seems downright degrading. I personally haven't dismissed alien genetic intervention, and propose taking a long, hard look at the human genome just in case.

Carl Sagan lamented Fundamentalists' distaste with the idea that humans were, ultimately, forged in the nuclei of exploding stars. Sagan found the idea awe-inspiring, eclipsing the sense of the numinous claimed by the religiously inclined. An agnostic, I share Sagan's sense of wonder. Which is partially why I wince at the tactics of so many self-proclaimed debunkers, who act not in defense of truth, but to deify contemporary paradigms at the exclusion of all else.

Sure, it's nice that they trash Creationists. But why the Pavlovian need to dispel legitimate unknown phenomena?

26 SEPTEMBER

In the not-so-distant future, the majority of titles on bookstore shelves will be written by pretentious assholes who can't write (which, now that I think about it, sounds just like now). Once reputable reviewers like *Kirkus* start reviewing self-published books for a fee – which is already happening – it's only a matter of time until a bigger "fee" wins the author a better review. Which means bigger sales to the lit-trend pseudo-intelligentsia.

Within a few years, authors who prospered (or at least made ends meet) under the old system are back to reading their work in ill-lit coffeehouses while the independently wealthy throw huge signings and cruise around in limos tossing free copies of their novels/memoirs to the sullen masses on the sidewalk.

Erickson. Pynchon. Womack. Gibson. Vonnegut.

Who?

27 SEPTEMBER

On Thursday the Republican Party owned up to sending mass mailings to residents of Arkansas and West Virginia demonizing homosexuals and predicting liberals would ban the Bible if the Democrats won in November.

See, this kind of crap is why I don't give a fuck. Four more years? Bring it on. I have ceased to care; politics are for the terminally unimaginative. I refuse to play along.

I guess I'm "un-American."

Damn.

28 SEPTEMBER

I've just discovered that Dr. John Mack, Pulitzer Prize-winning Harvard psychiatrist and author of two controversial books on the "alien abduction" phenomenon (*Abduction*, *Passport to the Cosmos*) has died in London, apparently the victim of a drunk driver.

Mack's death didn't exactly capsize me, but it did take some wind from my sails on what otherwise might have been a very good day. I went to see *Sky Captain and the World of Tomorrow*; right as the movie started I developed stomach pains, which robbed some of the enjoyment from an excellent movie. Among other things, *Sky Captain* is the closest thing to a "steampunk" film I'm likely to see. I think mainstream critics are missing out with their predictable "the effects are great but that's about it" treatment.

Hey, here's something kind of weird: You know how when you screw your eyes shut you see vague geometric patterns? For the last couple days I've been seeing quite elaborate stuff – glistening bio-mechanalia and trippy cross-hatching. I close my eyes and, more often than not, I've got this funky kinetic tapestry waiting for me. It was cool at first. Now it's getting annoying.

Jeez – I must sound like Philip K. Dick with his account of "violent phosphene activity." Actually, I attribute my "visions" to circadian fluctuations and disturbances in caffeine intake.

So, are The Authorities lying about Toutatis?[47] Does the world end today? If it does, there's one comfort to be taken: John Mack didn't miss out on a whole hell of a lot.

29 SEPTEMBER

Who says "God" – given that it exists – is necessarily alive? More than likely, "God" isn't a "thing" at all, but a process. Then again, that's what life is: a self-perpetuating pattern in an ocean of disorder.

But if you're going to look for "God" in the biological domain, I think you're best off starting where our ubiquitous belief in it is most readily apparent – our own brains.

To be read in your best William Burroughs voice:

I hereby found the Institute for Neurotheological Taxonomy. We seek to isolate this so-called "God virus" so that its effects can be studied, catalogued for the benefit of posthuman scholars, and ultimately *eradicated*. Dr. Benway enters the laboratory wielding a bonesaw and a dismembered vacuum cleaner. He descends on the comatose patient's shaved skull with a wanton smile. Back in Kansas City the laptop computer's keys have grown warm with captive electricity. "I'm

---

[47] 4179 Toutatis is an asteroid with a chaotic orbit. Toutatis makes frequent close approaches to Earth, with a currently minimum possible distance of just 0.006 AU (2.3 times as far as the Moon). The approach on September 29, 2004, was particularly close, at 0.0104 AU, which made it a subject at the time of some conspiracists and fear-mongerers. See: www.echo.jpl.nasa.gov/asteroids/4179_Toutatis/toutatis.html.

gettin' outta here, man."

30 SEPTEMBER

Astronomer David Darling was on late-night radio a few days ago. He was fascinating, every bit as articulate about anti-gravity UFOs and ET supercomputers as his book *Equations of Eternity* is about cosmology.

One of the ideas he discussed was his personal conviction that consciousness is a field "tuned into" and individualized by organic brains. In other words, we're tapping into a universal commodity with organs evolved to do just that. We normally perceive such a small piece of reality because the hyper-awareness implied by disembodied, "raw" consciousness is simply unnecessary, and even potentially harmful, to organisms such as ourselves. Our bodies require constant physical attention; if we could access the entirety of the universe, many of us would probably keel over from sheer information overload. Of course, this is a species that can't even handle Dish TV.

The transhuman imperative, as I see it, is to upload ourselves into this vast, barely tapped reservoir of awareness. I think advanced aliens have taken a similar evolutionary route, originating as carbon-based life on rocky, terrestrial worlds and eventually learning how to transcend gross matter while retaining something of their individuality, whatever "individuality" might entail for nonhumans.

This juxtaposes the "afterlife" debate with the SETI debate in a most unfashionable manner. But that's part of the fun.

Meanwhile, this just in:

"Researchers are saying that caffeine withdrawal should now be classified as a psychiatric disorder."

I have a weird relationship with caffeine. It seems I can drink unlimited amounts of coffee/espresso at any time of the day or night without appreciable effect. More interestingly in light of the above headline, I've found that I can stop at any time without fear of the slightest "withdrawal" symptoms. No headaches. No more irritability than usual.

My craving for coffee drinks is purely habitual. I like drinking coffee not because I get a "fix," per se, but because I like drinking coffee. I like the feel of hot ceramic. I like the endearing way in which cardboard "java jackets" tend to slide off if not properly secured. I like the short-lived floral patterns on the surface of my latte.

I am not mad!

Chapter 22
October 2004

1 OCTOBER

Perhaps I've inadvertently managed to hack my brain's operating system. For whatever reason, my mind is conducting what amounts to a synaptic ink-blot test. If I lived in a Paleolithic culture, I imagine I'd scrawl my impressions on cave walls for others to wonder at. Because they'd obviously be signals from the gods, or the elements, or Gaia, or whatever – full of portent and significance.

In my opinion, their being the product of my own brain makes them no less intriguing.

2 OCTOBER

Some guy on the street gave me a check. No kidding. He just handed me a check and thanked me for accepting it! I have it here in front of me as I write. It's from an organization called "The Bank of Eternal Life," and it's made out to "Whosoever Believeth," which I guess is me, although the sum ("Eternal Life") has me a bit confused. Especially as the check doesn't appear to be signed, although it does bear the printed name of one Mr. Jesus Christ.

You know, the more I look at this the more skeptical I become. What do you want to bet it bounces?

3 OCTOBER

There are intriguing online whispers of a plan to fake a biblical Armageddon using insidiously clever special effects. What better way to immobilize enemy soldiers than showing them a stirring "vision of God," right before gunning them down?

A similar campaign could be waged domestically, possibly using

313

archetypical projections of apparent "aliens" and "angels" in an effort to subvert belief systems. Maybe that's what the flying triangles are actually up to when they're caught hovering over suburbs and interstate highways.

"Quick: Was that an extraterrestrial biological entity or the work of a thoroughly corrupted black-budget military-industrial complex?"

4 OCTOBER

I'm reconciled to the very real threat of ecological apocalypse in my (natural) lifetime. But a lot of people, especially Americans, whose "news" media virtually ignores environmental issues, are going to be even more frightened than I am when humans start dying by the hundreds of millions.

5 OCTOBER

Pioneering astronaut Gordon Cooper has died. A news report notes, "In his post-NASA career, Cooper became known as an outspoken believer in UFOs and charged that the government was covering up its knowledge of extraterrestrial activity."

And now that he's safely dead, the mainstream media will even acknowledge it!

7 OCTOBER

News headline: "Space Tourism Faces Regulatory Hurdles."

I would have liked to have seen humans make the move off-planet without the ubiquitous red tape we're so fond of here on Earth, but it doesn't look like it's going to happen.

14 OCTOBER

I think the brain's "idling" is spent manufacturing reality, perhaps even literally, by collapsing enormous numbers of quantum waveforms and thus selecting a single intelligible world-line out of the multiversal froth. "Psychic" phenomena such as premonitions of disaster may be caused by a sort of bleed-through between closely related universes, manifested sub-atomically in the central nervous system.

If the brain can be "tricked" into pronounced psychic activity during altered states of consciousness, it's certainly conceivable that direct neural interfacing could produce a potent, and reliable, organic quantum computer able to peer into the "future." And maybe even into the past.

A similar mechanism is described in Robert Charles Wilson's excellent novel *Blind Lake*, in which the eggheads in charge of the fictional "quantum telescope" technology don't know how it works. Ultimately, the unique perspective it provides becomes a two-way street and alien contact (of a sort) is accomplished.

Has something comparable already happened in the real world? My answer is "yes."

15 OCTOBER

It seems to me that gospel "witnessing" is on the rise. Twice in the last week I've contended with guys getting in my face quizzing me about the role of Jesus in my life while I'm trying to window-shop. I can't prove it, but I think the rise in "witnessing" – if there is one – is connected to the upcoming fake election. There's a certain fervor in the air, an apocalyptic vibe, and the primary symptom is desperation. These God-freaks feel they need to rope in as many converts as they can, and I get the disquieting feeling their time-table is more or less that of the Bush vs. Kerry campaign feud, perhaps triggered by the "debates."

16 OCTOBER

I read in *Vanity Fair* that model Gisele Bundchen is 24 years old. 24?

Good Christ – I'm not sure I even remember 24! I'd never given Bundchen's age much thought, but if I'd been forced to guess I suppose I might have volunteered 30 or so. Not because she necessarily looks any older than I do, but because something in me recoils slightly at the thought of her being younger. It's oddly emasculating.

Supermodels inhabit this strange liminal reality where concepts such as age become peripheral or meaningless. They don't exist in the same chronological matrix as you and I; they simply are.

Of course, the media wouldn't have it any other way. But that doesn't mean I have to like it.

17 OCTOBER

News item: "Betty Hill, the Grandmother of UFOlogy, passed away this morning, October 17, 2004, at the age of 85."

First John Mack. Then Gordon Cooper. Now Betty Hill.

18 OCTOBER

I've revised my online classified ad. I'm not paying anything for it, mind you. And I'm not actively looking for people to contact, as that costs money (and an appalling amount of time that could be more productively spent). So it's up to the women of Kansas City to write to me, in which case, depending on my mood, I might pay for full access and write them back (if they're sufficiently interesting).

The problem is that no one is ever "sufficiently interesting." And the feeling is, apparently, mutual. It makes me almost physically nauseous to think of the time I've spent over the years trying to link up with someone who might conceivably turn out to be a love interest.

The purpose of this post? To officially declare that I'm dealing myself out of the match-up game for the foreseeable future, because the dice are loaded and there is no paper-trail.

Even at my most optimistic, I've known the urge to seek out compatibility is hormonally mandated. I am a conglomeration of DNA sequences, all desperate to express themselves. Some personality types can skillfully exploit this seeming paradox, like a surfer riding a particularly gnarly wave; there's certainly nothing inherently wrong with being a creature built from selfish molecules.

But I think the option to opt out of this aspect of human existence, to the extent that such is psychologically possible, is fundamentally one of conscience, and mine is gasping for relief.

I don't expect this to be easy or pleasant. But it's imperative in the same way that removing a malignant tumor is imperative. I suppose I could launch into a screed about transhumanist automorphism, but my heart's not really in it. This isn't about redefining the human condition; it's about acknowledging an existential void that threatens to bisect my sanity if I allow it to continue unchecked.

20 OCTOBER

A guy named J.L. King is coming to Barnes & Noble. King is the author of a talk-show circuit book called *On the Down Low*, which purports to be about the world of "straight" men (presumably black) who sleep with other men. Confused? You're not the only one.

My question: Who's going to come to this signing? If you're on the "down low," that means it's a secret, right? It would seem to me that anyone "on the DL" (King actually uses this inane abbreviation) would make a point not to be present at a book signing for an author and self-professed expert on the subject. You can tell King is an expert, because the book cover is a somber black-and-white portrait of him looking very grim and serious, wearing the kind of expression that says, "We need to talk."

I have half an urge to make the scene just to see who, if anyone, is there, but I'm afraid someone might mistake me for being "on the DL."

The truly galling thing is that King is making a killing off this fictional social malady. Not that there aren't bisexual men of all races who cheat on their spouses. But all King has done is slap an Oprah-friendly name on it. By now, judging from his silly cover portrait, he probably believes he's a patron of humanity on a par with Gandhi.

21 OCTOBER

I need to do laundry but I'm one quarter short.

Damnit.

I suppose I could ask the cute girl down the hall for one, but she might read that as evidence that I just want to talk, and I really do need the quarter. And if I did ask her, assuming she's even home at the moment, I'd probably feel obligated to talk, since I don't exactly see her every day. So she'd definitely think the bit about the quarter for the laundry machine was a ruse, and I certainly don't want her thinking that. I mean, yeah, I'm weird, but not stalker-weird.

On the other hand, I have a mounting pile of laundry that requires mechanical attention. And to be honest, doing some laundry right now would actually make me feel productive. Or is that just the sublimated urge to talk to the girl down the hall messing with my mind?

Yes, she has a boyfriend.

Meanwhile, I had a long, thoroughly arresting semi-lucid dream last night. Essentially, I was "shadowing" people who lived in a near-future American society, watching everything they did, the people they met, the problems they encountered. I seemed to be holding an invisible camera, as if the participants were actors, and my role was limited to observing.

The overall milieu was a bit like that of a Bruce Sterling novel, or Wim Wenders' *Until the End of the World.* Exotic futuristic cars, one with what looked like liquid crystal graphics emblazoned on the exterior; grown-on-demand designer medications that resembled plump, brightly colored insect larvae; high-end apartments conjoined seamlessly with vast shopping malls.

At one point a woman took a panoramic picture with a holographic camera. The subjects had to tilt their heads awkwardly as laser-light played over their faces.

There was a pervasive psychiatric disorder among most of the children, a kind of undefined autism. With a few exceptions, the adults I "met" were detached, brooding, almost schizoid.

I ended the dream as I sat in the backseat of a car watching decrepit glass-paneled houses and schools scroll by outside. I sensed that I had traveled a few years farther into the future. The once-fastidious suburbs I had seen earlier had lost their luster; scabrous concrete littered abandoned lawns.

Glimpses of rusted steel mesh. Hardly any traffic, as if the world had been abruptly depopulated.

22 OCTOBER

"Asexuality" isn't exactly unappealing. There are times when it would be an eminent relief to jettison all the deoxyribonucleic baggage that accompanies mammal-hood. I've read that men think about sex six times a minute (or something like that). It's probably close to the truth, and there's nothing wrong with it. But think of all the things a brain could be doing instead of rehashing copulation scenarios. It's like having a computer with too many programs running in the background. The end result is sluggishness, and the risk of a system crash. In this context, "asexuals" might be a genuine evolutionary upgrade.

Sometimes I fear that an omnipresent sex-drive saps creativity by siphoning "willpower" (for lack of a better word) from the brain. Then again, maybe sex and creativity are innately linked. After all, sex is ultimately about creation. A person who uses some future therapy to eradicate his sex-drive in hopes of becoming more productive might be shocked to find himself creatively bereft, his imagination effectively neutered. Conversely, imagine a Viagra-like pill for writer's block. Would the patient find his/her creative prowess enhanced or diminished?

23 OCTOBER

Damn it, I don't have any quirks than can be construed as "charming." No, I'm afraid with me the apparent social dysfunctions are just that.

24 OCTOBER

I have this wretched, maverick urge to – maybe – vote in the presidential election. I'm confessing to it; that's the point of this post.

And although I haven't properly confronted it, I suspect part of me is almost enjoying the Fall of America (which will certainly continue regardless who "wins," thereby dampening my wholly unexpected urge to take part in the election). Politics have outlived their nominal usefulness; seeing the system disintegrate wholesale is paradoxically reassuring.

With luck, we might wake up to the real issues that shadow virtually everyone on this planet, issues that have gone blissfully un-whispered throughout the entirety of the campaign we Americans have been so steeped in.

26 OCTOBER

You know what I'm really sick of? People who like to inform me that it's my "duty" to vote.

Come again?

Listen: If you want to vote, go fucking vote and leave me alone. If voting's your thing then by all means get to it. But don't adopt this cloying, more-patriotic-than-thou pretense that you're somehow a more informed, responsible person because of it, because it doesn't wash.

I'm a creative person. I like making things and seeing how they fare in this strange, buzzing construct we like to think of as the "real world." So I take real offense when one of these vacuous drones assumes that because I don't vote then I've basically forfeited the right to be taken seriously.

"I voted today!"

Rah, rah, rah!

Good for you. Now go back home and watch TV, you pretentious fuck.

27 OCTOBER

Weird thought for the day: What if Homo floresiensis is the tip of an anthropological iceberg? Imagine a long-forgotten technological civilization of these creatures: Might it account for the persistent worldwide folklore of "little people" – and maybe even modern-day extraterrestrials?

Homo floresiensis is described as three feet-tall; so are a lot of "ufonauts," especially the "Grays" of abduction fame. Any connection? I doubt it. But…

28 OCTOBER

News item: Scientists warn of 'ethnic weapons.'

"In theory, experts could engineer organisms to attack genetic variations commonly found in, say, Chinese or German populations."

Or imagine a Muslim extremist concocting a virus that mostly kills people of Jewish ancestry. Or an Arab-killing virus "accidentally" set loose in the Mid-East and subsequently chalked up to a natural mutation. A genetic "heat-seeker" virus needn't be a weapon of mass destruction. If its designers are savvy enough, it could be incredibly selective, operating with the precision of an assassin.

30 OCTOBER

I drove to my parents' this evening. They live in the suburbs, which, for the uninitiated, are vast tracts of land devoted to ugly housing where minds can rot unmolested. Campaign signage is everywhere, like thatches of red, white and blue weeds. I yearned for a machete.

While there, I watched some TV. *The Matrix* was showing on a cable channel as part of an extended Army recruitment infomercial. I kept seeing a black-clad Keanu Reeves juxtaposed with machine-gun-wielding soldiers and commercials for Sony PlayStation. Has all television become this surreal or did I just stumble upon a particularly postmodern moment?

I've watched all of 12 hours of TV in the last five years, and most of that has been on tape, where at least I can fast-forward through the commercials. It's strange how jarring it is to watch after abstaining for so long. It's like a physical blow to the head, and not in a good sense, inasmuch as a blow to the head can be a "good" thing.

I am absolutely convinced from personal experience that television viewing dampens cognitive ability. Want your IQ to go up 10 points? Stop watching TV. I'm serious. You won't necessarily be any happier, but you'll be more receptive, with a heightened immunity to bullshit.

31 OCTOBER

I'm not claiming to have any weird psychic powers, but it seems to me the zeitgeist has turned downright menacing. People seem robotic, the mass media appalling in its absurdity. The suburbs sulk under a marinating haze of spite; the sky is the color of fading newsprint.

Religious cults are prone to bouts of incipience in which they know that "something," usually catastrophic, at least for unbelievers, is going to happen. I'm getting that same sort of vibe now, broadcast from the depths of a thousand anonymous skulls. The dead reptilian scent of imminent disaster.

On the stereo: Bowie's "We Are the Dead." A furtive waitress with teeth ground to points. Canned personalities gesticulating in electronic silence. Malignant headlights swelling in my rear-view mirror.

Untranslatable premonitions pressed against the inside of my head like electrodes fashioned from rusted corkscrews.

Chapter 23
November 2004

2 NOVEMBER

One of the biggest hurdles to cryonics at present is that the patient must be declared legally dead before cryonicists can set to work reducing cell damage. This invariably results in destruction that could be prevented if cryonicists were allowed access to a terminal patient before clinical death.

Long-term biostasis might bridge the schism between mainstream medicine and the cryonics community because it eliminates actual death ("de-animation"). A person suffering from an incurable disease might choose to have himself put into hibernation until such time as a cure is developed. It's the same gamble made by cryonics patients, of course, but cryonics must deal not only with curing present-day maladies, but "reanimating" patient's "dead" bodies, presumably with the help of nanotechnology of the sort described in K. Eric Drexler's *Engines of Creation*. Hibernation – if we can achieve it – does away with the need for quasi-exotic cell-repair technologies.

In college, I spoke at length with former CryoCare president Charles Platt (author of *The Silicon Man*) about my prospects as a cryonaut. Truthfully, I imagined that I'd be signed up by now. So why aren't I?

Good question.

4 NOVEMBER

If cloning ever becomes medical reality – and I hope it does – imagine the dissent from the radical religious right, who just won't get it no matter how many times it's explained to them that the bodies are simply life-saving tissue cultures in anthropomorphic form. There will be rioting and bombings. Geneticists will be killed. Fundamentalists will line up at the gates of biomedical clinics wielding inane placards and those sloppy wheeled crosses that are becoming more and more a part of the post-Dubbya cultural landscape.

Meanwhile, those of us actually wearing new custom-tailored bodies will glance furtively at each other and wonder how long till the stoning begins.

5 NOVEMBER

I've become transfixed by images from an imagined future forty or fifty years from now, maybe less. Most of the "creative process" has been purely subliminal; I'm piecing it together from images harvested from dreams. Only occasionally do I indulge in wide-awake extrapolation.

I'm surprised how old the future looks, but perhaps I shouldn't be. Right now we're in the midst of a continent-wide suburban boom. New strip-malls, entertainment complexes and stand-alone stores crop up in endless profusion, sterile and oddly welcoming, only to be razed and supplanted by their Darwinian successors. Consequently, everything looks new, with an almost CGI luster.

This phase won't last. The present riot of consumer sprawl will wind down as resources become scarcer. Very soon, the available real-estate will be consumed and the fervor that fueled expansion will be forced to find new channels. The present obsession with prefab architecture will become a near-maniacal need to retrofit, fulfilling William Gibson's sly prophecy that "the street finds its own use for things." The commercial sheen of today's store and restaurant interiors will become dingy by comparison with our own – age-scuffed and time-battered utilitarianism seeking to subvert its millennial origins.

This reinvented world is hushed, stagnant; the excesses of today's fast-forward commercial ecology keep the population in virtual submission. It's not necessarily that there are fewer people; it's simply that humans will find themselves dwarfed by structures whose function seems to balance on the razor's edge of obsolescence. Ever seen a deserted shopping mall slated for demolition? Imagine a whole country with that same sad, desiccated atmosphere; a world thrown rudely upon the concrete shores of its own past.

A man sits on the shore, bracketed by clammy concrete walls, and sips rice tea. He watches the tide, warm and strangely odorless, rush in, crashing against the fortified seawall with a peculiarly electric sound. Lukewarm spray beads the asphalt between his feet.

I am watching.

6 NOVEMBER

Maybe I could be the next James Bond.

I'd be the perfect spy; no one ever notices me. Just the other day I walked up to the Starbucks counter at Barnes & Noble and the teenage baristas just kept on talking. Like I was invisible. I could have looted the cash drawer and no one would have seen me.

I'd be an exceptionally useful James Bond if the mission required infiltrating a complex of beautiful women. Women, especially, never notice me.

You know, something's telling me this just isn't box-office material.

7 NOVEMBER

Occasionally you hear of a scientific finding that will supposedly make Creationists think again.

Get real.

"Creation Science" has nothing to do with science, name notwithstanding. The belief virus will trump rationality every time, given half a chance, and "Creation Scientists" are in the business of giving it all possible chances.

9 NOVEMBER

On an environmental note, I've become exasperated by people

who take great pride in reminding us that "Our children are the future."

No they're not.

We are.

Our children just get saddled with it, and by the time they take over it's conceivable it might be too damned late to make an appreciable difference. Equating the next generation with the future is a thinly veiled attempt to escape the sheer fucking immediacy of the problems that haunt us now.

Bush's dubious election is indeed a huge step backward that may well be looked back on with an exceptionally fierce breed of Galan's "rage and recrimination." But what too many of us miss is the fact that we're living the "good old days."

Right now.

The life we experience, as dystopian and threatening as it is, will seem acutely idyllic in 30 years. Of course, that makes it all-too-easy to slack off, to wait serenely for the last possible moment.

The biosphere is running through our fingers like fine sand. It's becoming clear that politics are not the answer, as we become increasingly mired in the solipsism that is the lifeblood of the New World Disorder.

These are the days of stagnation; these are Giancarlo Galan's "wasted years."

12 NOVEMBER

Did you know there are vast "dead zones" in the oceans of this presumably living planet? There are. Because the planet is losing the race to keep up with us. It's tiring; it's near-breathless. But it's not yet powerless. It still holds us in its fierce ecological grip, a grip that as conditions inexorably worsen seems less and less welcome and more like a threatening imposition.

There's a mechanism nature employs when it loses a race against a particularly virulent species. It's called "dieback." It's not a word you hear a lot because, fortunately for us, dieback is a relatively rare occurrence. Typically, the Earth exists in equilibrium, the hard-won prize of resilience.

Humanity has reached a point in its technological trajectory in which its future resists even the best efforts at extrapolation. The maps aren't large enough, the calculators too feeble. Mathematicians call this novel post-historical state "nonlinear," a deceptively poetic word that smoothly dispenses with entrenched notions of control and dominion. It means that we don't know what comes next, that things have escaped our control, a position that humans will resist and cunningly refute until they find themselves jarringly translated into the new, nonlinear environment.

Crashing Antarctic food chains and rising waters are nodal points quietly heralding the emergence of a nonlinear world. Like constellations seen by primitive ocean-borne voyagers, they lead us to a new world, a world of terminal uncertainty and potentially catastrophic entropy, a world we may not like or even survive. There are no promises, no certainties. Only the nodal points, dim beneath the taut fabric of our dreams.

14 NOVEMBER

A nuclear blast in the Heartland, such as Kansas City or Chicago, would polarize the country against the perceived Al Qaeda menace as no coastal city attack could. It would clearly communicate that the country has been infiltrated, that our geographical borders are transparent and our leaders incompetent to enforce them.

The good news: If I'm vaporized in a nuclear blast, I suppose I can stop worrying about the Greenhouse Effect.

16 NOVEMBER

If our universe is a simulation engineered by a superhuman intelligence, how can we realistically expect to be to be able to discern the very inconsistencies that would betray its actual nature? Sure, the universe is complex. But perhaps only to us, and of course, according to simulation cosmology, we're enmeshed in the construct.

I'm reminded of a powerfully lucid dream I had a week ago. I was walking up a sidewalk (based loosely on an actual sidewalk not far from my apartment) reveling in the narcotic realization that everything I was experiencing was "simply" a dream. I actually stopped and looked around, every bit as purposeful and "conscious" as I am while awake, savoring the dreamness of it all.

Later, I tried the same mental exercise while awake. And for a moment it seemed like everything around me had the same ontological substance as the sidewalk in the dream, threatening to dissolve. Of course, it didn't; that's why I'm here typing this. But who's to say some other mental state couldn't shatter the programming of the "real" world, assuming that all of this is a clever technological illusion capable of being "hacked"?

17 NOVEMBER

Apparently it's not annoying enough that most of the population can't venture five feet from their ugly suburban homes without whipping out their cell phones; we have to have constant music in all public places as well, lest someone actually have an uninterrupted thought. I'm pretty good at tuning ambient music out, but tuning it out takes a certain learned skill, and sometimes, for whatever reason, I'm just not up to it.

I can't read in the coffee shop because they're blaring 80s retro on satellite radio.

The bookstore? Don't even think of it, because they're piping the music section's entire stock through a thousand unseen speakers.

Maybe a restaurant? Wrong! Because they've got satellite radio, too, and they want you to know it. Some of the places where I live even play music outside, ostensibly for the entertainment of potential patrons.

And chances are, if you listen carefully, you'll hear the insipid susurration of "adult contemporary" at your place of work. No escape!

What's wrong with turning the music off once in a while? Is there some federal mandate in effect that requires everyone to stumble along in a prerecorded daze day after day?

A side-effect of this deluge of songs is that, occasionally, you'll hear one you actually like, and it loses some of its subjective value. I love R.E.M., but I don't want to hear "Losing My Religion" when I'm shopping for cat litter. And with the 80s retro trend in full-swing, it's near-impossible to navigate the already-unnerving consumer landscape without having a backlog of classics thrust down your ears. Only "thrust" isn't the right word; the hidden speakers of stores and restaurants don't broadcast music so much as ooze it, leaching it of resonance, craftily stripping it of the very nuance that makes a good song something to be treasured.

I don't want an iPod for Christmas.

I want a pair of industrial-grade earplugs.

18 NOVEMBER

The world population is now so staggeringly high that scientists realize we can't go on unless we radically minimize our birth-rate or colonize space. One estimate demands that we colonize the equivalent of two new Earths or else our planetary resources will be impoverished in a mere 50 years. If we fail, humans (among countless other species) may find their numbers decimated by food and energy shortages.

Wisely, China is beginning to lurch spaceward, with plans to mine the Moon for energy-rich Helium 3. The Western world will follow, but perhaps only at the last possible moment.

The culture that triumphs over the coming eco-debacle will inherit a new world, perhaps even a newly accessible solar system.

But at what cost?

20 NOVEMBER

The 20th anniversary edition of William Gibson's *Neuromancer* is out. It seems like last month I was buying the 10th anniversary edition.

I read *Neuromancer* in my junior year of high school, before the Internet existed in recognizable form. I wouldn't send an email for two entire years. Experiencing Gibson's world was a jarring experience, a literary epiphany that totally altered my reading habits; although I had encountered Philip K. Dick, I had yet to read Burroughs (or Sterling or Rucker or Delany or Shirley).

While I was very much a science fiction reader, my diet had consisted primarily of classics from an altogether different era – Clarke's *Childhood's End* comes to mind. I was drunk on the dying promises of the Space Age, virtually unaware that the Information Age was beginning to cast its first portentous shadows.

Gibson changed all that. I even remember the bookstore where I bought my copy of *Neuromancer*, a modest store along Florida's Space Coast, the slowly fossilizing turf so knowingly visited by proto-cyberpunk J.G. Ballard, a writer I wouldn't encounter for several more years.

I cite Gibson as my single-most important creative influence, despite the fact that I've only written two books, and of these only one is fiction. This is far from an original claim; Gibson has become a sort of god-king among those aspiring to write "literary" science fiction, a force as omnipresent, and unremarked, as today's consumer ecology of software-packed cell phones. Imitation is the sincerest form of flattery. For better or worse, our world has taken on the texture, if not the historical trajectory, of Gibson's prophecy.

I admire a lot of authors, many of them fabulously prescient. But the early 21st century belongs to William Gibson. We are the unwitting offspring of his fictional zeitgeist.

We are all cyberpunks.

26 NOVEMBER

Today is one of the ugliest days of the year. I plan on making myself scarce.

27 NOVEMBER

Wouldn't it be weird if you were walking along with a friend, minding your own business, when suddenly – CRACK! – a grain-sized meteorite impacted your friend's skull, exiting the forehead and sending a spume of semi-liquefied brain all over the sidewalk?

Maybe if I'm really lucky I'll get to see that someday.

28 NOVEMBER

When people start to talk about Extraterrestrial artifacts, I think, "Uh-oh. Dangerous territory."

If we're dealing with a highly advanced extraterrestrial intelligence, equipped with an appropriately advanced technology, then it's probable interstellar communiques will be rather more interesting than simple "messages inscribed onto physical matter."

For example, they could be artificially intelligent, able to respond to their environment and even home in on habitable worlds, a trait that sounds tantalizingly organic.

Already, machines on Earth are becoming more and more like living things. And experts such as Ray Kurzweil and Hans Moravec insist this trend will continue. So maybe we shouldn't be terribly surprised if our first message from space takes the form of a sophisticated intelligence of some sort, infinitely richer in information than any plaque or gold-plated record.

29 NOVEMBER

Interesting. I picked up a postcard advertising an art exhibit the other day. The name of the artist is Max Fearing, which I read as "Mac's Fearing."

Which I suppose I am.

30 NOVEMBER

SETI co-founder Frank Drake writes:

Planets might not even need stars. No one has directly observed a rogue planet, but we know they're out there; astronomers have discovered more than 130 extra-solar planets, and their orbital motion tells us that during the formation of a solar system, extra planets get dumped into the star or kicked out of the system. The castaways wander in the great empty spaces between the stars, the orphans of the Milky Way. In theory, if the rogue's crust contained radioactive elements, their decay could keep the surface warm enough for life.

Who says you even need planets? It's possible a civilization could arise on a proto-planetary body such as an asteroid if conditions were right. Or maybe even on the surfaces of depleted stars. It's weird out there. I'm not quite ready to quarantine hypothetical aliens to planets, even bleak, sunless ones.

Chapter 24
December 2004

8 DECEMBER

I just checked my Mars book's Amazon.com ranking and discovered, to my dismay, that I'm unwittingly helping to advertise, among other things, *The Passion of the Christ* DVD and a website all about Revelations and the end of the world, Fundy-style.

The problem: poorly written software. Amazon's pages are smart enough to detect keywords in a book's title and connect them to other items of possible interest, but they lack a sense of context. Thus, a book about Mars (that happens to have the word "apocalypse" in the title) generates a list of "related" products, even if they have nothing to do with it – indeed, even if they appeal to an opposing demographic.

I know Amazon can do better because I took a quick look at Blogger's "get paid for ads on your website" scheme and they're careful to hype their software's context-recognition ability. This must be fairly new, because I remember when BlogSpot sites hosted unsolicited ads in place of a proper nav-bar, I'd sometimes get hilarious results. While chronicling the wad of airbag fabric known as the "bunny" after the Mars Exploration Rovers landed, for example, I'd see recurring text-ads for rabbit slippers. Or I'd post a harangue about Precious Moments figurines and within minutes *Posthuman Blues* had been turned into a virtual billboard for the damned things.

10 DECEMBER

Someone instant-messaged me the other day to ask for my ideas on cattle mutilations. While I don't claim to know what they're all about, I'm satisfied that some of them are indeed mysterious, but not necessarily due to an overarching alien agenda. My best guess is that a "black-ops" government project is monitoring the spread of toxins and/or diseases by sampling cattle.

The guy I was chatting with posed the obvious question: If it's the government doing a clandestine study, why scare people when it could buy its own cattle-land for research? After all, who would know?

My answer is that people would know. They might not be aware of the ultimate purpose of the project, but sooner or later they'd be curious, and asking uncomfortable questions. Keep in mind that Area 51 was a tourist destination long before it officially existed. Hiding research projects in the Southwest isn't nearly as easy as one might assume.

So rather than risk snooping researchers who might expose a frightening secret, why not simply do all research "in the field," using made-up UFO scare-stories to keep the project safely protected behind the "laughter curtain"? I wouldn't be in the least surprised to discover that some of the UFO reports associated with cattle mutilations were actually staged to confuse the issue, and perhaps even frighten away potential witnesses. Inevitably, there are unsubstantiated rumors of grisly human mutilations, supposedly the work of cattle-snatching alien biologists.

Aside from remaining invisible, albeit with its handiwork in plain view, the project could expand its sample population by plucking cattle and horses from disparate locations. This makes sense if the goal is to actively track contaminants as opposed to studying them in the privacy of a lab.

My question: What, exactly, are they tracking? And how dire is the threat, assuming there is one?

12 DECEMBER

I had an interesting "visionary" experience while drifting to sleep last night. It was similar to other recent episodes in that it had the feel of a lucid dream (although I was awake with my eyes open) but different insofar as it seemed like I was interacting with an actual technology of some kind.

In front of my face, at reading distance, there appeared to be multiple rows of compressed text, each word encapsulated in an ellipse. Each row moved rapidly from the right to the left, too fast for me to make out any sort of narrative, but acutely responsive, so that I could visually choose a specific word-balloon and have it persist for a moment before vanishing, instantly replaced by a stream of words with similar connotations. It was like looking into the mind of a language database or some futuristic heads-up display word processor. It also had the feel of a timed quiz or test of some sort; I can see something like it eventually becoming a high-bandwidth Web application.

Perhaps significantly, I seem to have experienced increased hypnogogic phenomena like this since I suffered a retinal occlusion a few months ago, temporarily blotting out the sight in my right eye. Maybe my retina (technically, part of the brain) healed with heightened sensitivity to the phosphene activity most people experience when they close their eyes in a dark room. My subconscious could be amplifying ocular "noise," allowing me to experience certain dream imagery while not fully asleep.

15 DECEMBER

Fun fact: In a few short weeks this blog will celebrate its second-year anniversary, which is rather surprising when I stop to think about it. I wasn't sure if I'd "take" to the blog medium or not; when I started, I was pretty much doing it as a self-centered writing exercise. So it's very cool that I've picked up a few readers along the way – that was unexpected.

16 DECEMBER

I think humane assisted euthanasia should be available to anyone, regardless of medical condition. We're so afraid of death that we've effectively criminalized it, as if it's something unutterably obscene;

consequently, we're unable to deal with it in any productive context. Ironically enough, you run up against the same ideological paralysis when you talk about extending healthy life spans; suddenly death ceases to be abhorrent and becomes natural, even "sacred."

We're afraid of dying; we're afraid of living forever. So most of us settle for the willful oblivion of organized religion, television-watching and flag-waving. It's not death – not quite – but it certainly isn't living, insofar as "living" implies some capacity for productivity.

And suicidal people are supposedly unbalanced? At least they know what they want, which is vastly more than you can say for most.

17 DECEMBER

Have you ever been around people who are functionally dead? People whose lives have become so automatic and uninspired that they're miserable and simply don't realize it?

You find high concentrations of these people in the corporate/political world. They're typically cloyingly religious and, for simple lack of a better term, total assholes. But they've got this craving for justification; deep down, something in them requires validation. On some level they know their "purpose," if one can call it that, is to stick out their genetically allotted time on this planet before keeling over from disease or age. So they become self-righteous, arrogant, and deeply boring.

These people suck the very prospect of vitality out of the air. Their presence induces fatigue, depression, anxiety.

And they own the goddamned planet.

18 DECEMBER

Ignorance is a tenacious enemy. Will we triumph, in the long run? The odds are stacked against us; I would be quite surprised if we survived our technological adolescence and went on to become a robust space-faring civilization. As a species, we appear to lack the sense of perspective so direly necessary if we're to redefine our role in the Cosmos.

20 DECEMBER

You know how professional wrestling comes with the disclaimer "sports entertainment" – meant to discourage the credulous from thinking the matches are anything but rehearsed skits? In a similar vein, I think certain kinds of music should be labeled "music entertainment." "Young country" is one of them. It's always been stupid; now Dubbya's Iraq War has pushed it hurtling past the threshold of self-parody.

Rap, generally artless and formulaic, is another form of "music entertainment." "Gangsta rap" devotees buy Snoop Dogg CDs for image, not aesthetic virtue.

Britney Spears? More "music entertainment."

Same with Marilyn Manson and other contemporary "goth": sheer gimmick with little or no redeeming substance.

21 DECEMBER

I like to think of how I'd explain the world of 2004 to a citizen of the 1940s or 50s – someone with a good grasp of science for whom descriptions of ubiquitous marvels like DVD players and global positioning systems would seem like technology, not fantasy or mysticism. Nevertheless, a daunting task.

Let's say I've got only a couple minutes to sum up the post-millennial zeitgeist. Where should I start?

Even a typical street scene is liable to sound like bad science fiction, what with people coasting by on Segways as they prattle into cell phones that double as cameras. To say nothing of those drinking $2.50 cups of organic coffee as they establish wi-fi connections with their laptops, which they use to "surf" this enigmatic thing called "the Web" and transmit messages that dance across the globe in fiber-optic cable.

Blogs.

Depleted uranium.

The search for Hawking radiation.

9-11-01.

Stem-cells.

Global warming.

Computer viruses.

Mars rovers.

Chat-rooms.

Dish TV.

MP3s, PDAs, GMOs, SUVs and MRIs.

The Higgs boson.

Quantum encryption.

Transgenic art.

Dirty bombs.

Solar sails.

Google.

22 DECEMBER

An article I read today about some politician who wants to "save society from moral destruction" makes me wonder: isn't it great that politicians are so eager to help us? I find it boundlessly encouraging that some total stranger is going beyond the call of duty to protect me. I mean, the utter selflessness of it![48]

Last week, Dubbya's base introduced a bill that would ban the use of state funds to purchase any books or other materials that "promote homosexuality".

Seriously: I don't "get" homophobia. I suspect that just as there are biological conditions that predetermine if one is gay or straight, there are genes/hormones/enzymes that kick in to make people homophobic. And I have a hunch this biological mechanism is tied to religion, another irrational phenomenon with known neurological aspects (thus the burgeoning field of neurotheology).

---

[48] Gary Taylor, "We Have to Protect People," *The Guardian*, 9 December 2004. www.guardian.co.uk/books/2004/dec/09/gayrights.usa.

In other words, there are sets of factors, intrinsic and cultural, that conspire to turn people into assholes. You might not actually find the term "asshole" in the neurological literature, but perhaps it should be there just the same. Assholes, like the "shits" scorned by William Burroughs, appear fundamentally unable to mind their own business. So they become politicians and corporate hotshots, careers that allow them to make a profitable living screwing with other people's lives in the name of "morality," the worst possible form of ersatz altruism. These are the "functionally dead" people I mentioned a few days ago. They're everywhere.

As far as I'm concerned, they might as well belong to some virulent alien species. And yet, far too often, the rest of us willingly play by their rules. We cow-tow to them. We make it easy, consoling ourselves with the costly fiction that casting a vote once every four years might make a difference.

Meanwhile, the planet goes to hell.

I don't think the rest of the world realizes how profoundly twisted things have become in the US. To Bush and his pals, the end of the world is eminently desirable because that means Jesus is on his way, complete with flaming sword. So global warming and other serious environmental threats are unflinchingly neglected.

It's not a relatively simple matter of choosing to look the other way for fear of what might be seen; those in control actively want this.

Mind-blowing?

Certainly. But then again so was Dubbya's "re"-election. We should be practically numb to absurdity by now.

Meanwhile, I got this email today:

hello! my name is Elena, I'm from Russia. I looked your profile on dating site. So, you are look like as my type. let's get acquainted! It's probably you'll like me if you see my pics and find out a little about me. Please write me back!

Sounds like a teaser for an erotic website, doesn't it? The weird thing is that I think it could possibly be for real. I've had two Russian single women email me to profess their desire to meet American singles, and, to my surprise, both turned out to be real people. How serious they were about "dating" is another issue, but they weren't hawking porn or asking for money.

So I wrote "Elena" a quick message in reply just to see where this goes, which is probably nowhere fast. The bone-chilling irony is that I probably have a better chance at meeting someone in Siberia than in my own hometown.

Insert Morrissey lyric here.

24 DECEMBER

I'm always reading about the quest to join science and spirituality. The popular assumption is that reconciling the two, if possible, will be an unquestionably good thing. To be sure, it has a nice ring to it; it's not as if the appeal is obscure. But why do we assume we need to bridge the gulf between science and spirituality? For that matter, who says the "gulf" even exists? It could be a perceptual anomaly, an intellectual mirage.

This might sound stodgily materialist, but maybe the only way to humanize science is to do more science. As we continue exploring the frontiers of neurology and quantum cosmology, the "bridge" so many of us are looking for may begin to reveal itself with increasing resolution.

25 DECEMBER

Be very afraid.

A new poll in *Newsweek* shows that sixty-two percent say they favor teaching creation science in addition to evolution in public schools; 26 percent oppose such teaching, the poll shows. Forty-three percent favor teaching creation science instead of evolution in public schools; 40 percent oppose the idea.

Newsweek is at glaring fault here for using the condescending term "creation science." Biblical Creationism isn't science; it's not even close. But Fundamentalists know perfectly well they need to work the "s"-work into their agenda if they're to wield political clout; flaunting Creationism as some sort of overlooked field of objective study is nothing but a prudent gimmick. And of course once they've accomplished their mission of subverting the public education system they'll abandon the pretense altogether.

Meanwhile, the mainstream news media obligingly endorse the fiction that there's something scientific about Creationism.

Welcome to Jesusland.

26 DECEMBER

A year or so ago Stephen Hawking predicted the human race would go extinct within 1,000 years unless it expanded into space. Between global bio-warfare, nuclear proliferation, rogue asteroids, and ecocaust, we don't have much of a chance unless we take radical measures.

I've always thought Hawking was being naively optimistic and generous; 300 years seemed a more likely figure. Now, in my mind if nowhere else, that figure is dropping to somewhere between 50-100 years. The veil of optimism, the smokescreen of contrived hope, is in tatters, and I suddenly realize what a bruising my psyche has taken while trying to keep up a positive front.

Maybe this is what psychologists call "externalization." Maybe things aren't all that dire, but my frustration with myself, my uncertainty, is superimposing itself on the outside world. Or maybe people are saner and kinder than I assume. Or just maybe the environment can take an unprecedented artificially instigated pounding and still keep a human population of billions alive and in reasonable health.

Is it any wonder Christian Fundamentalism has made such an appalling cultural and political comeback? I honestly suspect most of us harbor an unrecognized visceral certainty that we're on the brink. Maybe I've been out of the loop all along, while the Fundies have enjoyed something like prescience.

The irony stings.

29 DECEMBER

The BBC reports that cell phones alter human DNA.[49]

Good. Maybe cell phone addicts will keel over from insidious mutations. I'm utterly exasperated with the cell phone thing; I blame their popularity, in part, for my ailing social life. For example, the other night I was doing laundry and a girl I'd never talked to was there, talking on a cell phone while tossing bales of wet clothing into the steel maw of a commercial Maytag. I've found that cell phones make people genuinely unapproachable. Same with iPods. And Segways – what, you're too lofty to share the pavement with the rest of us?

The irony is that I'm healthily technophiliac. But my requirement is that new technologies fulfill some useful role, and the gadgets that people are so enamored of these days are generally just costly toys.

Don't misunderstand. I like Segways; I think they have the potential to redefine our relationship with our increasingly congested cities. But that doesn't mean taking walks is an obsolete concept.

And what's with this sudden pressing need to have DVD players installed in cars?

Do I really need to point out the danger here?

30 DECEMBER

Here's a weird dream I had about a week ago: I was at the news-stand at Barnes & Noble and a magazine caught my eye. It was *Time* or *Newsweek* or something – a major mainstream news monthly. The cover showed the barely lit limb of the Earth, apparently taken from orbit. And across the image was the sentence "WE ARE CAMERON DIAZ-LESS" in commanding white capitals.

"Huh," I remember thinking. "Cameron Diaz must have died."

---

49 "Mobile Phones alter human DNA," *BBC News*, 21 December 2004. www.news.bbc.co.uk/2/hi/health/4113989.stm.

31 DECEMBER

I don't usually make New Year's resolutions because I think the concept is dumb. But I'm making one for 2005 (and posting it here so readers, if so inclined, can call me on it if I slack off).

Here it is: Get to serious work on my oft-mentioned yet unfinished novel, *Women and Children First*. Maybe even finish a first draft before '06. The down-side is that I won't have as much free time to read. And it's possible, but not terribly likely, that I won't blog quite as frequently. I simply don't know.

One of the reasons I'm in a hurry to write this depressingly eco-dystopian story is because some of the basic themes are coming true much faster than I expected. And this sounds off-puttingly messianic, but maybe if the final product is good enough and I find a publisher, perhaps it will actually do some good. Michael Crichton (an author I've loathed since wading through the consummately unoriginal *Jurassic Park*) just came out with a thriller titled *State of Fear*. The premise of *State of Fear* is that environmentalists are dangerous lunatics, a sort of tree-hugging Al Qaeda.

Most intelligent readers are likely to see through Crichton's propaganda; already, more than a few are actually wondering who, ultimately, gave Crichton the green light for this latest delusional offering. Popular fiction's potential as a political instrument shouldn't be underestimated, especially with the current neo-con freak-show expediently spreading its roots.

Best wishes to everyone for the best possible 2005.

May reason prevail.

Bibliography

Atwood, Margaret. *The Blind Assassin*. McClelland and Stewart, 2000.

_____. *The Handmaid's Tale*. McClelland and Stewart, 1985.

Ballard, J. G. *Crash*. Jonathan Cape, 1973.

Bell, Art, and Whitley Strieber. *The Coming Global Superstorm*. Pocket Books, 1999.

Benford, Gregory. *In the Ocean of Night*. Dial Press, 1977.

Brunner, John. *Stand on Zanzibar*. Doubleday, 1968.

_____. *The Sheep Look Up*. Harper & Row, 1972.

_____. *The Shockwave Rider*. Harper & Row, 1975.

Burroughs, William S. *Naked Lunch*. Grove Press, 1959.

Clarke, Arthur C. *Childhood's End*. Ballantine Books, 1953.

Coupland, Douglas. *Generation X: Tales for an Accelerated Culture*. St. Martin's Press, 1991.

_____. *MicroSerfs*. HarperCollins, 1995.

Cremo, Michael. *Human Devolution: A Vedic Alternative to Darwin's Theory*. Torchlight Publishing, 2003.

Darling, David. *Equations of Eternity*. Hyperion Books, 1993.

Darlington, David. *Area 51: The Dreamland Chronicles*. Holt, 1998.

Dick, Philip. K. *Solar Lottery*. Ace Books, 1955.

_____. *VALIS*. Bantam Books, 1981.

Drexler, K. Eric. *Engines of Creation: The Coming Era of Nanotechnology*. Doubleday, 1986.

Egan, Greg. *Permutation City*. Millennium Orion Publishing Group, 1994.

Fukuyama, Francis. *Our Posthuman Future: Consequences of the Biotechnology Revolution*. Farrar Straus & Giroux, 2002.

Gaiman, Neil. *Neverwhere*. BBC Books, 1996.

Gibson, William. *Count Zero*. Victor Gollancz, 1986.

_____. *Neuromancer*. Ace, 1984.

_____. *Pattern Recognition*. G. P. Putnam's Sons, 2003.

Hesse, Hermann. *Siddhartha*. New Directions, 1951.

Hopkins, Budd. *Intruders: The Incredible Visitations at Copley Woods*. Random House, 1987.

Hopkins, Budd, and Carol Rainey. *Sight Unseen: Science, UFO Invisibility, and Transgenic Beings*. Atria, 2003.

Hoyle, Fred, and N. C. Wickramasinghe. *Diseases From Space*. Harper & Row, 1980.

Hubbard, L. Ron. *Dianetics*. Bridge Publications, 2007.

Huxley, Aldous. *Brave New World*. Chatto & Windus, 1932.

Jung, C. G. *Flying Saucers: A Modern Myth of Things Seen in the Skies*. Routledge & Paul, 1959.

Kafka, Franz. *The Castle*. Trans. Anthea Bell. Oxford University Press, 2009.

———. *The Trial*. Trans. Idris Parry. Penguin Modern Classics, 2000.

Keel, John. *The Complete Guide to Mysterious Beings*. Main Street Books, 1994.

———. *The Eighth Tower*. Saturday Review Press, 1975.

———. *The Mothman Prophecies*. Panther Books, 1975.

Kerouac, Jack. *Book of Blues*. Penguin Books, 1995.

Kesey, Ken. *One Flew Over the Cuckoo's Nest*. Viking Press, 1962.

King, Stephen. *Dreamcatcher*. Scribner, 2001.

Kunetka, James, and Whitley Strieber. *Warday*. Holt, Rinehart and Winston, 1984.

LaHaye, Tim. *Left Behind: A Novel of the Earth's Last Days*. Tyndale House Publishers, 1995.

Lethem, Jonathan. *Gun, With Occasional Music*. Harcourt Brace & Company, 1994.

Mack, John. *Abduction: Human Encounters With Aliens*. Scribner, 1994.

———. *Passport to the Cosmos: Human Transformation and Alien Encounters*. Crown, 1999.

MacLeod, Ken. *Cosmonaut Keep*. Tor Books, 2001.

———. *Dark Light*. Tor Books, 2002.

———. *Engine City*. Tor Books, 2003.

Mieville, China. *Perdido Street Station*. Macmillan, 2000.

Nietzsche, Friedrich. *Twilight of the Idols and The Antichrist*. Trans. R. J. Hollingdale. Penguin Classics, 1990.

Nugent, Ted. *God, Guns & Rock And Roll*. Regnery Publishing, 2000.

_____. *Kill It & Grill It*. Regnery Publishing, 2005.

Orwell, George. *Nineteen Eighty-Four*. Secker and Warburg, 1949.

Platt, Charles. *The Silicon Man*. Tafford, 1993.

Randles, Jenny. *The Truth About the Men In Black*. St. Martin's, 1997.

Rucker, Rudy. *Software*. Ace Books, 1982.

_____. *Spaceland*. Tor Books, 2002.

_____. *Wetware*. Avon Books, 1988.

Sagan, Carl, and Ann Druyan. *The Demon-Haunted World: Science as a Candle in the Dark*. Random House, 1995.

Spinrad, Norman. *Agent of Chaos*. Franklin Watts, 1988.

Stephenson, Neal. *Cryptonomicon*. Avon, 1999.

Strieber, Whitley. *Communion: A True Story*. Avon, 1987.

_____. *Confirmation: The Hard Evidence of Aliens Amongst Us*. St. Martin's Press, 1998.

_____. *The Communion Letters*. Harper Prism, 1997.

_____. *Transformation: The Breakthrough*. William Morrow & Company, 1988.

Talbott, Michael. *The Holographic Universe*. HarperCollins, 1991.

Tevis, Walter. *The Man Who Fell To Earth*. Gold Medal Books, 1963.

Thompson, Richard. *Alien Identities: Ancient Insights Into Modern UFO Phenomena*. Govardhan Hill, 1995.

Tonnies, Mac. *After the Martian Apocalypse: Extraterrestrial Artifacts and the Case for Mars Exploration*. Paraview Pocket Books, 2004.

_____. *Illumined Black and Other Adventures*. Phantom Press Publications, 1995.

_____. *The Cryptoterrestrials: A Meditation on Indigenous Humanoids Among Us*. Anomalist Books, 2010.

Vallee, Jacques. *Anatomy of a Phenomenon: Unidentified Objects in Space – A Scientific Appraisal*. Henry Regnery, 1965.

_____. *Passport to Magonia*. Neville Spearman, 1970.

Vonnegut, Kurt. *Cat's Cradle*. Holt, Rinehart and Winston, 1963.

_____. *Player Piano*. Charles Scribner's Sons, 1952.

_____. *The Sirens of Titan*. Dell, 1959.

Watts, Peter. *Maelstrom*. Tor Books, 2001.

_____. *Starfish*. Tor Books, 1999.

Wiesel, Elie. *Night*. Hill and Wang, 1958.

Williamson, Jack. *Terraforming Earth*. Tor Books, 2001.

Wilson, Colin. *Alien Dawn: An Investigation Into the Contact Experience*. Virgin Publishing Limited, 1998.

_____. *The Outsider*. Houghton Mifflin, 1956.

Wilson, Robert Anton. *Cosmic Trigger: The Final Secret of the Illuminati*. New Falcon Publications, 1977.

Wilson, Robert Charles. *Blind Lake*. Tor Books, 2003.

Womack, Jack. *Elvissey*. Grove Press, 1993.

Wright, Susan. *Slave Trade*. Pocket Star, 2003.

Wyndham, John. *Day of the Triffids*. Doubleday & Company, Inc., 1951.

Zinn, Howard. *A People's History of the United States*. Harper & Row, 1980.

Index

C

S

Sagan, Carl · 99, 180, 203, 277, 308, 348

SARS · 50, 238

Savage, Andrew · 280

Scantlin, Melana · 169

Schwarzenegger, Arnold · 148

science · xviii, 9, 95, 115, 133-134, 137, 140, 144, 151, 153, 196, 198, 203, 225-226, 250, 295, 298, 302, 307-308, 325, 337, 340

science fiction · xviii, xix, 4-5, 30, 51-52, 54, 61, 78, 81, 101, 114, 125, 134, 144, 182, 225-226, 232, 263, 270, 289-290, 295, 330, 337, 361

Scientology · 181, 293

Segways · 141, 284, 299, 337, 342

Seinfeld · 6, 26, 188-199, 251, 293

September 11, 2001 attacks · xvii-xviii, 7, 13, 24, 38, 60, 113-114, 187, 245, 250, 259, 268, 271, 285, 288, 294, 338

SETI · 18-19, 231-232, 287, 297, 311, 331

Sheldrake, Rupert · 86

Shirley, John · i, xi, xix, 155, 223, 305-307, 330

Simon and Garfunkel · 154, 213, 253

skepticism · 49, 55, 97, 123, 134, 247, 307

sleep paralysis · 122

Smith, Will · 278-279

space exploration · xvi, 3, 7-8, 12, 23, 54, 78, 125, 151, 161, 177, 188, 190-192, 196, 248, 314, 329, 336, 341, 361

space shuttle · 7, 8, 24, 126, 191

Spears, Britney · 160, 212, 337

Spinrad, Norman · 101, 348

Starbucks · 4, 46, 87, 136, 148, 150, 192, 222, 231, 233-234, 242, 258, 266, 325

steampunk · 247, 309

Stephenson, Neal · 13-14, 348

Sterling, Bruce · 1, 4-5, 14, 318, 330

Stewart, Martha · 223

Stipe, Michael · 64, 167, 265

street preachers · 21, 24, 244, 313, 315

Strieber, Whitley · xix, 11-12, 15, 32, 62, 122, 134-135, 152-153, 187, 233, 258, 261, 274, 298, 345, 348

Stylites, Simeon · 280

suburbs, the · 72, 132, 195, 300, 314, 319, 321-322

suicide · 190, 236, 305-307, 335-336

Super Trouper · 280, 281

Supersize Me · 288

synchronicity · 11, 56, 150

T

Talbot, Michael · 134, 240, 348

television · 2, 5, 8, 14, 26, 28, 35, 41, 52-53, 70, 73, 76, 78, 125, 145, 147, 156-157, 169-171, 186, 189, 191, 204, 209, 217-219, 223-224, 244, 251, 274, 285, 290, 301-302, 311, 320-322, 336, 338, 361

terrorism · 7, 16, 42, 45, 70, 122, 132, 175, 178, 214, 239, 250, 253, 259, 321, 327

Tevis, Walter · 349

The Cryptoterrestrials · xiv, xvi

The Day After Tomorrow · 261

The Day the Earth Stood Still · 23

The Matrix · 17, 70, 72-73, 131, 135, 161, 201, 215, 321

The Matrix Reloaded · 65, 69, 72, 129, 161, 228

U

V

W

Z

ABOUT THE AUTHOR

 Mac Tonnies (1975 – 2009) was an American author, futurist, and journalist whose work focused on transhumanism, science fiction, space exploration, the paranormal, and the human condition. He grew up in Independence, Missouri, and graduated from Ottawa University with a Bachelor's of Arts in English Literature, after which he lived in Kansas City, Missouri, where he supported himself by working at various "nine-to-five" jobs while he pursued a career as a writer. Tonnies' first book, *Illumined Black*, was a collection of short stories published in 1995. *After The Martian Apocalypse*, a speculative look at the possibility of life on Mars, was published by Simon & Schuster in 2004. His third book, *The Cryptoterrestrials*, was published posthumously in 2010. Tonnies was a frequent guest on various paranormal radio shows and podcasts, including *Binnall of America*, *Radio Misterioso*, *The X-Zone*, *Strange Days Indeed*, and *Coast to Coast*. He was featured in the 2007 television documentary *Best Evidence: Top 10 UFO Sightings*, as well as an episode of the Canadian television series *Supernatural Investigator* in 2008. In 2007 he co-wrote the science fiction play *Doing Time* with Canadian filmmaker Paul Kimball. His popular blog, *Posthuman Blues*, was described by *The Pitch* in 2004 as "one of Kansas City's best blogs, filled with well-written, intelligent takes on offbeat news items and humorous rants from a left-leaning political perspective."

Mac Tonnies passed away in 2009 of cardiac arrhythmia at the age of 34. His personal website remains active, at mactonnies.com; *Posthuman Blues* can still be found in its entirety at posthumanblues.com.

Made in United States
North Haven, CT
10 June 2023

37583792R00209